Second Edition

Pitching from the Ground Up

Bob Bennett

ISBN: 1-58518-946-4
Library of Congress Control Number: 2005933073
Cover design: Jeanne Hamilton
Book layout: Jeanne Hamilton
Front cover photo: Al Bello/Allsport

Coaches Choice
P.O. Box 1828
Monterey, CA 93942
www.coacheschoice.com

Acknowledgments

Two of my former pitchers, Mark Gardner and Bobby Jones, were very helpful with the formation of this book. They demonstrated the drills and mechanics shown in this book. Both were All-American pitchers in college, and both played in the major leagues.

I was fortunate to have played for two outstanding coaches, Ollie Bidwell and Pete Beiden. Both coaches were outstanding fundamentalists. Their ideas were passed along to me and are the foundation for this book.

Teaching cannot be done without good students. The many pitchers whom I had the privilege of coaching have been a source of enthusiasm and energy during my coaching career. Their willingness to learn and to exchange ideas helped to develop the pitching program discussed in this book.

For all of these coaches and players I owe a debt of gratitude.

Foreword

In the two years that I attended Fresno State, I never once imagined that I would become a major league pitcher. With hard work and the coaching of Bob Bennett, dreams became reality for me. I am a firm believer in a good solid delivery that incorporates balance and a consistent release point. These are some of the small but important areas of pitching that are sometimes overlooked.

The art of pitching is broken down into many areas. In this book you will find all of those areas defined and illustrated for you. As you go through this detailed, but easy to understand book, you will find drills and techniques that will aid you to coach or perform better. When learning to pitch, I feel you should learn your craft well enough to be able to teach others. I found that it helped my pitching to be able to analyze others as well. This book is going to be an excellent teaching tool for the pitcher starting at square one or for the coach and pitcher just looking for a little help.

As I wrapped up my pitching career in baseball, I found myself looking back and remembering those days at FSU when pitching came together for me. It wasn't easy and nobody said it would be. I definitely have many thank-yous to give out for my career, but nobody deserves more credit for my technique, perseverance, and positive outlook in baseball than Coach Bob Bennett. He is the reason his teams and players excelled at FSU.

Mark Gardner
Former Pitcher
San Francisco Giants

Contents

Introduction

For the better part of five decades, I have been observing, catching, or coaching pitchers. This has given me an opportunity to evaluate many pitching techniques and a variety of teaching methods. Along the way I have observed very creative pitching coaches, non-creative pitching coaches, solid teaching methods, and poor teaching techniques. These experiences have helped me develop better teaching procedures. They were used to create a better system for learning.

True learning takes place when there is a need to know, a solid understanding of how to learn, and the realization that the goal can be reached. A learning system that identifies sequential learning patterns provides a learning environment.

A common system is what I refer to as "hit and miss" teaching. This is the act of throwing out information in all directions and hoping it will hit the target. Sometimes this system actually works. It may work because the pitcher is so eager to learn that he grabs the information and makes it work. This is not a tried and true method that produces consistent results. The pitcher simply sorts out the rubble and picks up the stray parts and puts together a workable plan.

Some pitching coaches believe that a pitcher's motion should not be changed. They believe that a change in technique will destroy the natural delivery of the pitcher. In other words, "he throws that way for a reason, so don't foul it up." Imbedded in this thinking is the idea that any success the pitcher enjoys may be negated by changes in the pitching motion.

A large number of coaches favor the notion that college or professional level pitchers are too far along to make changes. They do not specialize in teaching mechanics. They emphasize velocity, control, strategy, movement, or gamesmanship. Some are outstanding in these areas.

There are differing philosophies concerning competitors. Some coaches believe that a pitcher is either a competitor or he is not a competitor. Those who are competitors win. Those who are not competitors lose. This group believes that competitiveness is an inherited trait. Others believe it can be learned.

The teaching of pitching can be done successfully from any number of methods. Some offer clear and concise lessons. Others are difficult to understand. The purpose of this book is to provide a simple step-by-step teaching method. It is written with both the pitcher and the pitching coach in mind. Teaching and learning are simplified.

Pitching can be divided into five major teaching areas. They are: (1) Mechanics, (2) Control, (3) Velocity, (4) Stuff, and (5) Gamesmanship. Pitching coaches use one of these five as a base for teaching. A pitching coach who uses control as a base, for example, will coach the other areas. He will however, place major emphasis on control. The teaching base of this book is mechanics. Greater emphasis will be placed on that area.

Even though the base is mechanics, the others areas will not be neglected. In fact, each area is extremely important. Using mechanics as a base will make the other areas easier to learn. If a pitcher has sound mechanics, it allows him to maximize his ability. Good mechanics enhance balance and create better angles.

The first chapter describes with words and pictures, the pitching delivery. The teaching and learning process starts with the feet and moves upward, dealing with each body part. The pitching delivery is divided into three teaching areas. They are: (1) the feet to the knees, (2) the knees to the waist, and (3) the waist to the head. By starting with the feet and working up, the delivery is easier to understand. The learning process is done in phases. As each fundamental is learned, it paves the way for the next lesson.

Balance is one of the keys. The first phase of the teaching program deals with the push off and the stride. Developing good techniques at the push-off position gives the pitcher a sound starting point. Once that is accomplished, the proper stride is developed. Included in this teaching process is the first phase of the leg lift. All of this is taught in area one, the feet-to-knees area. Once this is learned, the pitcher is able to move on to area two.

The leg lift, elevation of the front hip, breaking of the hands and the leading of the front hip are taught in area two. As the pitcher moves to area two, he may experience difficulties with the push-off foot, the first phase of the leg lift, or the stride. If this happens, simply go back to the first area. Make sure this area is learned before moving on. Only when area one is successful, should the lessons in area two be taught. There is a sequence that should be followed. Once area two has been learned, the pitcher should move on to area three.

The throwing arm lift, the front arm, the chest, head, and follow-through make up area three. Again, make sure the pitcher is well schooled in the first two areas before teaching the third area. Each part of the delivery is important. If area one and two have been thoroughly understood, the work in area three will be much easier to accomplish.

A pitcher who goes through this learning system will understand the mechanics of pitching. He will develop a feeling for each body part and how it pertains to the throwing motion. This pitcher will be able to identify a flaw. He can move back and forth in the three areas and make corrections. With this knowledge he can identify and help a fellow pitcher.

The book will explain the necessity for sequential teaching patterns. It will demonstrate how to evaluate and pinpoint the various fundamentals of pitching. It shows how to develop teaching skills. The fundamentals of the pitching delivery are emphasized in several ways. Defining the fundamentals, showing how to teach the fundamentals, and the presentation of a step-by-step teaching method are valuable parts of the book. In addition, a pitching language and teaching tools are introduced.

Over the years, my observations tell me that the best teaching is done by those who simplify their messages. This will be done in the book by breaking down the pitching delivery and showing how to focus on these parts. A pitching language is developed that is clearly understood by both the coach and the pitcher. This speeds the learning process.

In order for success to be achieved in any field, the achiever must know what to do and how to do it. This is why we have identified the five areas of pitching. A good pitcher should excel in at least two of the five areas and be acceptable in the other three. Great pitchers are good in all five areas.

Good teaching requires a plan of attack. This includes a solid goal and the steps to attain the goal. With this in mind, it is necessary to develop a sequential pattern of teaching. Skill is taught. If the skill is learned, the lesson plan calls for advancement to a higher level. When success with a certain skill is not accomplished there should be a plan to back track, or to start over, or to try another method. In other words there should be a step-by-step plan of learning.

Most skills are learned through a number of repetitious drills. These drills should be illustrated clearly and their purpose should be defined. A good drill fits the skill level of the individual, and it is easily recalled. It should be made up of specific details, and should be challenging. Finally, the drill should help the pitcher attain success. The drills in the book qualify under the above definition.

Good teaching skills call for the coach to be specific and to deal with the job at hand. A good teacher does not beat around the bush. The following chapters will show

how to focus on particular details and demonstrate how to work in a persistent manner. This will keep the pitcher on track and focused keenly on the goals.

Teaching skills, like any other skills, are both learned and instinctive. Each of us has some instinct, but most skills are learned. There are specifics involved in teaching. For instance, timing, setting, motivation, and understanding are all to be considered. This book will show how these are used in the teaching of pitching.

Follow-through and getting on top of the ball are often discussed among pitching coaches. Pushing off of the rubber and releasing the ball too early are of equal concern. Developing rhythm is of interest to pitchers and pitching coaches. These are all covered in this book. Correct mechanics and common flaws are thoroughly discussed. Properly executing skills will be beneficial to the pitcher. Statements are often made about the skills involved in pitching. Sometimes the statements are factual but often they are not. We will carefully analyze the fundamentals of pitching.

This book is written in a simple and plain style that can be understood by pitchers and pitching coaches at all levels. Our particular aim will be to offer a pitching system. This will help those who are presently using the "hit and miss" system. The pitching system developed in this book can be used for pitchers from little league to retirement.

There are many ways in which this book is designed to help the pitcher and the pitching coach. It can serve as a guide to teaching and learning. By showing a step-by-step approach, motivation is enhanced. It introduces methods of communication that speed up learning. Pitchers and pitching coaches can learn how to pinpoint flaws and learn how to correct them. Finally, it will break pitching down into segments that can be learned and taught in a systematic manner.

The uniqueness of this book as a teaching tool is the manner in which the pitching delivery is segmented. The three teaching areas of the pitching delivery are clearly defined. There are specific starting points and goals set in each area. This makes teaching and learning easily attainable.

1

The Pitching Delivery

The pitching delivery is an extremely important factor to the pitcher and the pitching coach. Sound fundamentals of throwing should be one of a pitcher's most important goals. Using proper techniques will help the pitcher to get the most out of his pitches and allow him to throw longer with less effort. Seeking fundamentally sound body mechanics creates an exciting and thought-provoking adventure. Commitment to sound movements is a commitment to long-term pitching success with a minimum of injuries. Adhering to proper pitching mechanics enables the pitcher to maximize his abilities. Good mechanics allow a pitcher to properly align his body, to accelerate in rhythm, and to properly store and use his energy for the task at hand.

Improvements can be measured when a systematic approach is used in pursuing proper mechanics. Proper movements are concrete things. They can be taught, evaluated, and measured. The pitching delivery is not a mysterious accident that some attain and some do not. There are very specific and exact motions or acts which, if done correctly, cause the pitcher to throw more efficiently. It is quite possible that some pitchers will already do many parts of the delivery with proper mechanics. These are the gifted athletes. Others are not so fortunate. Proper mechanics can be learned, however. Even gifted athletes should take careful notes and remember what causes "good feel" and better efficiency.

Freedom of movement is a result of good mechanics. A consistent and fundamentally sound delivery reduces strain on the pitcher's arm and shoulder and minimizes injuries. This freedom creates an opportunity for the arm to fully accelerate through a full range of motion and to follow through without stopping or slowing down at the wrong time. A good delivery provides the pitcher with the angles, alignment, and rhythm to get the most out of his ability.

The pitching delivery is the base for all other pitching activities. Perfecting each pitch is much easier when the delivery is sound. Competing is done better and more consistently when the delivery is solid. Maintaining speed over a longer period is more prevalent with those pitchers who have good deliveries. Control is more available to the pitcher with good balance and good feel. And finally, pitchers with fundamentally correct deliveries are able to extend their careers. Operating from a strong base—the sound pitching delivery, the pitcher and the pitching coach will have a mutual point of reference. In this instance, when a problem is discovered, a return to the pitcher's "home base" and a careful check-up of the pitcher's mechanics provide the information necessary to take the corrective measures.

A well thought-out, mechanically sound delivery will provide a foundation for both the pitcher and the pitching coach. This foundation will not only serve to help correct problems, but it will become the dispensing point for all learning. The pitcher seeking to refine his skills will start here. The pitcher looking to maintain the skills he already has will have a point of reference.

The pitching delivery is the vehicle the pitcher uses to attain success. It is extremely important to build the vehicle for efficiency and endurance. Keeping the delivery in working order will require both physical and mental input. An intelligent pitcher never stops learning about his craft. When flaws are discovered, the smart pitcher tries to correct them. When the delivery is rhythmical and sound, the good pitcher works to maintain his good timing and rhythm.

Taking on a real study of any subject will require a solid commitment by those involved. Remember, an individual can pitch without using correct mechanics. If his ability level is high, his flaws may not result in failure. In other words, pitchers can get by, though they have major flaws in their delivery. Because of one or two special factors they have going for them, they may enjoy success. As a general rule, however, the flaws increase a pitcher's chances of being injured, or are magnified when the competition level rises. With this in mind, a pitcher should seek and attain long-term goals. The pitcher who commits to a good delivery will have a home base in which to explore and correct problems. As a result, his reliance on a hit and miss approach will be cut to a minimum. Since he has schooled himself in fundamentals, he will take the guesswork out of pitching. The pitcher who makes no study of his craft and strives on quick fixes often falls prey to illogical or spur-of-the-moment solutions.

Where do the pitcher and pitching coach begin? Since most beginning pitchers will have many flaws and much to learn, it is important to be selective and to begin at a point that will help his balance. This will automatically help some of the other aspects of his delivery. Often both the pitcher and the pitching coach attempt to correct too many flaws at one time. Learning motion skills not only requires understanding the motion, but the learner must also develop a feel and rhythm for the activity. Pitchers should focus on one part of the delivery at a time and should not be discouraged by the number of deficiencies or flaws in the beginning stages. It is important to simply begin with the most obvious problem and continue until the delivery is sound.

Both the pitcher and the pitching coach should begin by evaluating the total delivery and the skill level of the pitcher. Teaching units will be developed with the pitcher's skill level in mind. Coaches should prioritize on the basis of what is needed to give the pitcher better balance and good angles. This system calls for the pitcher to start with the feet. The pitching mechanics have been separated into three major areas: feet-to-knees, knees-to-waist, and waist-to-head.

Generally speaking, feet-to-knees is first on the priority list. However, from time to time, good judgment calls for the pitcher or the pitching coach to move out of the area of priority in order to reference other material that may help tie all the parts together. For example, it is necessary to talk about the separation and movement of the hands and the angle of the arm because these movements play a role in rhythm. It is important to remember that sound pitching is the final goal. Even though a system for teaching is being stressed, that system should not be so diligently followed that common sense or interest in the final goal is overlooked.

When a pitcher's interests involve an area of pitching not being emphasized, the coach should take advantage of this interest by connecting it to the lesson plan. It is also necessary to connect the three areas. So while emphasis remains in the priority area, it is often necessary to involve movements in one or both of the other areas. This is not an endorsement for skipping around indiscriminately. It is absolutely necessary for the pitcher and the coach to be committed to the lesson at hand and to stay focused on the area of priority.

There are specific fundamentals in all three areas that need to be developed. All of the movements in each of the areas should be considered and explored with vigor. Beginning with the feet and moving upward through the head will pay great dividends. Not only does this provide a sequence of teaching and learning, but it helps align the body and develops balance. In the process of developing balance, which starts with the feet, some of the fundamentals involving the upper body will also show improvement. Correct use of the feet will also pay dividends with establishing proper angles and sound direction.

Mechanics Feet-to-Knees

Starting Stance And Push-Off Foot

Establishing a solid base that allows for a consistent and forceful push-off is extremely important. The push-off foot should point straight ahead and be placed so the front cleat is over the front edge of the rubber. The back foot should be pointed straight ahead and should be behind the front foot and about even with the heel of that foot. The feet should be less than shoulder-width apart. The correct distance will be between 6 to 12 inches.

The straight-on position cuts down unnecessary movement. The pitcher who positions himself in a "side-saddle position" (one that is between a stretch and a wind-up) increases body movement and makes a consistent and balanced push-off and leg lift more difficult. The side-saddle position causes more movement, creates a need for adjustment to begin the leg lift, causes an adjustment to be made from side to side, and makes it more difficult to establish a consistent height in the leg lift. In other words, it is more difficult to gain and maintain balance from this position. On the other hand, the straight-on position simplifies the movements, keeps the pitcher aligned with the target, and also uses less energy. The straight-on position enhances balance.

At this point the pitcher should practice a slight rocking movement. This is the shift of weight from an unlocked front knee to a locked back knee. When the weight is shifted to the back leg, the head should not go backward beyond the push-off foot heel. This will keep the weight over the back leg and eliminate too much back-and-forth movement. This shift allows for the proper placement of the push-off foot on the pitching rubber without long or undue movements.

In the parallel position, the push-off foot is placed parallel to the rubber, toe ahead of heel. The back foot should be relatively close to the front foot.

There are two correct methods of foot push-off position from the rubber. One method is the placement of the foot at a 45-degree angle. This method calls for the front and inside cleats to drop down and over the edge of the rubber and the outside cleat and heel cleats to rest on top of the rubber. Most commonly used, though, is the parallel position. In this procedure, the push-off foot slides in front of the rubber but remains in contact with the rubber.

The key to foot placement is to push-off from the ball of the foot. A fundamental phrase that should be strictly followed is "to keep the toe ahead of the heel." When the toe moves behind the heel it shifts the weight toward the back of the foot, which creates a weak push-off position. When weight shifts to the back of the foot, balance is affected, which essentially results in pushing off with the heel of the foot. If the weight shifts to the heel as the leg is lifted, the pitcher is forced to make adjustments in balance at that point, making it more difficult to successfully pitch.

Although the push-off foot placement appears to be rather elementary, it is extremely important. When done correctly, it dramatically simplifies the weight transfer and the push off; when not followed, balance, push-off, and other pitching movements are affected. Often these factors are affected enough to interfere with control, stuff, velocity, and ultimately, confidence. Focusing on the weight transfer and push-off position will definitely pay off as the pitcher moves further into the delivery.

The short stroker style.

Short Stroker Or Long Stroker

What happens to the hands during the shift? There are basically two styles of arm action in the wind-up and two types in the stretch. We call one style "long strokers" and the other style "short strokers."

During the wind up, the short stroker simply starts with both hands in front of his body and makes a slight bouncing motion with the hands, stopping at the waist or slightly above the waist. The movement starts as the weight

The pitcher begins the wind-up by facing the target.

The pitcher's belly button should be toward the target. The elbow should be in and the hands together, slightly above the bill of the cap.

shifts to the back foot and should be completed when the push-off foot is placed in its proper position.

At this point, it is necessary to discuss the hands and what role they have in aquiring proper timing. The priority is still the feet-to-knees area. In either, the wind-up or the stretch, the hand movement should be consistent and should follow a path in the middle of the body and perpendicular to the ground. This action helps keep the parts compact, which creates a more consistent pivot. Many problems result when the hands do not follow this path, such as breaking, rhythm, wrapping the arm, and over pivoting.

Working with the hands deviates from the normal sequence of teaching, but it is necessary to establish the type of stroke the pitcher will use. This approach will help a pitcher develop the necessary rhythm as he progresses through the fundamentals. Coaches must simply establish the type of stroke with each pitcher, discuss it briefly with him, and move back to those movements pertaining to the area from the feet to the knees.

The weight shifts to the back foot, which is only a few inches back of the rubber. Some pitchers will need to take both hands to the back of their head. In some cases, this action helps with rhythm.

Leg Lift Stretch Position

The feet should be in a closed position. The front shoulders should be closed to the base runner at first base. Both knees should be "unlocked," with the back knee slightly turned in toward the hitter.

The space between the pitcher's feet is very important. The feet should be relatively close together. Ideally, the distance should be about six to eight inches and should not exceed the width of the shoulders. With the feet close together, the front foot travels less distance during the leg lift, resulting in a quicker release for the pitcher.

The pitcher should lift the heel of the front leg with the toe leaving the ground last and then pick the knee up in a line directly toward the right outside part of the chin. The leg lift is soft and relatively quiet. As the front foot is picked up, the toe should be relaxed and pointed toward the ground. The outside cleats of that foot should be slightly elevated and the toe should be kept away from the body. In fact, as the pitcher looks down the front leg, he should be able to see the thigh, the knee, and the tip of the toe.

The pitcher should lead with his front hip. The front foot is relaxed, the front hip elevated and the front shoulder closed.

With the shoulders relatively even and the belt line higher in front, the back knee should coil in toward the target.

The hands should drop softly with the fingers down as the knee drives down and inward.

Leg Lift from the Wind-Up

After rocking to a locked back knee with the hands at the top of the wind-up, the push-off foot is placed in one of the two positions mentioned earlier. When the weight shifts to the ball of the push-off foot, the lift of the stride foot is ready to commence. Similar to the stretch, the heel is picked up first and the toe is the last part of the foot to leave the ground. The toe should be kept pointed in a downward and relaxed position.

It is important to pick the leg up as opposed to slinging it up. A slinging action creates problems in consistency and rhythm because it is often difficult to control the height and direction of this type of movement. It is much easier to attain consistency because picking up the legs is a controlled movement.

Push-Off

A good push-off is essential to forceful throwing. However, the push-off is not solely done with the push-off foot. Much of the work is done by leading with the front hip and deactivating the bottom of the front leg during the first phases of the push or thrust.

If the weight is kept on the ball of the push-off foot and the drive knee is unlocked and turned slightly toward home plate, the elements for a sound push-off are in place.

Slight elevation of the front hip helps develop a pivoting action and helps create a rhythm of movement. The soft, minimal action helps build tremendous force in the arm and back side. From this position the front hip is driven down and toward the target. Pitchers should think of driving the front hip to the spot of the stride. Coordinating the front hip action with the push-off, the pitcher bends his back knee forward and toward the ground to create a powerful drive.

Deactivating the bottom of the stride leg during the early stages of the push-off was mentioned earlier. The reason for such emphasis is to maximize the driving action of the front hip and the push-off knee. To thrust with the bottom part of the stride leg is to break rhythm and timing. This thrusting action often uses energy too quickly and opens the body too soon.

Stride

As the stride leg knee comes to the top of the leg lift, the front hip should be slightly tilted above the back hip. The tilted front hip then starts forward ahead of the lower part of the stride leg.

Holding the bottom part of the leg back allows the front hip and the push-off leg to furnish the drive. The bottom part of the stride leg becomes very important as it

With relaxed hands, the pitcher leads with the front hip, and the back knee is unlocked.

The pitcher should keep his front leg up as long as possible, and keep striding with the front hip. The weight of the body creates a bind in the back of the knee that puts power in the push-off.

With shoulders closed, the hands break at the same place.

The hands should break softly, bottom out and move upward and outward.

lands. All of the weight and force is transferred onto the stride foot. How the foot lands will dramatically affect the throw. For instance, if the weight drifts to the outside of the front foot, balance will be hindered.

The foot should land in the same spot on each stride. When the stride is erratic, control is often inconsistent. Proper repetition with leg lift, push-off and stride will pay dividends. The pitcher should practice until he has control over the body parts controlling the stride.

After the initial contact with the ball of the foot, the remainder of the foot glides into contact with the ground, providing a solid base. Most of the weight is still on the ball of the foot, but certainly the entire foot should act as the foundation. There should be no spinning or rolling of the stride foot. Proper weight shift means good balance. Good balance leads to a stable and solid landing.

Many pitchers become overactive with the stride leg. Often this action causes a pitcher's weight to shift violently to the outside of the stride foot, or it causes a breakdown in his rhythm. It is extremely important for the pitcher to control the movement and timing of his stride leg.

The front toe is down and the foot is slightly closed. The pitcher should stride to the inside. The front knee is held inward and the hand is on the inside of the front foot.

The front knee is inward and the inside of the front knee should be inside the front foot.

The front knee is bent and "rides in," while the weight is on the inside of the front foot. The front foot remains stable.

Diligent work with the push-off, leg lift and stride will definitely pay dividends. Correct execution of fundamentals in each of these movements will provide a primary pitching foundation. Obviously, improvements in balance and timing will be enhanced, but many other parts of the delivery will start to take better shape as the result of work on these movements.

Knees-to-Waist Mechanics

In either the stretch or the wind-up, the pitcher should be aware of how the knees play a part in push-off, stride and balance. Locked knees create a stiff, non-powerful and awkward delivery. Unlocked knees deliver power and enhance both balance and freedom of movement. Therefore, emphasis should be placed on the delivery flowing from a bent back leg to a bent front leg.

The push-off leg starts to bend as the foot is placed on the rubber. As the foot is set, the weight should move slightly forward to the ball of the foot with the knee bent and pointed inward. This action allows the weight of the body to cause a natural drop, which provides a good position to start the push-off.

The push-off knee remains pointed inward as the stride knee is brought up and back into the coil or push-off position. The front knee should be lifted to a height relative to the timing and body style of each pitcher. For the sake of a starting point, the belt can be used as a general marker. Although such a distance is an acceptable guide for a relatively normal leg lift, it is not an exact or correct height for every pitcher. The most important factor is to develop consistency in the height of the leg lift.

The knee of the stride leg should be bent and inside the stride foot. Weight should be on the inside ball of the foot, with the toe slightly closed.

The stride foot should be slightly pigeon-toed, and the knee of the stride leg and the inside of the stride foot are bent.

The knee should be lifted to this consistent height and toward the throwing arm side of the chin. A slight holding pattern in this position as the front hip starts the stride is important. Even a slight lift as the front hip starts forward will offer a helpful timing pattern for some pitchers.

Mechanics At The Waist

At the top of the leg lift, the belt line should be slightly tilted with the lead hip higher than the back hip. This alignment helps to start the driving action with the front hip. If the belt line is straight, the pitcher generally drops through the first part of the push. This approach causes problems in timing and leads to difficulties for the pitcher in raising his arm into a throwing position.

The hands should separate at or near the waist. The separation, or breaking point, of the hands should be executed at the same place on each throw. The breaking point should be the same in the stretch as it is in the wind-up. Separation of hands, leg lift, and any other movement make up the total rhythm package. Inconsistencies with any of these movements lead to problems in rhythm.

Similar to the leg lift, the belt line for hand separation is simply a general guideline. Adjustments must be made with each pitcher to accommodate size, technique and feel. The adjustment area should be from slightly above the belt line to the crotch area.

Before the hand separation takes place, the hands should travel a path together in a straight line. This path should lead directly in front of and at the vertical midline of the body, and should be perpendicular to the ground. Keeping the hands at this midline helps to compact the coiling action. Moving the hands away from this midline tends to drift the pitcher away from a solid pivot by bending his body parts to that position in segments.

The hands should be held in comfortable position that is not too close or too far away from the body. A general guideline is to have a pitcher keep his elbows resting comfortably on or touching the pads above the waist. The hands remain in front of the body even as the pivot is executed. They will break as the driving action begins. As the throwing hand moves down and back to the ready position, the glove (hand) will often trail the throwing hand for a few inches. This breaking action should be soft and relaxed. Because power is being built at this point, it should not be expended yet. Relaxing or softening this separation will allow the hands to separate, drop, and start a natural movement back and up. A harsh movement either down or back at this point breaks the natural flow and forces the pitcher to bring his hands back to a proper throwing position.

To illustrate this point, the pitcher can simply stand in a stretch position, raise his hands about three inches and let them drop softly down the vertical midline until they bottom out. The hands will drop, separate and start back up again. Next, he will take the same stretch position with his hands in front, raising them about three inches. This time he should make a quick and forceful movement with the throwing hand down and back to prepare for the throw. Pitchers will find it takes a longer time to raise the arm. This mistake is repeated over and over with many pitchers in an attempt to throw harder, or get rid of the ball quicker.

As the hands separate, the throwing hand should leave the glove with the fingers pointing toward the ground. The fingers should remain in that position as the arm moves down, back and then up into throwing position.

Even as the hand is moving up into the throwing position, the fingers should remain pointing toward the ground. This requirement keeps the wrist in a "forward" or "cocked" position that allows for maximum wrist snap and proper extension. This action is similar to reaching back from a pivot position, picking a ball up from a batting "T" and raising the ball to throwing position with the fingers pointing toward the top of the batting "T."

Waist-Through-the-Head Mechanics

Working with the top half of the body is very critical. Some of the mechanics have already been improved if diligent and forceful effort have been made with work on the feet, knees and waist areas. A coach should keep in mind, however, that overemphasizing the upper parts of the body without first establishing a sound foundation of the lower body is not very wise. For example, a pitcher who gives undue attention to the top half of his body without proper work on his feet may suffer arm injuries and have difficulty developing balance and rhythm.

The Front Arm

As the hands separate, the front arm will drop down the vertical midline with the back arm and start to reach out. This movement should be a soft maneuver. Overactivity with the front arm opens the body too soon, breaks a sound rhythm package and often leads to the destruction of control and loss of power. The front arm is a guide arm. It is the meter or measuring device for distance and speed. It is the sight guide or the direction finder. It is also a balance lever and motion control monitor.

Since the front arm is so important to the throwing delivery, a good deal of work and understanding should be explored in this area. Overemphasis or overzealous attention without proper understanding may create additional and very serious problems. On the other hand, giving the front arm less than the work it needs is an equally unsound approach.

With a forward wrist, the fingertips point downward and the front arm reaches out toward the target.

The front arm is soft and the back of the glove is to the target. The ball should be brought to a height above the head.

The chest is barreled, the front arm pulls in and the chin stays up.

Often a lecturer on pitching will make a comment that "the front arm doesn't throw the ball, therefore why worry about it?" This statement makes about as much sense as saying "the legs don't throw the ball, so why worry about them?" Ignorance has never been a partner with learning. Without question, the front arm can play a critical role in proper delivery. On the other hand, if a pitcher does not know what to do with his front arm and is unwilling to learn, he should just throw, letting the front arm do whatever feels natural. Coaches should also remember not to experiment with the front arm or overanalyze its movement. Overemphasis or foolhardy use of the front arm may result in rhythm and control problems.

The front arm action will vary according to the build, size, and ability of each pitcher. There are some basic elements common to all pitchers and to the pitching delivery.

After both hands bottom out, they begin to start outward and upward into the throwing position. The front arm drops downward, then begins to come up and reach out toward the target.

As a general rule, the front arm will reach out farther when throwing harder or longer. A clear example can be seen by watching a shortstop throw from the outfield to home plate on a relay throw. The height and length of the front arm when the shortstop makes a short throw to first base from a position on the infield grass will be shorter.

Attention should also be paid to the height of the front arm. For example, an outfielder who is throwing 280 or 300 feet will raise the front arm higher in order to gauge and aim for the distance. He is adjusting his body for the flight trajectory of the ball. The pitcher must throw the ball as hard as the outfielder but his target is lower and much closer. He must adjust the height of his front arm to correlate with the type of throw to be made. Basically, the glove of the pitcher should not be raised higher than the chin.

The action of the front arm is not harsh. It is very much a controlled maneuver. The best term to use in describing the activity of the front arm is to "place it out and bring it in." Following this advice will help the pitcher train himself to control and guide the path and timing of those movements. If allowed to relax, the front arm will get in sync with the throwing arm and greatly aid in almost every aspect of throwing.

There are basically two methods used to place the front arm out. One approach calls for the pitcher to use the back of his glove facing the hitter as it reaches toward the target. The other method entails reaching toward the hitter with the palm of the pitcher's glove toward the batter. It really does not matter which method is used, as long as the arm follows a correct route.

The back of the glove should face the target and the thumb should be up.

The thumb then moves down in a palm-out position.

The palm toward the hitter method is advocated by many pitching coaches and is used by many pitchers. After reaching out with the palm toward the hitter, the pitcher should turn his palm up and should place his arm in a position to be drawn back in close to the body. Often this method causes the glove to drop too low and causes a sweeping action. This action moves the front arm to a position which is much too far to the side, thereby forcing the delivery to open prematurely and causing the pitcher's front side to open too far.

The back of the glove to the target method appears to be an easier and more functional approach. The back of the glove is placed out toward the target. When it reaches the proper extension, it is ready to open and help the throwing arm get the maximum freedom, speed and extension. The pitcher simply turns the palm up, raises the heel of the hand higher than the fingers, and brings the arm toward the chest, letting the elbow brush the fat pad above the hip. This action should continue until the throw is completed. The elbow of the front arm should be visible from the home plate area. It will appear as a chicken wing and will show just above the back of the pitcher at the completion of the follow-through.

The route the front arm travels should coincide with the angle of the throwing arm. The overhand delivery calls for the palm of the glove hand to be facing directly upward at the extension point and drawn back in close to the body. Should the delivery be a three-quarter motion, the palm of the throwing hand will face upward as much as the palm of the glove hand and should relate to the three-quarter arm action. A side-arm pitcher should turn the hand even less. The glove hand will turn only to point the thumb upward, causing the palm to face toward the side of the body.

The correlation between the palm of the pitching hand and the palm of the glove hand is relevant. When drawing the glove hand in toward the side of the body, the palm of that hand should be directly facing the palm of the throwing hand. Following this pattern, the arms will be moving in the same plane.

Rhythm, energy, and function are dramatically curtailed if the front arm is routed for a different delivery than the throwing arm. Many pitchers pay little or no attention to this factor. As a result, their effectiveness is often minimized and, in many cases, their careers are shortened.

Regardless of the delivery method, the front arm should be brought back in toward the chest and kept close to the side as it completes its route. This action will help keep the shoulders, chest, and head in a balanced and forceful position.

The eyes should be parallel to the ground and toward the target. The bottom of the chin should be parallel to the ground and the head should be directly in line with the target. The right-handed pitcher will follow a right to left action with the throwing arm, and the elbow should finish to the outside of the thigh.

The Chest

The chest should turn, or coil, with the front leg. Care should be taken to create a springing action with the entire body. The chest and the head should remain relatively straight as they are brought directly over the ball of the push-off foot.

As the front hip strides down and toward the target, the top part of the body stays closed. The feeling at this point is that of holding the top back while striding forward with the front hip.

The chest will begin to follow the stride. Because the front arm opens the body, the forceful action of the throwing arm is then brought into play with the help of the chest. Reaching out to the target with the chest will greatly increase the length of the throwing lever and allow unrestricted freedom of movement.

The elbow should be up and the chest should be out. The eyes move to the target and the front arm stays close to the side.

The eyes should stay level, the chin stays up and the front elbow pulls back close to the target.

All forces should be directed toward the target. Any part of the delivery which takes a different route interferes with the individual pitch. In order for the chest to be directed toward the target, both breasts should stay parallel to the ground. The back should be arched, and the chest should assume a barrel-like status. There should be a feeling of throwing the breasts to the target.

The chest remains barreled and continues out in front. The bottom of the barreled chest should extend and come down and squeeze against the top of the stride leg thigh. At this point, the throwing arm is free and well to the outside of and free from the stride-leg knee and thigh. Following this pattern, the energy supplied for the throw is delivered directly over the thigh.

A common mistake made by some pitchers is to throw with a concave chest. If the chest is not barreled, the throwing motion will be drastically restricted. The concave position shortens the throwing arm, brings the throwing arm to an abrupt stop at the end of the throw, and forces part of the body to be directed away from the target. In effect, a concave chest will result in a recoiling action. This action causes injuries and loss of rhythm. Extra energy is used at a very fast rate when the pitching delivery is not rhythmic. Injuries and poor results often follow.

The arm follows a right-to-left action and the throwing-arm shoulder moves toward the target. The back arm is in a "chicken wing" position. The pitcher should keep his chin up and his eyes to the target.

The pitcher should reach to the target with a barrel chest.

During both the coiling action and the driving action, the shoulders should be relatively parallel to the ground. The back shoulder may drop and the front shoulder may lift slightly, but neither shoulder should move significantly away from this flat position. If there is an appreciable drop in the back shoulder or a dramatic lift of the front shoulder, the direction of the throw will not correlate with the desired target. A great deal of compensation needs to be made in order to deliver the ball to home plate. Again, extra energy, risk of injury, and poor results often accompany this approach.

Pivoting the shoulders and timing their closing and opening with the hip are essential to good pitching as well. A curveball is often left hanging high and over the plate because the shoulders open too soon. The fastball is occasionally high because the shoulders opened too soon. Often the ball does not break, or it continues on a course to the outside of the pitcher's arm. This result is caused by overpivoting the shoulders.

The shoulders should be kept level and closed until the throwing arm starts forward. This action will allow them to be placed in the proper direction when the front arm rolls over and is drawn in towards the body. This approach also keeps all body parts moving toward the target and uses energy more efficiently.

Chin

"Keeping the chin up" is not only a positive mental statement, but it is also a physically correct statement. Keeping the chin up allows the chest to extend toward the target. "Chin up" means to keep the bottom of the chin parallel to the ground as the drive starts toward the plate. It is also a good idea to think in terms of sticking the chin out toward the target. Where the head goes, the rest of the body will follow. This action simply helps align the body parts in the proper direction. A chin up and out also helps the chest and arm reach forward, creating a much longer lever. When the arm moves in a longer arc, more power and freedom of movement are generated.

Eyes

The eyes lead the way to the target. They should be parallel to the ground and thrown out toward the target. In fact, a practice of making the eyes bigger and "bugging them out," or taking them right into the catcher's mitt is a good practice for many pitchers. This practice not only serves as a reminder to keep the eyes level while helping improve the alignment of the body parts to the target, but it also provides the pitcher with a method to pinpoint the target.

Level eyes afford a better visual delivery service for the pitcher. Tilting the head throws the eyes out of their proper alignment, thereby affecting mechanics and the visual image. Tilting the head also creates improper angles, increasing the chance of injury while negatively affecting control and velocity.

Throwing Arm

Leverage, power and flexibility are words closely related to actions concerning the pitching arm. How the arm is used will complement or hinder each of these factors. To properly gain the best advantage, the pitching arm should go through a range of motion that maximizes leverage, produces the greatest power and aids flexibility.

As the hands separate, the throwing arm should drop down, bottom out, reach back, and then move upward into a throwing position quickly. It is extremely important to come out of the glove softly since a soft movement allows the arm to drop, reach back, and start up quickly.

A harsh, hard movement at separation causes a quick movement downward but a slow movement upward. The quick movement down generally creates a stop, or complete change of direction, thus slowing the total action. The softer action allows for

With the chest out, the knees should point inward. Weight should be on the ball of the foot, with the elbow inward. The elbow is at shoulder height, with the front arm close to the body. The glove should brush the side and the chin should stay up.

As the arm extends toward the target, it pulls right to left for a right-handed pitcher. The arm extends through and finishes on the outside of the front thigh. The front knee should be bent and ride in during delivery.

a flowing natural motion. To best illustrate this, coaches should have a pitcher simply stand in a stretch position, bounce his hands up slightly, and drop them softly. He should let his hands separate at the bottom. They will move apart in opposite directions and begin to move upward. Next, he should take the same stance and move his hands down harshly or quickly. His hands will stop at the bottom. Before the hands are brought outward or upward, another action must be started. The soft, relaxed movement allows the hands to change direction at the bottom more easily. In fact, the hands will naturally start out and up at the break if the movement is not harsh.

Arm Action and Follow-Through

The fingers should remain on top of the ball as the ball is brought out of the glove. Upon separation, the back of the thumb will face the side of the leg. As the hand reaches back, the wrist rotates outward, placing the back of the thumb facing away from the side of the leg. The fingers will still remain on top of the ball with the fingertips pointing toward the ground. This will place the hand in a flexible and cocked position, providing the arm quick access to the best throwing position.

The thumb should be in as the hand drops down to the bottoming out point. The fingertips should point toward the ground.

As the ball is lifted to throw, the fingertips should continue to point down. The thumb should turn toward the outside as the hand starts to move up into the throwing position.

It is important for the arm to be in a proper throwing position quickly. It is also necessary for the ball to be at a height above the head when the stride foot lands. At this height, the hand has the best opportunity to get on top of the ball and create a downward action to the throw. Leverage, arm extension and freedom of movement are maximized from this position. Power directed toward the target is best delivered from this position.

The fingertips point down until the arm lift is complete. The wrist should be forward and relaxed, and the ball should be higher than the head.

The ball should be above the head when the stride foot contacts the ground. The elbow should be at a right angle.

If the hand is not raised to a height above the head as the stride foot lands, many problems may follow. The most common problem is that of tilting the head to the opposite side of the throwing arm to allow that arm to move through a range of motion. This practice appears to move the arm up and into the throwing position. What really happens is a cheating action which shortens the arc and throws the head, front shoulder, chest and sight out of alignment. These parts should all be aligned directly toward the target if maximum power, flexibility and leverage are to be possible.

Shortly after the stride, the arm will move into a right angle. From there it is ready to drive forward with tremendous acceleration, while gaining maximum extension and power. At this right angle, the wrist is in a forward position.

As the elbow leads the way, the wrist drops to a backward or laid-back position. The arm continues with the wrist laid back as long as possible or until the arm reaches full extension toward the target. At this point, the fingers snap forward through the ball, creating even greater extension. The pitcher should have a feeling of his fingers leaving his hand and following the ball for a few inches.

The wrist starts to turn. The thumb begins to turn in toward the head. The elbows should be at approximately shoulder height.

The head should be out in front, and the arm moving with a right-to-left action (for a right-handed pitcher).

The elbow should be up, the knee in and bent, and the foot pigeon-toed.

The hand continues to make a long arc as it travels right to left (for a right-handed pitcher), finishing free and to the left of the stride knee. Often a pitcher will complain of hitting his arm on his knee. If proper mechanics are executed, the arm will be clearly away from the knee. The stride knee should be inside the stride toe.

The arm should follow-through and come to a natural finish with the hand relaxed. Abrupt stops, jerky motions and quick, unusual changes in direction are counterproductive to an efficient throwing motion.

The Feet at the Follow-Through

The stride foot should remain stable during the follow-through. The push-off knee will drive downward and toward the target for a short distance. Next, the foot leaves the rubber after a good forceful push and moves slightly upward and outward. It will then form a circle before coming to the ground in an area parallel to and a few inches greater than shoulder width from the stride foot. The greater the force directed to the throw, the further the push-off foot will finish ahead of the parallel position. It is important to finish with balance. An unbalanced finishing position indicates a problem with mechanics.

The arm should finish on the outside thigh, and the left arm pulls through with a "chicken wing" look. The pitcher should also keep his head up.

To gain a little extra force and freedom while allowing the range of motion to be fully completed, the push-off heel should turn over after landing. This action allows the front side to pull in and helps the throwing arm to move through an arc a few more inches. This result provides unrestricted freedom of movement, allowing energy to be released through the body without the occurrence of back lashing or recoiling.

Fielding Position

The throw should be finished before the pitcher assumes a fielding position. Pitchers who worry about fielding before the delivery is completed often are forced to field more balls than the pitcher who finishes each throw. If the pitcher's mechanics are sound, he will have finished close to a fielding position. Basically, he will need to square up with both feet in a parallel position, his weight on the balls of the feet, and his knees unlocked. His hands should be up and in front of the chest, with the thumbs facing inward and slightly upward, and the total mind and body in a ready position.

Summary

Working from the ground up to teach the mechanics of pitching is both simple and sound. It provides an organized and systematic approach to teaching the basic fundamental of pitching. The feet provide balance and direction. A concerted effort in establishing a consistent and sound push-off foot and stride foot gives the pitcher a good foundation.

Focusing on the three basic areas of mechanics gives the pitcher and pitching coach specific points of reference from which to work. As a result, this approach simplifies the learning process. Establishing a sound base and working from the ground up, the mechanics of pitching can be taught in sequence.

2

Stretch Position

The basic reason a pitcher assumes the stretch position is to hold runners close to the bases. Not only does a sound fundamental stretch position help reduce stolen bases, it also keeps runners from breaking up double plays, reduces the opportunity for them to take an extra base, decreases their chance of scoring from second base on a base hit, increases the opportunity for the defense to get a force out, and serves as the greatest weapon for defusing the offensive bunting game. A pitcher who has poise and concentration while holding runners on base proves to be a tremendous asset to his team. Controlling the runner is a key ingredient to effectively defending the opposition's offense.

Some relief pitchers choose to throw from the stretch position even with no one on base. This practice has merit if the pitcher has better control and power from that position since it does not require as much preliminary movement. Therefore, it may be wise for some pitchers to adopt this less complicated position.

Since much of the game is played with men on base, it is highly recommended that the pitcher practice from the stretch position approximately fifty percent of the time. During each bullpen workout, he should alternate between the wind-up and the stretch positions. He should not throw half of the drill before changing to the stretch position. Shifting back and forth will more closely resemble the actual game conditions.

The stretch position also offers a less complicated set of beginning movements than the wind-up. Therefore, when drilling on specific details, the pitcher may be better served by employing the stretch for those purposes. By using the stretch on an elementary movement, the maneuver is simplified while the pitcher becomes accustomed to its use. This familiarity will help him gain poise and confidence in future situations.

Generally, pitchers who have dramatic differences between the stretch and the wind-up are not equally successful from both positions. It is recommended that the same fundamentals be stressed, regardless of the starting position. Adjustments made to accommodate quickness to the plate should not be major. If a major change is necessary to attain success in the stretch, then that same change should be made in the wind-up.

The glide step has become a very popular move with some pitchers. This step nearly eliminates the leg lift and is usually a very different motion than the particular pitcher uses from his wind-up. While the glide step has its place, it should only be used under certain circumstances. There are more conventional methods for successfully speeding up the motion. If there is a highly successful base stealer in a very favorable base-stealing situation, the glide step would be an acceptable choice, provided its use did not decrease the pitcher's effectiveness. A dramatic change with leg lift often affects timing, push-off, and hip action. There is also much more reliance on the arm, meaning the pitcher should not use this as a standard stretch position move.

The pitcher should be able to deliver the ball to home plate within 1.3 seconds. The time begins with the first movement by the pitcher and stops when the ball touches the catcher's mitt or contacts the bat. Corrections or adjustments in the delivery should not only accommodate the quickness from the stretch but must also benefit the total motion.

If the speed to home plate is too slow from the stretch position, the pitcher's mental approach should be examined. Coaches should think about speeding the motion by letting the pitcher mentally compute a quicker action. It is not uncommon to take 1/10 to 2/10 of a second off the original time by this process. The same mental computation should be used from the wind-up in order to keep the rhythm similar in both starting positions.

The next step is to quicken the physical actions. Because a relaxed body moves faster than a tense body, the pitcher should soften the separation of the hands and work to get his arm up faster. Movements should be coordinated with those of the stride leg. By relaxing the stride leg, the pitcher can attempt to quicken its movement to match the timing of the throwing arm. Timing changes should be incorporated into the wind-up position, as well.

If the time to home plate is still not satisfactory, previous practices can be continued with consideration now being given to lowering the leg lift. It is recommended that adjustments be made in small increments. Lowering the leg lift by two or three inches should help speed the delivery to home plate. With corrections in the leg lift, the original timing will also be disrupted and may cause problems in other areas. This point needs to be remembered as corrections are being made.

In one or more of the three adjustments in the preceding paragraphs, the pitcher will find results in improving his delivery to home plate. He must be able to retain power, stuff and control from the stretch position.

Feet

The stretch position offers obvious differences from the wind-up position: the starting position, and concentration shifting from holding the runner to successfully pitching to the hitter. All other movements in the delivery should be similar, regardless of the starting position. Keeping all movements similar will keep mechanical problems to a minimum.

The push-off foot is set at either a 45-degree angle (Figure 2-1) or a parallel position (Figure 2-2), with the toe ahead of the heel in either foot-position method. The feet should be approximately six to eight inches apart, with preference going to the lesser distance and the front foot closer to the hitter. The feet should never be farther than shoulder-width apart because when the feet are too far apart, it takes longer to execute the leg lift and to properly coil to throw.

Figure 2-1. The 45-degree angle.

Figure 2-2. The parallel position.

If the pitcher has difficulty picking up (i.e., seeing), the runner from the closed position, he should open the stride foot toe but keep the foot closed in relation to the push-off foot. Opening the entire front side will place the stride foot further from the pivot position, creating much the same problem that a wide stance presents.

Knees

Both knees should be unlocked with the push-off knee pointed slightly toward the hitter. This will help initiate a proper drive and push-off position. Unlocking means a slight bend at the knees. The pitcher should not squat or flex the knees too much during the stretch position. Squatting breeds tension, and tight legs do not push-off or stride well.

The leg lift, or height of the knee raise, should be similar to leg lift in the wind-up. Some pitchers lower the lift slightly when pitching with runners on base. The variation should be slight, otherwise the pitcher is dealing with two completely different motions. To vary the leg lift is to vary the rhythm. Even though some pitchers are capable of succeeding with this practice, it is not fundamentally sound.

Waist

The movements at the waist area should resemble those in the wind-up. The hands should separate as they do with no one on base.

Occasionally pitchers will tend to over-pivot from the stretch. This practice, of course, should be avoided. Over-pivoting creates poor throwing angles and interferes with rhythm.

In establishing a stretch position, the elbows should stay close to the body, coming to rest over the oblique muscle group on each side of the body (Figures 2-3 to 2-6). The back of the glove should face the hitter, with the throwing hand hidden in the glove. The glove, at the set position, should be somewhere between the letters on the jersey and the crotch area. Each pitcher should locate his own set position and that spot should remain constant. The belt area serves this function for most pitchers.

Tightness should be avoided. Hands held too close to the body create a cramped and uncomfortable feeling. Hands too far in front of the body give the feeling of reaching or stretching out. The set position should allow for relaxation, mobility and consistency.

Figure 2-3. The pitcher begins the stretch position with his hands relaxed, and not too close to the body.

Figure 2-4. The long stroker's hands go high and then back down.

Figure 2-5. The short stroker's hands move up slightly and then settle at a set position.

Figure 2-6. The front shoulder should be closed. The front foot should be closed and the feet should not be too far apart.

Shoulders

It is important to keep the front shoulder closed (Figure 2-6). An open front shoulder slows the pitcher's action to home plate. If the front shoulder starts in an open position, the pitcher must throw to the plate when the shoulder begins to close. It must close to be in proper throwing motion. An open shoulder must travel farther to activate a throw than a closed shoulder. A closed shoulder with a closed stride leg economizes movement and truly quickens the motion to home plate.

Holding Runners on Base

Picking a runner off a base is only one of the many reasons for throwing to an occupied base. Often a quick pick-off move shortens the lead of a runner or changes the strategy of the opposition. A complete stretch system executed well by the pitcher will force the opposition to operate with care. Refined work from the stretch will lead to a better defense of the bunt, the hit-and-run, and the steal. In addition, it will also create more force outs and minimize runners taking an extra base.

Looks

Along with the importance of the time it takes the pitcher to deliver the ball to home plate, another variable which can be used to aid the pitcher is the number of looks he gives the runner before throwing. Often a runner times the looks of a particular pitcher. If the pitcher has a pattern, the runner is able to steal almost at will. A good pitcher will vary the number and kind of looks he gives a baserunner, looking at the base runner one or more times before making a delivery. Before each throw, the pitcher should make sure there is some difference in looks. Often, a different way of looking, and a difference in the length of time before each delivery are other ways of disrupting the runner's timing. Moving the chin from side to side, or up and down, along with variation of counts or timing will add further complications for the base runner to consider.

Timing

Nothing can really happen until the pitcher throws the ball. Accordingly, a pitcher should remember that he controls the tempo and establishes the timing of each play. It is the job of the pitcher to control the timing of the runner. To do this he should vary the amount of time before delivering the pitch from the stretch position. By delivering the ball quickly after coming to a set position, the pitcher may eliminate the opportunity for the runner to establish a good lead. Alternating from set-and-throw to delivery of one, two, or three counts before the pitch will prevent the runner from accurately timing the pitcher's move.

Different Moves to First Base

No stretch position can be complete without sound methods of delivering the ball to first base. The pitcher should have at least two types of moves—a set-up move and a competitive move. It is not recommended to throw just for the sake of throwing. The throw should be made for the purpose of picking the runner off or forcing him to concede ground.

There are several effective and fundamentally sound pick-off moves. The right-handed pitcher does not have the benefit of looking directly at runners like the left-hander does, but this does not mean a right-hander cannot be as effective.

Short Stroker (Right-Handed Pitcher)

The pitcher who uses the short stroke method finds his deception through the quickness and cleverness in his moves to first base. This method calls for simply bringing the hands together at the set position, with little or no preliminary motion.

The short stroke stretch minimizes excessive movements, thereby letting the pitcher concentrate on the essential movements. Generally, a pitcher who is extremely wild will profit from this method. On the other hand, because of its simplicity and its effect of eliminating some preliminary movement, any pitcher may find it profitable.

The left-hander is also advised to use this procedure in most situations. The longer preliminary movement usually involves extra activity, which pays little dividend because it is in full view of the runner on first base. The left-hander will find greater dividends in developing a solid move to first or to home plate from the simple set position.

Spin Turn

The spin turn is the most common of all turns. It requires the pitcher to lift his heel enough to clear the rubber, then spin on the ball of the push-off foot and throw. Keeping the shoulders closed until the stride foot is ready to open and stride toward first is one of the keys to a successful move.

Having the hand up and in the throwing position during the spin turn is another key to achieving success. The hands should move in the same pattern as when throwing to home plate. Many pitchers move their hands in a different manner on a pick-off move. A good base runner will discover the difference very quickly.

Pitchers should always look home before each move and alternate between looking home and throwing to first base and looking home and throwing to home plate. This practice will eliminate one of the baserunner's clues. Often pitchers will form a habit of looking to one particular place and then throwing to the other. While the baserunner is looking for clues, it is up to the pitcher to not give him any.

Jump Turn

On a jump turn, the move is executed by a slight jump and a turn in the air which allows the pitcher to land in a stride position toward the base he is throwing. A jump turn to first base involves a quarter-turn. The same move to second base requires a half-turn. Even though it is a legal move, a balk may be called if there is an exaggerated movement before the turn is executed. Excessive movement with the hands, shoulders, and knees may result in the calling of a balk from any type of move.

To make the jump turn effective, the pitcher must learn to be quick and accurate. To accommodate this quickness and accuracy, the arm lift during the jump is absolutely essential. The hand should be ready to throw to the base as soon as the push-off foot touches the ground.

Step Off-Pause-Throw

To stop the baserunner's lead or disrupt his timing, the pitcher may choose one of his best options—stepping off the rubber. From this position the pitcher is considered an infielder. Since the pitcher is allowed to throw from this position without restrictions, the runner is forced to take a step or two back or return to the base.

Occasionally, a runner will keep his extended lead or take a step back and hold his ground. A good counter move for the pitcher is to step off the rubber, pause one second, then turn quickly and attempt a pick-off to first base. This move will serve to either pick-off the runner or give him cause to shorten his lead.

Barr Move

Throwing to first base without stepping in that direction is a balk move. However, if the back foot is off the rubber, there are no restrictions.

Jim Barr, a former pitcher with the San Francisco Giants, used a unique move during his major league career. Instead of stepping directly back to clear the rubber, Barr would step back toward third base (RHP). This move puts a pitcher's feet closer to a stride position toward first base. From this position, the toe of the stride foot is lifted, and a spin turn is used. This move entails a regular spin move with the push-off foot and a pivot off the heel of the front foot. This action is legal only when the push-off foot is off the rubber and in back of it. While Barr's method offers a good supplemental move, it is not meant to be a primary move.

Move from Left-Handed Pitcher

Some baserunners claim stealing is easier to execute against a left-hander than against a right-hander. This may be true, but it certainly should not be the case. The left-hander has a great advantage because he is looking directly at the runner, and has the choice of appearing to start his move toward home before throwing to first base.

An average or poor move is easy to read, but when a left-hander refines his activities to home plate and to first base, it becomes extremely difficult to run on him. Often the base runner is forced to break on the pitcher's first move. This situation absolutely works in the pitcher's favor.

The time from the pitcher's first movement to the catcher's mitt is not as significant for the left-hander if he uses his motion as the major deterrent to running. A pitcher with this motion either has an extremely quick throw to first base, or pauses and decoys the runner before throwing to home plate. If he does not excel in one of these areas, the quickness to home plate is as significant for a left-hander as it is for the right-hander.

Observations by coaches over the years have indicated that left-handers with good moves do exactly the same thing with their heads prior to each pitch, whether throwing to first or throwing to the plate. The looks from each pitcher may differ in number or style, but the last look before either throwing to first base or to home plate must be consistent. Left-handers also have the same arm action at the beginning of each pitch—the lead hip appearing to start home plate. In addition, left-handers possess a quick change of direction when throwing to first base. Essentially, a good move economizes activity and emphasizes simplicity.

The left-hander should give the runner at least two different looks from a timing point of view. These looks should consist of a set-up move, which is good enough to hold the average runner close, and a best move, which is a pick-off move or a move that controls the runner's lead. The point to be emphasized is that the left-handed pitcher should control the baserunner.

Step-Off and Throw

One move made by left-handers is to step back off the rubber with the push-off foot and make a quick throw to first base. This move is usually a side-arm throw and should be used as a supplementary or surprise move. It should not be used as a primary means of holding a runner close to the base. Pitchers who use this procedure generally do not possess a good standard move. Since this move is from a different arm angle and from an odd position, care should be taken to prevent injuries.

Summary

Pitchers should strive to become complete pitchers. Moving from the stretch to the wind-up should not reduce or enhance success. To win, the pitcher is required to meet the challenges from each position. To become proficient, the pitcher must work on each stance and gain confidence in dealing with all situations regardless of starting position. Lack of concern and careless practice habits are the main reasons for deficiencies in these areas. Pitchers should spend half of the practice time from the stretch position and work to refine both the move to first base and the move to home plate.

3

A System of Teaching Pitching Mechanics

In teaching a physical activity, it is necessary to create a system that is easily understood, is basically sound, has fundamentals that are recognizable to the students and if followed, will show results.

An athlete's body is a finely tuned instrument used to carry out intricate maneuvers designed by the mind in order to attain success in a game or an activity. To perform these maneuvers consistently, practice and repetition are needed. Even simple activities require repetitive practice in order to attain sound results. As an athlete's skill level rises, the demand for repetition will also increase.

The pitcher is required to heighten his skill level to a point where control, balance, power, timing and stamina are maximized. These factors are measured by the eyes of experts. The pitcher is challenged by qualified opponents, and success or failure may be decided by a single pitch. His skills are tested over and over. His success or failure also dictates the destiny of his teammates. For the pitcher to be successful, he must get his act together in all facets of the game. He must do this for several pitches and even several games. Over time, real success appears to be a by-product of consistency.

How can a pitcher attain this consistency? Certainly, his mental outlook and amount of commitment are factors. If both of these are sufficient, then the methods and knowledge of the daily work habits he employs are probably the most important factors.

Many pitchers work hard, spending hours striving to become better. If those same hours are spent perfecting something the pitcher knows to be correct, or something which is basic to a good performance, the time spent working will undoubtedly become beneficial. Practice does not always make perfect, but practicing something that is sound will tend to help improve a skill.

The system being introduced in this chapter is sound, easily understood, has checkpoints, and can be learned and taught by not only the pitching coach, but by each pitcher as well. In fact, the teaching may be a more valuable factor in the completion of knowledge than the basic learning mode. As teachers often note, when a student is asked to teach a unit, the learning process for that student often becomes more meaningful and lasting.

The Basic Approach

The first step in the basic approach to this pitching system is to locate the problem. Because a solid foundation is fundamental to the pitching motion, the first checkpoint is with the pitcher's approach to the beginning of the wind-up or the beginning of the stretch position. Identifying problems in this area is done by checking the stance from the wind-up and the stance from the stretch. Movements involving the stance should be concentrated on before moving on to other areas. Once the stance has been determined to be proper, coaches should then proceed to check proper positioning and balance of the push-off foot. After attaining sound placement and use of the push-off foot, coaches should next address those issues dealing with the leg lift, before proceeding on to the movement and placement of the stride foot. If proper attention is paid to these primary and basic movements, better balance will occur. This approach will prepare the pitcher to not only be able to identify proper mechanics, but to also enable him to create a sense of feel. This approach will also provide the pitcher with correct angles and balance, thereby helping establish a sound learning path for other lessons.

After appropriate work in the primary phase, the pitcher should move to the next step. This next step should not be attempted until the push-off foot and the stride foot are adequately controlled. This system encourages a step-by-step approach to the correction of flaws and the refinement of skills. Coaches must correct, refine, and move on, taking care of all the movements in the feet-to-knees area. When all of the mechanics in this area are deemed to be adequate, it is time to move on to the fundamentals of movement from the knees-to-waist. Subsequently, when the pitcher has sufficiently mastered the mechanics in the knee-to-waist area, the waist-through-the-head area should be addressed next.

Focusing on one area at a time will add consistency and specifics to the evaluation process. Problems are relatively easy to spot, provided the evaluator has knowledge of the fundamentals. Breaking the pitching delivery into three areas provides the evaluator with specific zones in which to focus his and the pitcher's attention, rather than a large zone that includes all of the pitching movements. Once the pitcher and the pitching coach are able to narrow the field of corrections, and the concentration is only on that area, the learning process is simplified and becomes more meaningful and lasting.

Once the problem, or problems, have been identified, the next step is to find a solution to each problem. The solution may call for anything from a simple explanation to a retraining or relearning process. Occasionally, the pitcher is able to make quick corrections or adjustments by identifying the problem. Others may need constant reminders and repeated practice to make a needed change. This approach calls for a commitment on the part of the pitcher to stay focused on the particular area until the job is accomplished. Perhaps, the most difficult pitcher to show progress is the individual who needs to reroute or relearn a particular skill. In any case, the coach needs to continue working on the particular area of concern until success is achieved.

Long-term results are the goal, and these results can be reached in many ways. A pitcher may be able to correct a problem by identifying and explaining the problem. The basic test is whether or not the implemented correction works in a pressured environment. If it works, he is cured; if it does not, he needs further explanation and a clear plan in which to attack the problem. Generally, this approach calls for explanation, understanding, planning, repetition, drilling without pressure, drilling with pressure, and finally, participation under game conditions. Another way to look at the learning process sequentially is to understand the fundamentals, to practice without pressure, to work in the bullpen, to apply mental or imaginary pressures, and then to move on to the final test, the game.

Throughout the lifetime of the pitcher, it will be a common practice for him to work in all the phases of the learning spectrum. Moving from a simple balance drill to a highly competitive environment, and back-tracking from a game situation to a simple drill are very common practices. In fact, these type of practices are necessary to both correct and refine skills. Often these procedures are used both to correct a flaw and to serve as a maintenance routine.

In correcting major flaws, it is a good idea for a coach to make a priority list. The coach should begin at the top of the list, but should concentrate on only one issue at a time. Not only will this shorten the list, but it will also improve the systematic approach to problem solving.

Minimizing difficulties with the feet will help eliminate problems in other parts of the delivery. Correcting balance helps put the body in a sound position to throw. Properly pushing-off and striding to a balanced front leg will certainly give the pitcher a base from which to work.

As stated earlier, identifying problems may not be difficult. With careful scrutiny, several problems will surface. This is especially true of young pitchers. The key is to identify the flaws that most interfere with the freedom of motion, and then set out to eliminate them one at a time.

The problem-solving procedure is to identify, prioritize, drill, work under pressure, increase the pressure, and test it in a game. If this procedure works, the coach should move on. If it does not, the coach and the pitcher should move back a step at a time until an acceptable level of success is again reached. As soon as success at that level looks solid, then the previous process should be repeated before proceeding to address the next flaw.

Understanding the reason for the remedy is the key to learning. If a pitcher sees greater results in speed, control or stuff, and also enjoys success in the win column, the need for learning will be apparent. Understanding the process of learning should be a lifelong friend to the pitcher. A solid knowledge of how to pinpoint problems, how to correct them, how to prevent them, and how to rely on oneself will not only enable a pitcher to develop his skills, but will also dramatically increase his level of confidence.

Fit the Work to the Solution

Coaches and pitchers should set short-term goals and solve each goal before moving on to the next one. They must carefully examine each goal, then carefully match their effort to achieve the desired solution.

Many coaches use the "machine-gun approach" to problem solving. This approach calls for itemizing as many problems as possible and throwing out dozens of tips, hoping the tips will match the problems. In theory, if the pitcher is smart enough to sort out and select the correct remedy in the proper order, the desired results will occur. Even though the coach may be right in his assessment of the many flaws, the "machine-gun approach" does not usually succeed. The problems may be identified, but the answers, even though correct, may be too much for an individual to grasp at one time. This often leads to confusion and despair.

Better, longer-lasting results are brought about by diagnosing the problem and drawing up a plan for a solution that is carefully explained to the pitcher. This plan should also have learning steps that can be identified by both the coach and the pitcher.

Motivation is an important factor in learning. Few things motivate as well as success. Keeping this in mind is extremely important in helping the pitcher evaluate and establish a problem-solving plan.

The pitcher's commitment is the most important piece of the learning puzzle. Without this commitment, most successes will be short-term. Ultimate responsibility for improvements should rest with the pitcher. When the coach assumes the pitcher's responsibility, he robs the pitcher of confidence, self-assurance and creativity. Depending on the situation, the coach has to become a counselor, a resource person, a drill master, or even an expert. Regardless of the circumstances, however, the coach should insist that the pitcher take charge of his own development.

Many drills and exercises should be done without the help of the coach because too many pitchers rely on the coach to watch every movement and evaluate each activity. At some point, the pitcher will be required to be on the mound all by himself. Ultimately, he will be totally responsible for getting the job done. Practicing self-sufficiency will help him on these occasions.

Matching the work with the problem speeds learning, increases interest, adds to the coach's credibility, and helps the pitcher to truly refine his skills. Each workout should have a purpose. Workouts should be designed to achieve one of three primary objectives—maintaining skill levels, improving a skill or correcting a flaw. It is extremely important for the pitcher and the coach to focus on the job at hand and be on the same page in order to facilitate the educational process. It will often be necessary for the pitcher to develop a certain technique or movement before moving to the next step. A lack of communication, a short loss of energy, or sloppy work habits may curtail the pitcher's progress.

It is absolutely imperative that the pitcher understand the assignment before undertaking the work. If the drill or movement does not feel correct or if the explanation does not make sense, it is foolish to continue until there is understanding. Often a pitcher will comprehend a fundamental at the outset only to find road blocks as he moves into the lesson. Honesty, patience and a sincere desire to find the correct answer will make this time very valuable. The pitcher must ask questions, describe feelings, visualize sound fundamentals and evaluate his mechanics.

The final, and perhaps the most important, step in the learning process is the pitcher's commitment to perfect his mechanics. A solid work ethic is unbeatable. The simple goal is to work until a good-and-sound delivery is achieved. Without the desire to pursue excellence, lessons become little more than ways to spend time.

Building Blocks to Prevent Problems

Preventing mechanical problems is a worthwhile endeavor for anyone planning to pitch. The first step in prevention is knowledge. The pitcher should learn about and know his own body. He should know his arm. He should make a study of how he feels after a workout or after a game. He should learn the reasons for each movement and evaluate the results when his mechanics are flawed or when his mechanics are correct.

Routines developed in a daily workout should enhance both the physical and mental sides of pitching. If a pitcher exhibits natural enthusiasm and general eagerness toward the daily work, the coach should let the pitcher simply go about his daily work, using this natural high to accomplish what must be done. However, the coach has to make a mental note of the feeling and realize that there will be "off days" when it will be necessary to manufacture this type of enthusiasm. On such "off days," the pitcher will need to push himself if progress is to be continuous. This objective will be achieved through self-discipline and the need to improve.

A serious list of a few "things to do" on a daily basis helps organize and bring about a good work day. It is easy to "just practice." Coaches must make sure there is a point to their practices. Following this advice will greatly minimize the development of new problems. A well-organized and meaningful practice will result in improvement. Practice without a purpose often creates bad habits and promotes low standards.

Rhythm, control, concentration, enthusiasm, energy level, and feel are all factors in pitching. Since no one has ever attained perfection in all or even one of these factors, it will not be uncommon to see a pitcher perform somewhat inconsistently from day to day. With this in mind, it is most important to develop a pattern of work that tones, polishes, and maintains the skills required to deal effectively with these factors.

A daily regimen of work on the pitching delivery is necessary. This guideline can often be a problem because of arm fatigue; therefore, a simulated throwing activity may substitute for the actual throwing routine. The dry-run pitching drills enable the pitcher to work on his delivery without throwing the ball. Simulating the proper pitching motion may be the most valuable of all drills. The process can be repeated many times without harming or over exercising the arm. The repetition will help develop proper mechanics. In addition to developing the throwing motion, the drill will also offer a repeated visualization of throwing pitches for strikes.

Using the body parts in proper sequence is certainly the essence of good pitching mechanics. Just as an automobile requires maintenance, tune-ups, and use to function effectively, so does the pitcher's body. To prevent injuries, stay in rhythm, and remain successful, the pitcher must develop a working program that will allow him to recall, review, study, and repeat the pitching motion. Generally speaking, pitchers who study and work intelligently on mechanics have few real difficulties. They stay ahead of the game and realize that proper mechanics are the foundation for sound pitching.

Terminology—Developing a Pitching Language

Developing a pitching language is another extremely important factor in the learning process. The use of words has little or no meaning to the pitcher if the words are not understood clearly. Coaches must develop a language filled with pitching words. These words should be strong in enhancement recall. Strong words, or terms, may bring back memories, flash to a specific scene, or serve as a reminder to review important lessons of the past. Discipline words, or phrases, help the pitcher understand the point quickly. They vividly describe the fundamentals to be stressed. They add clarity and simplification to the task at hand. They cause the pitcher to see clearly, understand exactly, and discard extraneous information in the path toward learning. Words and phrases that suggest positive actions are also important. These verbal cues flash a picture of possibilities and probabilities to the mind. They create improvement and commitment.

Prior to the study of the pitching system, it is very important for the pitcher to understand the language that will be used. This language will be the vehicle for knowledge. Clearly understood words or short statements deliver the message quickly. Many times, teaching circumstances call for short, precise explanations. The pitcher may be slightly off course, which requires only a phrase or a word to remind him that he is straying from the learning path. If the word or phrase is strong, understandable, creates a vivid picture and points to the issue at hand, the path for correction is clear. Time spent in demonstration and definition of the pitching language will pay dividends.

The following words and phrases make up the pitching language that has developed over the course of several years. Since learning is a never-ending process, changes to the existing terminology and new descriptions are added each year. Regardless, the following pitcher's language has remained relatively constant over the years and should hold up to the test of time.

Definition of Terms

1. *Arm lift*: This term applies to either the front arm or the throwing arm. It is more commonly used to describe the proper action of the throwing arm after the hands are separated and the ball is being brought into throwing position. When the pitcher lifts his arm, it should feel like he is picking up an object with his fingers and leaving the fingers in that position until they reach an area above his head. This action is controlled, relaxed and quick. For this reason, the thought of lifting the arm, rather than slinging or forcing it into position, gives a clear and concise description of its duty.

2. *Back knee down*: The push-off knee driving toward the ground as the push-off foot drives from the pitching rubber.

3. *Balance drills:* A series of movements designed to improve and develop balance. The drills include work with both the stride foot and the push-off foot. These drills can be done with or without throwing.

4. *Bent front leg*: The stride leg should be bent during the leg lift and should remain bent throughout the push-off and the stride. As the throwing arm finishes the last

phases of the throwing motion, the front leg should be bent, with the knee of that leg pointed inward.

5. *Belly button to target*: At the beginning stages of the wind-up, as the push-off foot is placed on the rubber, the belly button should face the target. As the chest and the head reach out to throw, the belly button should also face the target. When the belly button is not in this position during these two stages, extra movement and undue adjustment must be made to correct the position of the body.

6. *Bottoming out*: The action of the hands after separation. Both hands should continue downward in a soft, natural movement until they reach full extension. If this action is done softly, the hands will fall to the bottom of the reach and automatically begin to swing apart and move upward into proper position. When the pitchers let their hands drop or fall, their hands become relaxed and quick. The bottoming out procedure helps move the throwing arm up and into a proper throwing angle.

7. *Bouncing hands*: The action prior to the hand separation. A slight lift of the hands shortly before the hands separate creates an opportunity for the pitcher to develop rhythm as his hands prepare for the throw. The bouncing action should not cover more than a few inches. This movement should help the pitching arm drop, reach back, pick up, and proceed to the top of the throwing arc with freedom and quickness.

8. *Break the hands softly*: Another way of describing the hand separation. The hands should be soft and relaxed as they separate. Relaxation and softness at this point help the pitcher better control both arms as they prepare for the throw.

9. *Chest out*: The chest as it extends toward the target during the throwing motion. The pitcher should assume a barrel chest and arch back position as he reaches to throw. Sticking the chest out, or throwing the breasts at the target, are other effective ways of describing the proper method. The breasts should also be level as they are thrown toward the target.

10. *Chicken wing*: The correct positioning of the front arm at the completion of the follow-through. This position means the front arm has been drawn in near the rib cage and continued back until the glove hand is even with the left breast (RHP). This practice places the elbow beyond the edge of the back. From a straight-on position, the elbow will be higher than the back after the pitcher bends to follow-through, giving the appearance of the chicken wing. This movement will help the pitcher complete the full arc and provide freedom throughout.

11. *Concave chest*: A negative term. It refers to the fact that the throwing arm shoulder and the front shoulder are squeezing toward each other. This shortens the throwing

arm and causes the arm to stop suddenly. The concave chest action is one of the major reasons for recoiling. This action is restrictive and may result in severe injury to the shoulder, elbow or back.

12. *Deactivate bottom of stride leg*: The first part of the stride. The pitcher should hold the lift leg up and avoid thrusting with the bottom half of that leg. He should try not using the bottom of the stride leg until just a few inches prior to the landing of the stride foot. Overuse of the stride leg causes a multitude of problems including overstriding, opening too soon, recoiling, broken rhythm and premature use of power.

13. *Downward angle*: The direction the throwing arm should travel after it assumes its maximum height. This term also describes the direction the ball should travel as it leaves the pitcher's hand and reminds him to be on top of the ball. A pitcher should feel as though he is throwing downhill.

14. *Elevate the front hip*: At the top of the leg lift, the front hip should be higher than the back hip. From a side view, the pitcher's belt line should be higher on the glove-hand side than on the throwing-arm side. This action improves the pivot and coiling position, along with enhancing the stride. This movement should not cause the back shoulder to drop. The shoulders should remain relatively level.

15. *Eyes to target*: This term reminds the pitcher to reach toward the target with his head. This practice helps a pitcher to keep his head aligned with the target. If both his eyes are taken to the target, the rest of the body will follow. This action also creates better extension for the throwing arm.

16. *Finger pressure*: The amount of firmness applied to the ball as the fingers grip the ball. Each pitch requires its own grip, and grips may be different from pitcher to pitcher. By applying more pressure with one finger than the other, the ball may rotate in one direction more than the other. It is extremely important for each pitcher to pay attention to the type of grip pressure on each of his pitches. Often, with a simple change in pressure points, a pitch can be improved. This factor is the key point in establishing control, speed and movement. A sense of feel and a knowledge of its significance to the pitch are essential to good pitching. Pitchers need to constantly make mental notes about the finger pressure used for each pitch, and develop the touch to be able to use finger pressure wisely.

17. *Fingers down*: The position of the fingers as the pitching hand separates from the glove. The fingers are also in this position as the pitching arm is lifted to prepare for the throw. The fingertips should be pointed toward the ground during this movement. This practice helps move the arm up to the top of the arc without undue strain, and also properly prepares the wrist for its duties.

18. *Forward wrist*: The wrist position at the top of the throwing motion. A wrist in this position is in a cocked or ready position, allowing the full snap as the arm is brought forward to release the ball. This action prevents slinging, or pushing the ball. The forward wrist is a relaxed position, ready to move quickly backward and then snap forward to complete a full wrist snap at the end of the release point.

19. *Front arm (take out and bring in)*: The method in which the front arm is used as the throwing motion is executed. "Taking it out" implies a controlled movement of the arm, which is exactly the proper movement. "Bringing it in" refers to the arm being guided, or drawn back in, rather than being jerked back. These actions create rhythmical movements and eliminate uncontrolled activities.

20. *Heel over*: The correct position of the heel at the beginning and at the completion of the follow-through. After the push-off foot has pushed, lifted, and formed a small or large circle, it will contact the ground with the foot at an approximate perpendicular position. From this point, the pitcher should continue rolling his heel to the outside. This action constitutes the heel-over position. The heel-over action allows the arm to complete the arc, resulting in better extension and freedom of movement. This action also prevents recoiling and keeps the pitcher's arm from making sudden stops. The unrestricted movement of the arm provides an opportunity for the pitcher to maximize his effort.

21. *High thumb*: The position of the thumb is important to the grip. The thumb usually helps balance the ball and helps the index and middle finger apply the proper pressure. On one type of curve ball, the thumb is used to push upward and help the middle finger create top spin on the curve. On this type of curveball, the thumb is under the ball and almost in line with the middle finger. This position is referred to as a low thumb. Occasionally, a particular pitcher will not have enough dexterity with his thumb. In this case, he should move his thumb up toward the left side of the ball (RHP). This action basically moves the thumb out of the way and allows the index and middle finger to do all of the work. When the thumb is adjusted upward, it is called a high thumb position.

22. *Inside the ball*: The position of the fingers as they release the pitch. To go inside the ball will cause the ball to take on a sinking, or screwball, rotation. This action may also help an individual correct the rotation of a certain pitch. For example, a pitcher who has a fastball without movement may gain the desired movement by taking his fingers to the inside of the ball at the release points. Going outside the ball will have the opposite effect. Taking the fingers to the outside at release of the pitch may improve the rotation on the slider or cut fastball. Like finger pressure, the pitcher should be aware of how the ball is released. He should learn to use the inside of the ball or the outside of the ball to create the desired spin and movement on the pitch.

23. *Inside to inside*: This term illustrates a balanced position. While in the stretch-position stance, the pitcher's weight should be balanced between the inside of the back foot to the inside of the stride foot. The push-off should be executed from the inside of the push-off foot, and the stride should be made with the weight transferring to the inside of the front foot. This term is also used in the stationary stride position, with the drills being dependent upon the pitcher transferring his weight from the inside of one foot to the inside of the other foot.

24. *Inward knee*: The back knee at the push-off placement on the pitching rubber, and the beginning of the driving action for the push-off. This term also refers to the position of the knee as the stride foot lands and then as the weight is placed on it to complete the throw. An inward knee at each of these points will encourage a more forceful push-off and a better balance with the stride and follow-through.

25. *Lead with the hip*: The beginning of the stride. The front hip should move first and drive toward the stride spot and target. This movement creates greater thrust and propels the body in the direction of the target. The pitcher should have the feel of striding with the hip.

26. *Leg lift*: This is the movement of the pitcher's preparation front leg that aids the coiling action and preparation for the stride. The leg lift should be controlled without the use of a swinging or slinging action.

27. *Level eyes*: The position of the eyes from the beginning to the end of the throwing motion. Keeping the eyes level insures proper angles, keeps body parts aimed toward the target, and prevents tilting the head.

28. *Locked knees*: This is a straight position with the legs, with no bend at the knees.

29. *Low thumb*: The position of the thumb as it grips the baseball. Low thumb refers to the thumb being gripped at the bottom of the ball. This position is common to the curveball and fastball grips. On certain pitches, such as a cut fastball or a slider, the thumb is forced further under the ball to aid the grip. Normally, the thumb is at the bottom of the ball and even with the middle finger on the curve. It should be under the ball and between the index and middle finger on the fastball, and pushed to the right of the middle finger on the slider and cut fastball. The use and position of the thumb will vary from pitcher to pitcher.

30. *On top of the ball*: The position of the fingers as they grip the ball. Generally, this term is used to encourage a proper angle at the top of the throw when the fingers should be on top of the ball. This term also describes the correct position of the fingers as the ball is lifted up into the throwing position. Other ways this term is used are to

describe the proper position for the fingers when throwing a curve ball, and to describe the position of the fingers to help aid in a better release of a particular pitch.

31. *Push-off*: The process by which the pitcher drives off the pitching rubber. Collectively, the push-off includes the pushing action with the push-off foot, the lead action with the front hip and the pitcher keeping the lift leg up as long as possible.

32. *Recoiling*: This word has a negative connotation. It means the throwing arm or the throwing motion is stopped abruptly. Usually recoiling is caused by straightening the stride leg, but it can also be caused by a weak front arm or a lack of push-off. Recoiling restricts movement and causes a backlash effect. It does not allow the energy to fully transfer to the thrown ball. The sudden braking action causes a vibration, placing undue and unreasonable stress on the body parts. Recoiling is a result of one or more mechanical flaws.

33. *Release point below the bill of the cap*: The correct "feel" for the release point of the ball should be below the bill of the pitcher's cap, well out from and directly in front of the eyes. The ball is not actually released at this point. The actual release is much sooner. Among the benefits of this "feel" are staying on top of the ball, maximizing the use of the fingers, and developing a sense of feel for the direction of the throw.

34. *Right to left (RHP)*: The route of the arm as it proceeds through the throwing motion. The arm should extend properly toward the target and travel in a right-to-left action in front of the body. This movement allows the throwing arm to continue through the arc with freedom, permitting a full follow-through. The elbow of the throwing arm should be touching against the outside of the stride leg thigh on the follow-through.

35. *Rotation*: The type of spin on the baseball. It is important for each pitcher to understand the type of spin required for each pitch. Grip, wrist angle, finger pressure, arm angle and release point are some of the major factors involved in rotation.

36. *Separation of hands*: The separation of the hands in both the stretch and wind-up positions. The separation is also referred to as the "breaking" of the hands. The pitcher should develop a consistent point for the separation and this point should be the same from the wind-up as it is in the stretch. This factor is important to the throw because, in reality, it is the beginning of the throwing motion.

37. *Soft out of the glove*: How the hands should separate. As the pitching hand leaves the glove, it should be soft and relaxed. A soft and relaxed separation creates a faster arm movement. This action helps guide the pitching arm up into the proper throwing position with speed and ease. This action also improves the movement of the glove hand and arm.

38. *Toe ahead of heel*: The correct position of the push-off foot when placed on or in front of the pitching rubber to begin the throwing motion. It also refers to the stride foot as it is planted upon the finish of the follow-through. The toe ahead of the heel enhances balance and thrust.

39. *Unlocked knees*: This term refers to a slight bending at the knees, that allows the weight of the pitcher to sink or for balance his legs to flex or thrust.

40. *Weight on inside of foot*: This term applies to either foot. Any time either foot touches the ground, the weight should be placed to the inside of that foot. The bulk of the ball of that foot serves as the focal point. Starting the push-off with the weight to the inside provides the pitcher with better thrust and balance. Landing on the inside and keeping the weight there through the finish of the throw improve a pitcher's balance and creates better angles.

Summary

In this chapter, further analysis of pitching mechanics and the pitching delivery were discussed with the introduction of a pitching language and an emphasis on teaching methods. The terms and definitions of the pitching language that should add to the teaching and learning processes for both the coach and the pitchers were also received. The point was emphasized that repetition is a key to effective learning.

4

Step-by-Step Approach

Careful examination reveals that there really is no beginning and no end when it comes to teaching or learning about the pitching delivery. However, for purposes of practicality, it is necessary to develop sequential learning patterns. Certain movements require prerequisite information before their execution is perfected. This point explains the reason for dividing the pitching motion into three areas. By developing a system and moving orderly through the steps, learning is simplified, and each step enhances the ability of the individual to concentrate on a specific area.

Concerted effort in perfecting the fundamentals from the feet-to-knees area will fulfill the requirements necessary to move on to the next phase. In fact, some fundamentals in the other two areas may be corrected by the work in the feet-to-knees sector.

Coaches should move on to the knees-to-waist area when work in the feet-to-knees phase is satisfactory. Some aspects of the feet-to-knees area may show signs of deterioration when concentration is shifted to new concerns. If these breakdowns appear critical, it will be necessary to return to work in the preceding area. It's all right to move back to the knees-to-waist as long as progress is being made and the skill level in the previous area is maintained. Coaches can move back and forth, focusing on one problem at a time until satisfaction is attained in both areas.

Moving on to the waist-through-the-head area should reveal progress, and give both the pitcher and the coach a clear picture of how the preceding lessons have been learned. If moving to this area creates problems in the previous areas, the coach and the pitcher can simply move back and correct the problems. Eventually, adhering to the step-by-step approach will finally move the pitcher through all three areas.

During the teaching system just described, attention to detail is very important. Commitment to following the steps correctly is paramount. Shortcuts or lack of interest in one area will create problems in all three areas. Establishing a good foundation will serve the pitcher in all aspects of pitching.

Many details make up the total pitching motion. It is the job of the pitcher and the coach to pay proper attention to each detail. A sloppy habit that is overlooked or ignored is often the invitation to a variety of slumps and negatives. A pitcher who wishes for long-term success must be meticulous with his mechanics.

Focus

There are many ways to watch a pitcher. In a general way, to watch a pitcher is to basically see him and notice the results. If someone were to ask a "general watcher" to evaluate the pitcher, general information along the lines of "he's doing all right," "he's winning," "he's struggling," or "he's throwing strikes" would probably be received. Focus in this setting is on total performance, not on specifics. Watching a pitcher in a general way gives the evaluator information in a broad area. This information is valuable because it takes in the total delivery. If something is wrong with the total picture, there is a sound and necessary reason to shift the evaluation procedure to a more specific and refined area. Checking details of the delivery in each of the three areas is essential.

The focus should be similar to a zoom lens on a camera. The lens allows the photographer to select a detail within the picture. Good coaching calls for this type of focus. For example, during a game the coach may be observing the picture from a total performance perspective, with great concern toward strategy, pitching to situations, sharpness of stuff, and overall results. If the pitcher is operating in a successful manner, the coach will continue to focus on the broader scope. If a problem suddenly appears, or the pitcher or catcher hint at a difficulty, then it will be necessary for the coach to begin "zooming" in on specifics.

Developing a checklist for the pitcher's mechanics is very beneficial for a coach. Starting with the feet and working up through the head is the recommended path. This approach is consistent with the aforementioned teaching patterns, because correcting mistakes in balance (feet area) generally leads to solving difficulties in the upper parts of the body.

Pitchers should learn to give quick check-ups on each other, as well. This practice serves both the pitcher checking and the pitcher being checked. Spotting difficulties forces the pitcher to learn more about the mechanics of pitching. Exchanging information creates friendship and interest for the pitching staff.

Another by-product of focusing on specifics is concentration. Watching an activity with the intention of picking up details requires concentration. To deal in details is to learn how to wade through peripheral activities and move on to the heart of the matter.

Helping a fellow pitcher is a form of teaching, and teaching is one of the best ways to learn. True teaching requires great understanding and an intense desire to know more about the subject matter. Within this setting, an opportunity for both teaching and learning is very high.

Teaching Touch and Feel

Most teaching techniques involve the senses of sight and sound. Pitching is aided by both, but relies mainly on motion. The pitcher must learn to feel every movement. Touch and feel are vital to the pitcher. Developing "feel" requires an understanding of the skills involved in pitching and the need for repetition.

Understanding a skill is not enough. A physical activity requires the participant to maneuver, move, and propel an object, while doing all of these with a high degree of success. Pitching skills are different to develop because they require a highly-tuned sense of feel. A pitcher without feel is not able to effectively utilize his abilities.

Upgrading the sense of feel will most definitely improve the pitcher's total performance. Practicing with specific goals in mind, and in a repetitious manner, will increase the sense of feel. Pitching is not a casual activity; it requires hours and hours of concentrated effort. Without repetition and constant concern, the feel will come and go. Consistency calls for a planned schedule, attention to detail and a repetition of proper mechanics.

Associating skills and techniques with feel and touch is highly suggested. Whether learning a new pitch or a new method, the pitcher should be very concerned with the feeling derived from the activity. Knowing how an athletic act feels, or how it should feel, is the meter or guide from which the pitcher operates.

Once an athlete has developed how fundamental skills feel, he places information in his memory bank. During competition he simply turns on his computer (memory bank), and allows it to feed back the information necessary for the task at hand. Subsequently, it is important for the pitcher to trust what his memory tells him and let the body free up to do the rest.

In any athletic endeavor, there is a desire to become successful. Once success has been attained, there is a comparable struggle to repeat. In order to continue at a high level of performance, proper training and attention to details of success are essential. Staying on top of skills calls for a steady diet of activities designed to improve and to maintain those skills. Improvement calls for a concentrated effort to reduce weaknesses and develop strengths. Maintenance requires regular check-ups and enough work on all areas of pitching to remain sharp. One of the pitcher's primary goals should be knowing what it takes to stay sharp.

In order to correct a flaw, it is necessary to develop a recall system. Everyone uses recall in one form or the other. Some have almost total recall, while others have very little. Practicing to remember is the first step in forming a system. Pitchers should associate each drill with the flaw it is correcting or with the skill it is refining. They should also pay attention to words and phrases and use them in association with points of emphasis to form an image or clear picture. By continuing this process, the subject matter will become familiar and have a natural feel.

The second step calls for the information to be filed, recalled and used during check-ups, maintenance or correction periods. Once data is filed in an individual's memory bank, it is important to use it periodically. This point is particularly true of something new. Freshly filed information should be recalled and used regularly. Within three to four days after filing the material, the pitcher should recall it and become familiar with it.

Step three is to practice the recall system on a fellow pitcher. Something the pitcher has used and filed will be of service to others. Pitchers may use their focusing techniques to pinpoint an area of concern on a fellow pitcher. They should pull out a drill or practice which matches the particular problem. This approach helps to keep the data fresh and usable. In a sense, the pitcher is practicing his mechanics as he presents information to the fellow pitcher.

The final step is to become more aware of mechanical details. Pitchers need to make a habit of evaluating other pitchers, opponents and teammates. They should visualize good techniques and faulty movements and correlate them with positive pictures that may be recalled for use at any time. To be aware of the regularly used information concerning pitching mechanics turns the pitcher into student of pitching rather than an idle watcher.

Relearning

Relearning a certain skill is very difficult. Often it is necessitated by an injury, prolonged lazy habits or a traumatic experience. Regardless of the reason, retaining a certain movement calls for thinking through the act as it is performed. The throwing motion is best executed when the pitcher is not thinking of details. The details are scrutinized and perfected enough during practice that the pitching motion can be accomplished without centering on specific parts of the throw.

To be classified as relearning, the difficulty would have to be serious enough to warrant changing major parts of the throwing motion. Problems, such as a prolonged pause in the rhythm package, a dramatic overemphasis in the stride or an unusual change in the motion, could be considered relearning subjects.

Analyzing the root of the problem is necessary if success is to prevail. The coach and the pitcher need to know the cause in order to find the solution to the problem.

If the relearning process is to be initiated, the pitcher must be absolutely committed. Without commitment, there will be no real progress. The pitcher needs to believe that the ordeal to be encountered will be worth the effort and that his effort will lead to a successful reward.

It is also essential to understand that in the relearning process there will be many setbacks, much elementary training and many hours of repetition. After all, relearning is basically starting over with a skill that was once familiar but is now lost. Often relearning is more difficult than the development of brand new knowledge.

Pitchers and coaches should concentrate on one item of correction at a time. They should simply prioritize points of emphasis, then eliminate each problem by starting at the top of the list. Working on more than one problem at a time tends to frustrate and cause concentration to be smothered with too many chores.

Each lesson should be simplified, and short-term goals should be set. Each goal should be completed before advancing and each movement completed until it can be done naturally. A simple test is to evaluate a particular skill while the pitcher is concentrating on another skill aspect. If that part of the activity is fundamentally sound, the pitcher has relearned a skill.

A lesson concerned with relearning should be taught in short spurts. Because the pitcher is somewhat confused and frustrated already, long periods of concentrated effort often appear to produce failure in the relearning setting. On the other hand, short periods with very intense centering are more conducive to reestablishing sound habits.

The pitcher should be responsible for both learning and relearning. His dependency on the pitching coach should only be for evaluation and resource. When the primary responsibility for concentrating on learning is shifted to the coach, only short-term success is experienced by the pitcher.

It is also important to note that regular check-ups, good maintenance and a solid effort toward improvement will help keep the pitcher out of the relearning process.

Teaching Each Other

Encouraging pitchers to watch each other and help solve each other's problems not only helps build rapport, but also helps the pitcher learn to deal with details. The system being taught will not only be repeated by the coach but also by each pitcher.

Teaching or advising will enhance the evaluation process. To evaluate a particular factor, a pitcher must know how to watch. He must learn to cut through the rubble and get to the heart of the matter. Each pitcher should be encouraged to become a good watcher, to recognize good mechanics and to pinpoint flaws.

Learning to evaluate pitching mechanics will give the pitcher practice in using the pitching system. He will learn to start at the feet and work through each of the areas. He should stop and advise when a problem is spotted. As the system emphasizes, he should not go any further until that problem is corrected.

Pitchers should be encouraged to simplify directions and explanations. Pitchers following this advice will automatically understand the advice they are giving because it will be arranged in a manner they understand. Using the pitching language helps an individual associate the words and phrases to the activity he is describing. Regular use of the pitching language will help pitchers visualize each mechanical movement and bring about better understanding.

Pitchers should be taught to minimize problems and use positive language when describing a flaw, and they should also identify only those flaws which are pertinent to the area of focus. They should keep the lesson focused on one area at a time and select only the most pressing issues in that area as points to be emphasized. They should not present more corrections than can be handled by the individual pitcher. By selecting and working on only the most glaring problems, they can focus on corrections or improvements in difficult areas that may clean up flaws in other areas.

When pitchers are helping each other, it should always be in the context of the pitching system, and it should always be with the consent of the coach. It is important for all pitchers to be on the same page with the pitching coach. The purpose of a pitcher helping another pitcher is to develop a full and sound pitching system. It is necessary for each pitcher to teach within the system and teach only in the area and on the specific subject matter being taught at the time. The coach should be close enough to the scene to make sure that proper skills are being taught.

Problem solving is an important part of the pitching routine. It is important for the pitchers to establish a routine designed for improvement. To do this, the problem must be identified and prioritized. The pitcher is responsible for the solution of any problem. The coach and the pitching partners will act as evaluators, resource people, motivators and guides.

Problem solving can be invigorating. To help a pitcher acquire a better curve ball or better control, or become more involved in the total process of pitching, is very exciting for both the pitcher and the coach. Excitement and enthusiasm are contagious. Becoming involved with the solution to a problem is not only gratifying, but it also activates the helper and serves as a confidence builder, as a reminder of the proper way to do things and as a method for self-examination.

One of the greatest advantages to encouraging pitchers to teach each other is that the teacher must learn in order to teach. Teaching requires thought and organization of the subject matter. Anything taught by a pitcher must be learned by that pitcher. The pitcher should first be encouraged to learn, and then asked to pass that knowledge on to someone else. Most people have an innate need to pass along information that has served them well.

A coach who implies that all problems can be solved also encourages pitchers to think in a like manner. There are many inherent obstacles. When a pitching staff approaches its job with the idea that pitching skills can be learned, and that no obstacle is too big to stop progress, then success is inevitable. Hard work may be one of the obstacles. Learning to share and to take an interest in others may be other hurdles. However, attempting to remove such road blocks places the pitcher on the path toward the development of better skills.

Summary

The step-by-step approach presented in this chapter is designed to aid in the total development of the pitcher. This method is designed to utilize the teaching knowledge and skills of the pitching coach, and to include the exchange of knowledge within the respective pitching staff. In no way should there be any inference that the teaching of pitching should be the responsibility of the pitcher. It is simply an approach that may include those pitchers who are willing and able to help with the teaching process. When a pitcher is skilled enough to teach, he will find this endeavor to be worthwhile for both himself and his benefactor.

5

Pitching Drills

Drills are valuable in the total development of the pitcher. A drill may be comprised of one or more mental practices, or it may consist of physical repetition. Most drills, however, entail the use of both the mental and physical skills.

A good drill is usually basic and easy to understand. In order for a drill to be the most effective, it should be clearly understood by the participant and should be designed to correct, refine or introduce a particular technique or strategy. Through such drills, enthusiasm and learning should take place.

The pitching delivery requires much work to become effective. Through sound repetition, the pitcher is able to maximize his abilities and minimize injuries. A pitcher who understands the specifics of a drill is more apt to show improvement than those who simply drill for the sake of practicing.

The following drills are easy to comprehend, and pertain to specific fundamentals. They are designed to help each pitcher and to enhance every movement involved with the pitching delivery. Selecting the appropriate drill to address a particular focus will most certainly result in a productive workout. Using these drills in conjunction with the step-by-step teaching approach will speed the learning process and provide lasting and meaningful knowledge to the pitcher about the proper mechanical movements. The pitcher should be able to recognize the value of these drills and find them useful for his immediate needs. He can also use them as a source to turn to when difficulties arise in the future.

The drills presented in this chapter have been developed to be used with either large groups, small groups, or an individual. Most of these drills can be used with or without the actual throwing of the baseball. They may service the tired-armed pitcher, as well as the individual who needs extra throwing.

Push-Off Drill

Most pitching coaches place a high priority on the push-off. The push-off is important but how it is accomplished is an even greater issue. The push-off is established by properly placing the push-off foot on the rubber and then shifting the weight to the ball of that foot. The knee should unlock, allowing the weight to flex the knee enough to produce a forceful push-off.

The push-off drill encourages the pitcher to lead with his front hip and to practice balance and weight transfer.

The pitcher should lead with his front hip, and direct the push-off knee to drive down. This will force the push-off foot to drive or push back before leaving the rubber. (You want to emphasize keeping the push-off foot on the rubber as long as possible.) As the foot leaves the rubber, it should lift up, move to the outside and form either a small circle or a large circle before touching the ground. The push-off leg and the front hip do the striding, not the bottom of the stride leg. Too much movement with the bottom part of the stride leg is undesirable. Overactivity at this point can cause overstriding, improper landing position, opening too soon, recoiling and a break in the rhythm pattern.

The front knee should remain bent upon landing. The weight should settle on the inside ball of the stride foot. This action forms a solid base that does not move.

Stride Foot Balance Drill

Balance is perhaps the most essential factor in establishing control. Balance is also an ally of power and movement. The stride foot balance drill is designed to improve the stride. This drill will help the pitcher develop a sound weight exchange and consistent landing position.

A proper landing allows the chest to drive out and over the thigh, with the pitcher's weight over the ball of his front foot. The foot should approach the landing position with a slightly "toed-in" or "pigeon-toed" angle. The weight should transfer from the inside of the push-off foot to the inside of the stride foot. The stride leg knee should bend as it lifts and remain bent, during and after the stride. In fact, as the weight shifts onto it, pushing or riding the knee forward is beneficial to the follow through.

During the stride foot balance drill, the foot should approach the landing position in a "toed-in" or "pigeon-toed" angle.

Leading with the front hip, pointing the stride foot toe down, and deactivating the stride leg from the knee down will facilitate the stride. When done properly, balance is attained. For purposes of this drill, the pitcher should hold the balance position for approximately three seconds. This practice is called balance and hang. Holding the balance for the prescribed time is evidence of success.

This drill is very practical and basic. It should be repeated until the stride is perfected. After perfecting the stride, this drill should be used periodically as part of a maintenance program.

Stride Foot Balance Drill with Chest to Thigh

A great deal of work is involved in the process of learning to balance and hang. After successfully accomplishing this phase, the activity should be increased to include squeezing the chest against the top of the thigh and touching the throwing elbow to the outside of the stride leg thigh. This practice will represent a complete throw with balance.

Success in this drill will pay dividends in other areas of mechanics, including the correct placement of the throwing arm, the chest, and the head.

Pitcher Isolated Feet Drill

By isolating the feet, the pitcher is able to concentrate on selected parts of the throwing motion without striding. The transfer of weight is a major factor in concentration. Without stepping to catch and striding to throw, the focus can be placed on the grip, the arm action, and any other selected phase of the delivery.

Even though the stride is not used in this drill, weight transfer is emphasized. By shifting the weight from the inside of the back foot and transferring it to the inside of the front foot, the pitcher is practicing balance and weight exchange in the same manner as when the stride is used.

The throwing distance in this drill is generally 40 to 60 feet. A range up to 60 feet is recommended when focusing on a specific part of mechanics. Longer distances are recommended for checking balance and strengthening the arm.

Stationary Stride Drill

The pitcher should simulate a throw without taking the push-off foot from the rubber, or the area in which the push-off foot begins. His feet are stationary in the stride position. This position permits the pitcher to shift weight from one leg to the other by eliminating some of the critical rhythm "grabbers" in the pitching motion. Rhythm is most often interrupted during the leg lift or during the stride. This drill eliminates the need for both the leg lift and the stride.

This is one of the most valuable of all drills. Arm action, separating the hands, left to right action, arm lift, chest out, chin up, chest-to-thigh and factors involved with weight exchange are some of the fundamentals this drill helps develop.

When the pitcher assumes the stride position, his front knee should be bent with the weight placed to the inside of the stride foot. Essentially, the pitcher is able to work on the stride without striding. This stationary foot position permits the pitcher to shift weight, properly bend the stride knee and better understand the feel of the stride. The recommended throwing distance is 40 to 60 feet.

Arm Lift Drill

The throwing arm should gain height in order to gain maximum power. "Getting on top of the ball" is a term often used by pitchers and pitching coaches. The maximum leverage is to be applied. The elbow should raise as high as the shoulder, and the hand should be higher than the head as the stride foot touches the ground. This position will provide a feel of throwing downhill.

The arm-lift drill helps the pitcher learn proper arm height, balance, and weight transfer.

A proper arc should be formed. The arc starts at the separation of the hands. The throwing hand should drop down, with the fingertips pointing toward the ground. The throwing hand then reaches back and is lifted up until the elbow reaches shoulder height. The fingers should remain in a down position and continue to lift until the hand is at or above the top of the head. The arc is completed by fully extending the hand toward the target and pulling down and to the outside of the stride leg thigh.

The arm lift drill emphasizes the break (or separation of the hands), the drop, and the reach back and the lift. A soft break is recommended because it adds to a pitcher's level of relaxation. It is important to remember that a relaxed arm moves faster than a tense arm.

Keeping the fingers on top of the ball and pointing toward the ground keeps the wrist in a forward position. This practice will create maximum wrist action. Pitchers should focus on keeping the wrist relaxed during this procedure.

The weight distribution from the push-off foot should generate from the inside part of the ball of that foot. The weight is then transferred to the inside ball of the stride foot. Therefore, the term "inside to inside" is derived.

Work begins with the feet isolated in the stride position. The pitcher should rock his weight back to the inside ball of the push-off foot and execute a throw while transferring his weight to the inside ball of the stride foot. This action can be done with a complete throwing motion, with or without the ball. It can be an actual throw or a simulated throw. Simulation is a good method for the pitcher who has just thrown in a game but still needs to work on his delivery.

Keeping the weight to the inside and on the ball of each foot will enhance balance. Working from a balanced position augments the learning process. An endless number of details can be singled out, emphasized and improved with this drill. This drill is an excellent way to establish the feel of weight transfer.

Front Arm Drill

The importance of rhythm is recognized by everyone in baseball. Rhythm promotes both control and power, and basically dictates the pitcher's outcome. One of the determining factors is how the front arm is used. It is the meter used to establish timing. The front arm aids the pitcher in opening the shoulders, assists in placing the arm in throwing position, contributes to the proper positioning of the chest, helps to get the chin up and out, benefits the hip action, and contributes to the freedom, extension, and follow-through of the throwing arm. The front arm guides these actions and serves as the direction finder.

The front arm is almost as significant as the throwing arm. The front arm should not be ignored. To throw with a weak front arm is to rob the pitcher of the opportunity to make full use of his ability. The improper use of the front arm also increases the chances of injury.

Pitchers often drop the front arm, making it virtually useless. When the front arm is not routed in the same manner as the throwing arm, the body is thrown out of rhythm and is misdirected.

Before embarking upon a program to improve the front arm action, there is need for caution. Since the front arm is such a factor in establishing rhythm, it is essential for

With a forward wrist, the front arm is soft, and the back of the glove is to the target. The ball should be brought to a height above the pitcher's head. The chest should be barreled.

both the pitcher and the pitching coach to have a sound understanding of its significance and use. A pitcher's balance and rhythm are disrupted if the movement of the front arm is exaggerated.

When using the isolated stride drill, emphasis should be placed on proper front arm action. After separating the hands, the pitcher should direct the front arm up and out toward the target, extending until the body is ready to open. When ready to open, the palm should be turned up with the thumb over, while the heel lifts and the arm is brought in close to the body as it proceeds to brush the side.

To say exactly how much the arm straightens is very difficult. The amount of extension will depend upon the ability, timing package and body build of each pitcher. The distance and speed of the pitch is also related to front arm extension.

Attention should also be given to the distance between the elbow and the side of the body as the front arm is brought in toward the body. If there is considerable distance between the elbow and the side of the body, the body will be pulled off course. The front arm should pass relatively close to the body to allow the shoulders to stay parallel and to keep the chest and head in proper alignment. Too much space between the side of the body and the elbow at the pull-through will cause the pitcher to fall to the side and move to the outside of his stride foot.

The pitcher should think about placing the arm out and bringing the arm in toward the body. The term "throw the arm out and pull the arm in" is not recommended because it often creates a setting for exaggerated movement. Overemphasis on either movement tends to cause direction and timing problems. The speed at which the front arm operates is directly related to the speed of the throw. Careful attention to details and repetition with this drill will pay dividends.

Chin Up-Chest Out Drills

A concave chest presents many problems for the pitcher. This position shortens the throwing lever and causes a recoiling action. Arching the back and reaching out with the chest is a position which creates better extension and better angles, while allowing for freedom of movement.

Working from the "isolated stride position drill" places emphasis on keeping the breasts parallel to the ground and throwing them toward the target. The chin should stay up, with the eyes being kept directly in line with the target. When the chin tucks in, the chest becomes concave and the back bows. This position shortens the arc of the throw.

Repeating this drill, with special attention placed on either the chin or the chest, will facilitate arm extension, freedom of movement, and follow-through.

Heel-Over Drill

The back hip and the push-off leg play a significant roll in producing power, balance, and freedom of movement. The push-off phase should feature a push down with the back knee. The push-off foot should drive with the knee, then lift up and form a circular motion to the throwing-arm side, culminating with the heel rotating over after landing.

To better understand the heel-over action, the pitcher should execute a number of throws by keeping his push-off foot on the rubber. Instead of bringing it up, out and over, he should simply push the back knee toward the ground and roll the push-off heel over toward the outside. This practice allows the chest to reach, the arm to extend, and the entire top of the body to continue on and complete the follow-through. The push-off foot remains at the starting point. Its function is to roll over to allow the body to rotate and the arm to complete the throwing motion. By keeping the push-off foot in one location, the push-off action is simplified. Emphasis is placed on the rotation of the hips and the push-off heel.

By operating from the stationary stride position, the actions are simplified. When the weight shifts from the push-off foot to the stride foot as the throw is executed, turning the heel over is somewhat easier, and the proper feel is developed. This stationary position reduces many complications and makes the focus on the heel paramount.

The heel-over movement may also be practiced from the regular throwing motion. The pitcher should push the knee down and toward the target. His foot should then push toward the target until it has completely cleared the rubber. The foot should then lift up, move to the throwing-hand side, form a circular motion, and come to rest approximately parallel with the stride foot, completing the movement with a rotation of the heel to the outside.

Chair Drill

This drill is designed to develop the feeling of throwing downhill, while encouraging the chest to be out and down. This drill will also refine the movement of getting the throwing elbow to the outside thigh, while improving the follow-through of the hips and promoting getting the heel over. Basically, this drill is the heel-over drill with a chair.

With the arm up, the back foot should start flat, with the inside of the foot on the chair.

With the front foot out, the stride foot is in place. The front knee is in, with weight on the ball of the foot. The chin is up, and the chest is out.

With the chin still up, the elbow should be to the outside of the front thigh. Rotating the foot over allows the arm to pull all the way through. The heel rotates over, while the front elbow should be visual from a front or side view.

The pitcher should place the inside of the push-off foot on the chair seat and assume a stride position. The chair should be in the area where the circular motion is made after the push-off. The weight should be shifted in the same manner as performed in the isolated stride foot position, which is inside to inside. The pitcher executes a throw, leaving the foot on the chair. He finishes the throwing motion by turning the foot over.

This drill is outstanding. It places the pitcher in a position representing the delivery at the point after the push-off foot has left the rubber. Repeating this drill not only enhances the follow-through, it also helps other aspects of the pitching motion.

Stride Foot Fence Drill

Often, pitchers lift the stride foot and pull the heel of the foot in toward the push-off leg. Anytime either leg is too tense, the tension spreads throughout the entire body. It is important for the pitcher to relax the stride leg. Picking the leg up, as opposed to slinging the leg into position, augments relaxation.

A fence, screen or similar object is necessary in order to carry out this drill. The fence is used to momentarily contain the front foot long enough for the front hip to lead the way.

The pitcher should work from the stretch position with the fence or screen in front of him and far enough away to enable the lift foot to touch it when the lift leg is at the maximum height during the lift action. This distance should be determined by the pitcher and the coach. The stride foot should remain relaxed as it is lifted. The toe of the stride foot should point downward, reach out and lightly touch the fence. The toe stays in that position until the front hip starts the stride. The toe should follow the front hip, brushing the fence as the foot continues to the stride position.

This drill is designed to slow the bottom half of the stride leg, thereby helping the pitcher to stay closed, which will result in a better stride. The pitcher should not reach with the stride foot. The front hip and the push-off foot should do the work. The fence acts as reminder to perform the motion properly. The pitcher should also avoid forcing his foot against the fence and should not allow his foot to roll under as the push off begins. The shoe laces should point upward and slightly toward the push-off leg as the foot brushes the fence. The outside cleats should be slightly visible to the batter. This position will help to lift the knee and hip at a proper angle.

In a proper stride, the stride foot is not overactive. The front foot catches the pitcher and provides balance and a solid base.

Trajectory Drill

Most shoulder, elbow or other arm injuries are probably the result of poor throwing mechanics. A very common cause of many sore arms is the failure to elevate the throwing arm. Not placing the throwing hand above the head by the time the stride foot lands is certainly a major contributor to arm injuries and poor pitching results.

For this drill, the pitcher needs to start from a "stationary stride position," with emphasis on throwing downhill. The throw should begin with the throwing arm at the top of the arc. The glove hand should be extended. The pitcher will execute the throw from this position. Part of the throwing motion is purposely eliminated in order to concentrate on the last phases of the throw.

The pitcher should make five or six throws from this position, but should not expect much power because only part of the motion is being performed. As the pitcher becomes accustomed to the feel of proper trajectory, or downhill action, he should establish a new starting point back and a few degrees lower. This point should be within the arc of the lift phase. A slight lift before reaching the top of the arc adds a little power and allows the pitcher to learn the proper procedure by practicing in phases. The pitcher should continue the process until he has worked backwards in increments to the separation of the hands. Next, he should separate his hands normally and take his throwing arm through the proper arc to see how smoothly a correct trajectory is achieved.

This drill is excellent for developing proper angles and helps create a good release point.

Rotation Drill

The purposes of this drill are to create awareness of how the ball rotates, to determine the effects of finger pressure, to develop methods of correcting inconsistent movement and, in general, to improve the rotation on each pitch.

This drill may be executed in one of several ways. One method is to isolate the feet so they are even with and parallel to the shoulders. The pitcher should not stride, but shift his weight from the inside of the push-off foot to the inside of the stride foot. By eliminating the stride, the concentration is focused on both arm action and grip (which produces rotation).

The pitcher should play catch with a partner who is stationed 30 to 40 feet away. While throwing, he should pay close attention to the rotation of the ball. Both the partner and the thrower should become acutely aware of how the ball spins and make suggestions to each other. They should help correct flaws and be equally willing to point out good rotation. The partner approach holds each partner accountable to understand and pay attention to the flight patterns of each pitch thrown. The coach should observe each pitcher and make appropriate suggestions.

The pitchers and the coach should be on the same page during the drill. Each pitcher should express his intentions and state the kind of movement and methods to be employed. The coach and the pitcher should be able to give advice based on these intentions.

Basic throwing grips can be introduced from a parallel isolated feet position. However, more serious work with various pitches is best handled from a stationary stride position.

A pitcher who has mastered a certain pitch is valuable as a teacher and as a demonstrator. Recognizing good rotation is part of the learning process. A pitcher with good rotation on a pitch can help others focus on some of the details involved in rotation.

It is recommended that one day per week be set aside for educated experimentation with grips and rotation.

Leg Lift Drill

Lifting the stride leg in a correct and controlled manner enhances balance and rhythm. The route and height should be consistent. Varied heights and different angles force extra energy and concentration in compensating for these inconsistencies.

The leg lift drill encourages the pitcher to be consistent in the height and direction of his stride leg.

The pitcher should be able to see the toe of his stride foot as he looks down his leg.

In the early lessons, the stretch position offers a simpler starting point than does the wind-up, so this drill should begin from the stretch position. The pitcher should lift the heel of the stride foot and keep the toe pointed as it leaves the ground. He should then lift the knee toward the outside of the chin (throwing arm side), keeping the stride leg relaxed and the stride foot in front of the body with the toe of that foot extended slightly beyond the knee. As the pitcher looks down his leg, he should be able to see the toe of the stride foot. He continues with the throw, coordinating the leg lift with the throwing action. The drill can be used to simply improve the leg lift. In this case, the proper lift and placement of the stride foot in its original spot should be repeated. In this setting, the relaxed and proper direction of the lift leg is learned.

This drill should also be performed from the wind-up position, making sure the stride leg is picked up and controlled in the same manner as executed in the stretch position. The pitcher should try to be consistent in height and direction with the stride leg.

Bottoming Out With the Hands Drill

A hard separation of the hands slows the throwing arm, creates tension and causes a delay in bringing the arm to its proper height. This action often results in several other flaws in the pitching motion such as shortening the arc, pushing the ball, pulling the head to the side to allow the arm to get through, opening the front should prematurely and breaking the rhythmic flow.

In a set position, the hands should be raised a few inches then dropped and separated at the normal position.

The hands drop softly until they bottom out.

The hands can now take a natural route outward and upward.

Relaxing or softening the hands at separation promotes speed and smoothness with the throwing arm. Bottoming out with the hands after separation encourages this freedom of movement.

Pitchers should use the "stationary stride position." They should then start with their hands at the set position, raise them a few inches, then drop and separate the hands at the normal position, letting them drop softly until they bottom out. At this point, the hands will take a natural route outward and upward. This relaxation allows the pitcher to have the throwing arc up quickly, and also aids the positioning of the front arm.

This drill is an excellent exercise to repeat in a "dry run" setting. Weight distribution, balance and timing are coordinated during the drill. As the hands separate, the weight moves to the ball of the push-off foot and shifts to the stride foot as the arm reaches the top of the arc.

Each pitcher will have a different separation point and will also exhibit differences in movement after separation. The "bottoming out" drill is excellent for developing consistency and success in separation of the hands.

Chest Out Drill

Arching the back and extending the chest to the target area will increase extension with the throwing arm and aid in the front arm action. Basically, this movement propels the top part of the body in a direct line to the target.

To execute the drill properly, the pitcher should use the "stationary stride" position, with emphasis on throwing both breasts directly toward the target. The breasts should be kept parallel to the ground and gain with the chest. With the back still arched and the chin up, the pitcher should complete the throwing motion squeezing the bottom of the chest area against the stride leg upper thigh. He should make sure the arm is finished well to the outside of the stride leg thigh.

This drill can be successfully performed in both an actual throwing setting and under simulation conditions.

Keeping the chest out helps the pitcher extend his throwing arm, and enhances his front arm action.

Chin Up Drill

As the chest arches to extend toward the target, the bottom of the chin should be parallel to the ground, which is referred to as the "chin up." When the chin is down, the chest becomes concave. This concave position shortens the throwing arm and generally restricts the throwing action. Allowing the chin to push down toward the chest is one of the causes of "recoiling."

Keeping the chest out helps the pitcher extend his throwing arm, and enhances his front arm action.

This drill is executed in the same manner as the chest out drill, with the exception of where the emphasis is placed. The priority simply shifts to the chin area. As the drill is repeated, pitchers should concentrate on keeping the chin up and directed toward the target.

This drill is a refinement exercise. Hopefully, some of the other drills will have already promoted good direction with the upper body. This drill will truly polish the "chest out" action and aid in the thrust and follow-through.

Eyes-to-Target Drill

This drill is similar to the chin up drill. In fact, concentration on taking the eyes to the target is a refinement of the chin up drill. In some respects, it is simply another way of emphasizing proper alignment of the upper body.

Pitchers who tilt or duck their heads will be helped dramatically with this drill. The head directs the body. When the head is thrown to one side, the body and arm will follow. Such a poor alignment increases the chance of injury and also contributes to a lack of control.

To carry out the drill, the pitcher should make sure his eyes are parallel to the ground. He should then open them widely, and produce the feeling of throwing them directly into the target. Good upper body alignment, better arm extension and better focus should result.

The pitcher's eyes should be parallel to the ground and feel like they are being thrown into the target.

This drill is designed to help with the pitcher's upper body alignment, arm extension and focus.

Screen Drill

Throwing into a screen is one of the best methods of improving mechanical skills. Such an exercise will provide an opportunity to concentrate on the mechanics of throwing, rather than where the ball is going. Often pitchers go to the bullpen to work on mechanical flaws only to hear a catcher or fellow pitcher remind him of another priority—control. Even the pitcher himself is often distracted when the pitch does not break enough or when it does not hit the target. The screen drill offers an environment for the pitcher to center on the priority he chooses with full concentration.

Using a screen helps a pitcher develop a sense of feel and helps him concentrate on the mechanics of throwing.

The screen drill is designed to teach independence and help the pitcher develop a sense of feel. The pitcher needs no one else for this drill. A partner may be incorporated, but it is not necessary.

The recommended size for the screen is at least four feet wide and seven feet tall. Other sizes are acceptable, as long as they are effective in stopping the ball. The recommended material for the screen is netting. This material will not damage the ball and will provide a view for the coach who may want to station himself behind the net and in line with the throw.

Watching the pitcher throw to a net is an excellent way to evaluate and make corrections. The pitcher is able to go through a full range of motion, but he is not required to throw long distances or with great velocity. This practice allows the pitcher an opportunity to repeat a movement many times without undue pressure or injury.

For best results, the screen should be placed approximately 20 feet from the pitcher.

Right-to-Left Drill

The purpose of this drill is to accentuate the throwing arm through the pitch. To do this, the right-handed pitcher should reach out toward the target and finish with his elbow to the left of the stride leg thigh. This action will help to drive the fingers through the ball, thereby maximizing movement and power. Proper extension, along with the right-to-left action, will help to produce better control.

This drill may be successfully performed from the stretch, the wind-up, or the stationary stride position. This drill is sometimes called the "elbow to knee" drill. The "right-to-left" term probably more truly defines the proper action.

The pitcher who finishes with a straight front leg, and does not bend his back or finish each pitch, will profit from this exercise.

Hop-Balance-Hop Drill

This drill is designed to improve agility and balance. The push-off and the stride should show improvement from its use. Balance is essential to consistent

Proper right-to-left action helps a pitcher produce better control.

athletic performance. Good balance at the push-off position indicates proper mechanics. Balance during the stride establishes the base for power and control.

The pitcher should begin the drill from a stretch position and pay special attention to the positioning of the push-off foot. The push-off foot should be placed at a 45-degree angle, with the toe ahead of the heel. He should proceed with a leg lift, making sure his weight transfers to the ball of the push-off foot. That foot should remain stable, and the pitcher should be able to have control of the body at this point. While on his right foot (RHP), the pitcher should execute a series of hops by landing on the ball of the push-off foot, Each hop starts and finishes at a 45-degree angle, with the toe ahead of the heel.

It is important for the pitcher to develop balance and agility at two key points of his delivery.

After successfully working on the push-off foot, attention should be transferred to the stride foot. To drill the stride foot, the pitcher will make a throw from the stretch position, making sure his weight is shifted to the ball of the stride foot. If the weight is properly distributed, the pitcher should be able to balance momentarily on the stride foot. At this point, he will again perform a series of hops, with each hop reestablishing a proper stride position. The stride foot should be stable at each landing.

After practicing the series of hops on each foot, the pitcher should then combine the work of each foot and add a balance phase between the hops. He should take three hops on the push-off foot, balance, and take three hops on the stride foot.

This drill is designed to help the pitcher's balance and agility at two very important points in the delivery.

Throwing from the Knees Drill (Knees Parallel to Shoulders)

Throwing from the knees serves the same purposes as the isolated feet, or stationary throwing position drill. Because it further eliminates various movements, this drill permits the pitcher to concentrate on upper body movement. It is also a good position from which to improve weight shift and balance. At close range (30 to 60 feet), specific details or mechanics may be practiced effectively. From distances of 90 to 120 feet, the pitcher is placed in a setting to improve balance and power.

Double-Catcher Drill

Occasionally a particular pitcher will have difficulties throwing to the outside part of the strike zone. This situation is generally the result of a mechanical problem, but when the mechanical problem is deeply rooted, a mental block is also often present.

Using two catchers, one stationed in the normal position behind home plate in the bullpen and the second stationed in the other home plate area to the glove hand side of the pitcher, gives the pitcher two targets. The home plates are usually eight to ten feet apart. If they are farther apart than ten feet, the plate for the second catcher should be ignored, and the second catcher should be stationed approximately eight feet from the normal target.

The pitcher should throw two to three times to the normal target and then two or three times to the second target, using the same stride. The stride should be the same on all pitches, regardless of the target. This procedure should be continued until the pitcher is successful in striding toward the primary target and successful in effectively hitting the secondary target. This drill will improve the right-to-left action for the right-handed pitcher or the left-to-right action of the left-handed pitcher. This drill will clearly demonstrate to a pitcher how much flexibility he possesses and how much adjustment is possible without changing the stride. It is also designed to illustrate the importance of extension and follow-through.

Exaggerated Target

Occasionally a particular pitcher has an unusual fixation with the plate as a target. He "freezes up," or over concentrates, to the point of complete distraction. As a result, he is unable to hit the target. In some cases, removing the plate as a target helps this psychological problem.

The catcher should be placed a foot or two on either side of home plate, making him the target. Home plate should be completely eliminated from the picture. Once the pitcher is able to consistently throw to the catcher, the catcher should move to the opposite side of the plate, with the emphasis again on the catcher rather than the plate. As the pitcher learns to throw to the catcher, the catcher may change his position, offering a target closer to the plate.

Over a period of several days, the target can be moved by small increments toward the plate area, while keeping the focus on the catcher. This practice is done until the catcher is able to set up directly behind the plate, and the pitcher is no longer adversely affected by the plate as a target.

Extremely wild pitchers frequently benefit from this type of drill, since a larger and more realistic target at the early stages of development is offered.

Strike Zone with Strings

This drill is an old-fashioned and simple control exercise that involves throwing to a strike zone made of strings. To make a strike zone, two strings should be attached to two standards or poles. One is the height of the lowest part of the strike zone and the other represents the highest part of the strike zone. Two more strings should be placed in a position running vertically to each of the horizontal strings, 17 inches from each other. This will provide a strike zone similar to that of an average batter.

The standards or poles should be far enough apart to provide safety for the catcher. The catcher should also use full gear when catching behind the strings. Although the strings will give when hit, a ball hitting one of them may be thrown off course enough to interfere with the catch. Throwing through the strings offers the pitcher a visual target and creates greater incentive to work toward better control. More sophisticated targets are on the market which serve the same purpose. Anything which encourages the pitcher to concentrate on the target is acceptable.

Stick Drill

The stick drill can be used to improve hand speed. Just as some hitters use a lighter, rather than a heavier, object to improve their swing, pitchers can follow a similar practice to improve the pitching delivery. Hand speed, particularly at the release point, is of paramount importance to the bite, speed, and location of the pitch. Speed with the hand through the release area almost assures relaxation, proper acceleration, and proper deceleration through the braking area. Improve the acceleration of the hand, and it is reasonable to contend that pitch velocity will increase and the delivery will be more energy-efficient. In addition, less strain will be put on the arm and shoulder.

The stick is a 3/8- to 5/8-inch dowel, cut to 18 to 24 inches in length. The dowel can be attached to a baseball by gluing the dowel into a drilled hole in the ball. However, it is preferable to use the dowel without attaching a ball. The hand action appears to be smoother and faster without the ball attached.

If a ball is attached to the dowel, the pitcher should grip the ball with the index and middle finger in a normal manner, but make sure the dowel is pointing in the same direction as the fingers. If the pitcher is using the dowel without a ball, he should place the dowel between the index and middle fingers, pointing in the direction of the middle knuckles of those fingers.

The drill can be done from a stationary stride position, or from the stretch or wind-up position. The pitcher should make a throwing motion and try to reach out and extend through the release point quickly. Repeat several times. Remember, the emphasis is on executing a correct throwing motion. Close observation is important to see that the pitcher does not alter the throwing motion because of the lighter object. The stick is lighter and should provide an opportunity to move the hand through the throwing area more quickly. The coach should be vigilant and stern concerning the proper motion during the drill.

Note: Be careful not to do so many repetitions that blisters will result. The stick does rub against the inside of the index and middle fingers, so be aware. (In most instances, 20 to 30 simulated throws with the stick could be done without producing blisters.)

Release Point by Sound—Stick Drill

Working with a stick also helps the pitcher get a "feel" for the release point and arm extension. It even helps to get the arm up and into a functional load position. Sound is the key to the drill. The sound from the whip of the stick moving through the release area gives the pitcher valuable information. The sound indicates where the ball was released. When he knows where the ball is released, even the beginning pitcher can determine the destination of the pitch.

Instruct the pitcher to simulate throwing a pitch down the middle at the knees while holding onto the stick. After the simulated throw, ask the pitcher the location of the pitch had he actually thrown a ball. Some pitchers will instantly associate the sound with the release point and produce the correct answer. If the sound made by the stick racing through the release point was to the right of a right-handed pitcher and above the pitcher's head, for example, the location of the pitch would have been up and into a right-handed batter. Have the pitcher simulate another throw with the same target in mind. Ask the pitcher where the sound from the swishing stick occurred. If you both agree on the area of the sound, then ask the pitcher to associate the sound with where he released the imaginary ball. Then have the pitcher associate the sound, or release point, with the location of the pitch.

Assign a spot in front of the pitcher for him to make the sound with the stick. After the throwing motion with the stick, ask the pitcher to evaluate the action:
- "Where did the sound occur?"
- "Where was the release point?"
- "What was the location of the imaginary pitch?"

Continue this routine until the pitcher can locate the sound, associate the sound with the release point, and associate the release point, or the sound, with the location of the pitch. Normally, the pitcher can recognize the association quickly. Both the pitcher and the coach can easily determine where the sound was made.

To establish a sound and consistent release point, the pitcher corrects and improves many of the other aspects of the delivery. Balance, separation of hands, getting the arm up and in throwing position, stride, and body angles are all aided by this simple drill.

Summary

This chapter discussed the fact that each drill should accomplish one or more goals. Drills should be used with specific purposes in mind, otherwise they have little value. Focusing on the task at hand and supplementing that task with a worthwhile drill may speed up the learning process. A proper drill for the occasion will also add interest and enthusiasm to the workout.

A pitcher who knows how to perform a drill and understands its purpose has the major elements of improving his skills. When drills are simple and clearly deal with important parts of the pitcher's game, they are more eagerly used. To improve any skill, repetition is necessary. Accordingly, not only should the drill should fit the goal, it should be utilized on a regular basis.

6

Dry-Run Pitching

Dry-run pitching is a method of pitching without throwing the baseball, although it may include throwing at minimal speeds. During a dry-run practice, each pitcher should have a baseball in his possession, and each drill practiced should include going through the desired movements while using a proper grip.

Perhaps the most valuable asset of this type of practice is that of perfecting and maintaining good mechanics. Dry-run practice can be done at almost any time. It is often difficult to work on the pitching delivery with a pitcher who has just finished pitching or a pitcher with a tired arm. During the course of a season, this situation is often the case. For the pitcher experiencing some mechanical flaws, the logistics of correction are very important. Dry-run pitching not only makes corrections possible, it also creates a learning environment which allows the pitcher to see and feel the various movements of the pitching delivery. This objective can be accomplished with little or no strain on the pitching arm.

Virtually any part of the pitching delivery, or even the entire pitching delivery, can be emphasized in the dry-run phase. This procedure blends with the sequential teaching patterns of this system. Each area can be isolated, and specific concentration can be applied to that area. When properly utilized, dry-run pitching drills will serve as both a valuable teaching method and a motivational adventure. The instructor is able to coach a large number of pitchers at one time and still point out positive and negative activities to a single pitcher or the entire pitching staff.

Dry-run pitching may also serve to develop leadership among the pitching staff by assigning experienced pitchers with teaching the skills they have already learned. This practice should only be done if the pitcher assigned is serious about sharing his knowledge with others. If the pitcher is capable and ready to do this, he will find his teachings to be not only beneficial to the learner but very rewarding and educational for himself. Many pitchers find the teaching of a skill to be more helpful to themselves than to the person being taught. Much thought is necessary in order to impart knowledge. The act of showing or telling someone how to do something often refines the skills of both parties. For example, a pitcher with a good curveball is proud of that pitch and finds it exciting to help a fellow pitcher develop his kind of curveball. That good curveball pitcher will make sure he emphasizes the correct way to throw the pitch and also describe those factors which cause problems for himself. While giving valuable information to his counterpart, he is also preaching to himself.

Repetition is absolutely essential in learning motor skills. It is also necessary in order to maintain and refine those skills. Dry-run drills provide such repetition. Any pitching fundamental may be repeated as many times as necessary without putting excessive stress on the arm. This repetitive procedure offers a setting for the young, inexperienced pitcher to practice new and sound movements, and also offers the experienced pitcher opportunities to refine known fundamentals. The dry-run procedure provides a stage for corrections. The pitching coach should devise a checklist of fundamentals for the pitchers. Each time the dry-run drills are used, both the pitcher and the pitching coach can review skills from the checklist. This practice provides concrete teaching and learning. A pitcher who has not fully learned a particular skill is made aware of his shortcomings, and the pitcher who becomes sloppy or lazy is also quickly reminded of his mistakes.

The regular use of the dry-run teaching station encourages and develops both discipline and sound work ethics. This practice leads to the establishment of long-term pitching results. On a regular basis, the pitching coach is able to impart ideas involving these areas to the entire pitching staff. A diligent effort and a steady focus on correct movements and a commitment to perform these movements well, will lead to not only a better delivery, but also will enhance a pitcher's level of desire and pride from his accomplishing his goals.

Dry-Run Drills

Any dry-run drill can be started by forming one or more lines directly in front of the pitching coach or the leader of the drill. Each pitcher should face the leader and should give himself adequate space to be able to make a full pitching motion. The pitching coach or the leader is better able to teach the group when the lines are no more than six pitchers across and no more than two deep. In this particular setting the coach is able to see each pitcher. Smaller groups are even more desirable. An experienced pitching coach will be able to work with larger groups by moving his central position back from the two lines to provide a more panoramic view.

STEP 1—All pitchers should face straight ahead with their belly buttons facing the target. They should start with their right foot (right-handed pitcher) in front, and should place their left toe even with the heel of the front foot, about 6 to 12 inches apart. The belly button remains facing the target. The weight shift should be practiced. The front knee should be locked, with weight placed on the front foot. Then, their weight should shift to a locked back knee and an unlocked front knee. The belly button now faces the target. The right foot turns and is placed with the toe ahead of the heel, in front of the pitching rubber (either the parallel position or the 45-degree angle position can be used). Next, the weight is brought from the locked back leg and placed on the ball of the front foot and the unlocked front leg, with the belly button still facing the target. The pitcher and coach should make sure the shift is done with smoothness and a minimum of excess movements.

Attention should also be paid to the pitchers' shoulders, making sure they stay parallel to an imaginary pitching rubber, which means the pitchers are making the shift by keeping their belly buttons facing the target. A premature pivot should not be allowed.

STEP 2—The step #1 movement should be practiced, but the coach should also include the coordination of the hands and arms with this movement. As the weight is moved to a locked backed leg, the hands are moved upward, using the long- or short-stroke technique. When the hands come to the top of the stroke, the front foot is placed, with the toe ahead of the heel, in either the parallel or the 45-degree position. The belly button should still be facing the target. As the front foot is placed into position, the weight is moved onto the unlocked front leg and the ball of the front foot. These moves should be practiced until a good shift is accomplished. As in step #1, extra movements should be eliminated.

As the hands are brought upward, the pitching hand should be kept deep and near the web of the glove, with the elbows no wider than the width of the pitcher's body. This movement should be soft and relaxed. Attention should be paid to the timing of the move. When the hands stop, the front foot should be placed into proper position.

This phase offers an excellent opportunity to review those simple movements that were emphasized in the feet-to-knees area.

STEP 3—From the step #2 position, the pitcher is ready to activate the leg lift. As the hands start down in front of the body, the front leg should begin to lift. With the weight on the ball of the push-off foot, the front leg continues to lift until the hands reach the point of separation. At that point, the leg lift ends. Simultaneously, the pivot, or turning, begins.

At the top of the leg lift and the end of the leg lift, the toe of a relaxed front foot should be pointed downward, and the front leg should be bent. The lift leg foot should be slightly ahead of the knee. In this position, the pitcher should be able to look down the thigh of his front leg and see the tip of his front toe.

The knee of the lift leg should be lifted toward the side of the chin nearest the throwing arm. At the top of the leg lift, the heel of the lead foot should be higher than the toe of that foot, and the outside cleats should be slightly tilted higher than the inside cleats. Pitchers should be careful not to reach toward the target during the lift.

Pitchers should practice the weight shift and the leg lift, making sure the leg lift is soft and properly directed. They should be particularly concerned with several factors, including how the front foot leaves the ground, the relaxation and softness of the leg lift, the distance of the front foot from the body and the timing of the pivot with the direction and coordination of the stroke.

It is also very important for the pitcher to keep his belly button facing the target until slightly prior to when his hands and front knee come together. The pivot should not begin too soon.

STEP 4—At this point, it is a good practice for the pitcher to repeat steps #1, #2, and #3 from the stretch, or set position.

The right foot begins in either of the correct positions, with the front foot closed about 6 to 12 inches apart. Both knees should be unlocked, and the weight should be on the balls of the feet. The ball should be gripped in the pitching hand and held behind the right leg (RHP), or the ball may be kept in the glove with the right hand behind the right leg. The glove is held at a point close to the belt area, or at the spot where the pitcher separates his hands in preparation for the throw. This spot varies with some pitchers. The correct area is anywhere from the crotch to the letters, but the most desirable and functional spot for most pitchers is the area near the belt.

Next, the pitcher takes a short rocking step toward the target with the front foot, and brings that foot back to its original spot. As the foot rocks forward, he should institute the desired stroking action (either the short stroke or the long stroke). The rocking action should correspond with the stroke. The stroke should be completed as the front foot is reset. At this point, the weight should be on the balls of both feet, and both knees should be unlocked. Slightly more weight should be on the push-off foot.

At the top part of the body, the front shoulder should be closed to the target, the elbows should be close to the body, the back of the glove should face the hitter, and the ball and the pitching hand should be hidden in the glove. The glove and pitching hand should be held slightly out in front and at the vertical mid-line of the body.

Pitchers should move through the step #4 movements until they can be done with smoothness and balance. While these movements are basic and elementary, they are extremely important in establishing a balanced and functional delivery.

STEP 5—From the stretch position established in step #4, the stride foot should be lifted by raising the heel first, making sure the heel remains higher than the toe throughout the lift. As the leg is lifted, the hands move upward in line with the vertical mid-point of the body. This hand action is a bouncing movement, but should be short and relaxed. he hands move up the mid-line of the body, and then move back down the same mid-line, where they separate at the top of the leg kick. The separation point should be exactly the same each time. In addition, the hands should separate at the same point in the stretch as they do in the wind-up.

The knee should be picked up toward the throwing arm side of the chin. The leg lift should be soft and relaxed. Quickness is also important. Constant practice will allow the pitcher to make this movement without extra or wasted motion.

At the top of the leg lift, the foot of the lift leg should be in front of the vertical mid-line, with the toe pointed toward the ground. As the pitcher looks down the thigh of the lift leg, he should be able to see the tip of his lift leg toe. This check point will assure a pitcher of how far away from the body the foot should extend. The outside of the lift leg foot should be elevated slightly higher than the inside of that foot.

Special attention should be paid to the width between the feet. Too wide a stance will create a longer distance for the lift leg to travel. The front foot should be in a closed position. The pitcher should also focus on the method in which the front foot leaves the ground and how it is positioned as the leg lift is executed. A balanced position, with both knees unlocked, is the correct starting position to make the movements efficient.

Initially, the stance should be practiced. Then, the pitchers should proceed through the total procedure until the movements are successfully performed.

STEP 6—Each pitcher should properly execute the leg lift from the stretch position, and when the knee reaches its desired height, the pitcher should hold that position. This action will serve as a balance checkpoint, and can be used as a prerequisite for the stride. This action should be repeated, with each pitcher holding the balance position for a count of three.

From this position, the coach should check the balance of the pitcher, making sure his weight is on the inside of the ball of the push-off foot. The toe should be ahead of the heel. At this point, the coach should also check the height of the leg lift, the position of the leg-lift foot, and the position of the hands and arms, making sure the push-off knee is unlocked.

STEP 7—From the wind-up position, step #6 should be repeated. Most pitchers will have more difficulty getting to a balance position from the wind-up position than from the stretch position.

STEP 8—From the stretch position, the pitcher executes the leg lift and holds it. Then he executes the stride. This action is done by deactivating the bottom half of the stride leg. He should not reach or stride with this foot at the outset. He should hold the knee lift and keep the stride foot in front of the vertical mid-line as long as possible. The stride should be started with the front hip. The front hip should lead the way. As the front hip moves toward the stride spot of the stride foot, the unlocked back knee should be pushed downward. Keeping the knee at its maximum height and deactivating the bottom part of the stride leg will provide an even greater drive.

The stride foot will want to reach. It is important for the pitcher to hold it up and back as long as possible. At the end of the drive with the hip and push-off knee, the stride foot should be placed with the weight landing on the ball of the foot as though landing an airplane. The ball of the foot acts as the front wheels of the airplane. After contact with the ball of the foot, the rest of the foot should be brought in contact with the ground. This position will provide a sound and solid base from which the pitcher can balance. As the foot lands, the outside of the stride foot should be slightly elevated above the inside part of the stride foot. This position properly places the weight on the ball of the foot. The stride foot should land in a slightly pigeon-toed position.

STEP 9—From the stretch position, the pitcher should again execute the leg lift. At the top of the leg lift, he should assume the balance position. From this position, he should then slightly elevate the front hip (three to six inches) and fall forward with the front hip leading the way. This action will give the pitcher the feel of the initial push-off movement.

While falling, the pitcher should hold the leg lift. This action will help him land on a bent front leg and the ball of the foot. For purposes of the drill and in order to keep from opening the front foot too quickly, he should keep the front foot closed while striding. This procedure will place the stride foot in a closed position at the landing point. This placement is not a correct landing position, but it will help the pitcher attain the proper feel of the push-off and the driving part of the stride.

The pitcher should make sure the front leg does not reach or extend. He should insist upon the front hip and the push-off knee doing the work. It is also important for the inside ball of the stride foot to make contact first. The weight of the pitcher should be brought over the ball of the stride foot.

STEP 10—At this point, it is important to make certain the stride foot is properly used. The stride foot should land pigeon-toed, with the weight on the inside of that foot. As the throwing action continues, all of the weight should settle over the stride foot with the pitcher's total weight balanced on it.

The procedure from step #9 should be followed, except focus should be on the initial contact of the stride foot. Instead of landing with the foot closed, the pitcher should simply open the toe shortly before it makes contact with the ground. To open the foot properly, he has to leave the heel closed and make a half circle with the pointed toe of the stride foot. He should also make sure the foot is not thrown to an open position.

Coaches should have their players continue practicing the contact point of the stride until they can make a consistent and properly positioned placement with the stride foot. A slightly pigeon-toed landing position with the weight on the ball of the foot, and the weight evenly balanced over the front foot, is a desirable goal.

STEP 11—From the stretch position, the pitcher will execute the leg lift and the stride. At the stride position, the pitcher should balance on the stride foot and hold this balanced position for a count of three. During this step, the pitcher should stride in the same spot and land on the inside ball of his foot in a pigeon-toed and solid position, with the stride knee bent. When the weight is brought through to finish the arm action, the top part of the body should be directly over the stride foot. The stride foot should not roll, slide or spin. It should remain solid. Such a position helps to maintain balance during the entire throwing action.

This drill is excellent for recognizing the need for balance. A balanced position at this point will correct many problems. Good balance at the stride position enhances proper angles and body direction, improves the consistency of the release point, helps distribute power properly and allows the pitcher to complete a full range of motion with freedom. Good balance with the stride will also help to minimize injuries.

STEP 12—From the wind-up position, the pitcher should practice the weight shift and the placement of the push-off foot. He should coordinate these elements with the stroking action and the leg lift. At this point, he should check the balance on the push-off foot, making sure the toe of the push-off foot is ahead of the heel. The back knee should be unlocked and pointed slightly toward the target.

This is a good time for the pitcher to review the starting stance, making sure his feet are no more than 12 inches apart, and the toe of the back foot is no further back than the heel of the front foot. The weight transfer should occur without taking a big step backward. The move back should be a slight rocking action, with the weight shifting to no more than a straight-up position. The rocking action should not drop the weight back to the heel. Such an action will carry the body away from the target.

As the leg is lifted, the pitcher should take care in controlling the leg, rather than slinging it into position. Coaches should watch the direction of the body as the leg is lifted. The body should remain quiet and in line with the target. The leg lift should not be allowed to cause the body to drift to the right or fall back to the left.

STEP 13—From the wind-up position, the procedures of step #12 are followed, with the exception of holding the balance position at the top of the leg lift. Pitchers should proceed from the leg lift to the stride by leading with the front hip and pushing down with the push-off knee. They should land properly on the stride foot and hold that position for the count of three. This action will allow the pitcher and the pitching coach to check the balance at the stride position.

Coaches should note the balance at push-off, the direction and rhythm of the body and the landing stride of the foot. If the pitcher lands in a balanced position and is able to hold for the full count, he is probably executing the movements efficiently for that position.

In the holding position, the pitcher should have a bent front knee which is in line with, or in front of, the toe of the stride foot. The stride foot should be slightly pigeon-toed and the weight should be on the ball of the foot, with the heel of that foot in contact with the ground.

STEP 14—This step involves executing step #13 from the stretch position. The coach should check the leg lift, making sure it is similar to the leg lift of the wind-up. The coach should also scrutinize the separation point of the hands, making sure they separate at the same point as in the wind-up.

The push-off and the stride execution from a stretch position should be similar to those of the wind-up. If the movements are not similar, the pitcher will develop two different deliveries, one from the stretch and one from the wind-up. To be effective, the pitcher should be able to move from one position to the other without a noticeable difference.

STEP 15—From the stretch position, the pitcher should move through the first part of the delivery, but stop at the top of the leg lift, pause for a count, then hop toward the target three times. While hopping, he should keep the leg lift at its maximum height, keeping the front toe pointed downward and relaxed. On each hop, the pitcher should relax, move with grace and balance and land with the toe ahead of the heel and the weight on the ball of the push-off foot.

STEP 16—From the stretch position, the pitcher should move through the delivery until the stride is fulfilled. At this point, the pitcher should hold the stride position for one count and follow with three hops on the stride foot toward the target. Coaches should pay special attention to the placement of the stride foot on each hop. The foot should land pointing toward the target , with the toe slightly closed.

On each hop, the stride knee should be bent, and the weight of the body should be balanced over the inside and the ball of the stride foot. The pitcher's head and chest should be pointed directly toward the target, and his throwing arm should be well to the left (RHP) of the stride leg. The arm should be relaxed and loose.

STEP 17—The pitcher should follow the instructions in step #15 from the wind-up position. Coaches should pay close attention to the pitcher's direction and balance.

STEP 18—The pitcher should follow the instructions in step #16 from the wind-up position. Again, the coach should pay close attention to the pitcher's direction and balance.

STEP 19—From the stretch position, the pitcher should go through the first part of the pitching delivery, should pause at the top of the leg lift, and then hop three times on the push-off foot. This action should be followed with a stride and throwing motion, allowing the arm to complete its motion while pausing on the stride foot. This action should be followed with three hops on the stride foot. All hops should be soft, graceful, balanced and directly toward the target.

This drill is an excellent method for coaches to check direction and balance. If the pitcher is able to execute these moves with agility and balance, he is ready to move on to the next step. If he has difficulty, the coach should make an assessment of the origin of the problem and go back to the step which solves that problem. It is important not to move on until the pitcher has mastered each particular step.

STEP 20—The pitcher should follow the procedures in step #19 from the wind-up position.

Summary of First 20 Steps

The 20 steps are basically concerned with the stance in the wind-up, the stance in the stretch, the push-off and the stride. The movements taught in these drills are essential to a sound pitching delivery. Spending quality time and carefully focusing on the movements will make other movements of the delivery easier to understand and to perform. Coaches should not go any further until their pitchers are able to perform these movements successfully.

Although it may be easy to overlook some of these simple steps, to do so would create even greater problems later. Even pitchers with sound deliveries should go through these steps. For the skilled pitcher, these steps serve as a maintenance tool and provide a solid checklist.

Every pitcher should know the purpose of each step. A pitcher should develop a feel for each step and recognize when that feel is not right. Not only should he be able to recognize what is correct for himself, but he should also be able to recognize and see what his fellow pitchers are doing right and wrong. These movements are concrete, absolutes that are visible to anyone interested in recognizing them.

STEP 21—From the stretch position, the pitcher should execute the leg lift and hold it. Before executing the stride, he should lift the front hip three to six inches and reach with the stride knee toward the throwing arm side of the chin. This movement will finish the coiling action and prepare the hip to drive down and toward the target.

The belt line of the pitcher should be higher on the glove-hand side than the throwing-arm side. A look from the side of the pitcher should reveal a three- to six-inch height differential.

The front hip initiates the stride and is aided by the downward drive of the push-off knee. It is extremely important for the pitcher to lead with the front hip. He should make sure the front hip elevates slightly before the stride begins, and he should pay attention to the bottom part of the lift leg. The leg should be relaxed, with the bottom half held back as long as possible. He should let the front hip and the back foot and leg do the work.

STEP 22—This phase is a repeat of step #21, only from the wind-up position.

STEP 23—From the stretch position, the pitcher should execute the leg lift, and hold that position at the top, making sure his hands move up and down the vertical mid-line of the body. From this position, the coach should check the position of the pitcher's hands and the position of the foot of the lift leg.

At this point, the pitcher should refine the hand position and the pivot. This objective can be done by the pitcher keeping his elbows close to the fat pads on the side of the waist, with his elbows not extending beyond the back. This placement will keep the hands out in front in a functional and relaxed position. He should keep his hands in line with the vertical mid-line of the body through the separation point. A pitcher's hands should be in front of the vertical mid-line and even during the pivot.

As the hip is elevated prior to the stride, the lift leg foot may go slightly to the throwing arm side of the vertical mid-line of the body. This movement will create a greater coiling position and provide a better driving action. Pitchers should not overdo this movement, however. To overemphasize this move may result in losing the coil and may also create an inconsistent arm angle. This action causes difficulties in placing the arm up into a proper position.

The drill is completed by striding and simulating the throw. The total process should be repeated until success is achieved.

STEP 24—This phase is step #23 performed from the wind-up position.

Stationary-Stride Position

The next few steps should be done from a position called the stationary-stride position. To form the stationary-stride position, the pitcher begins by making an imaginary throw with a normal stride with the stride foot. However, he should keep the push-off foot in contact with the ground at its original starting point. The pitcher stays in that position. This action will place the pitcher in a stationary position. During the next few drills the pitcher will not be required to move either the stride foot or the push-off foot; they will both remain in the stationary position.

This approach will enable the pitcher to concentrate on specific parts of the delivery without having to make the long movement and the difficult timing involved in the push-off and the stride. It basically allows him to better concentrate and to refine one or more priorities in the following steps.

The stationary stride provides greater opportunities for the pitcher to focus on specific movements and gives the pitcher a sense of feel for that movement. More attention can be centered on the movement in question without the added burden of having to perform the total series of movements.

STEP 25—From the stationary foot position, the pitcher should practice shifting his weight from the push-off foot to the stride foot. He does this by holding the ball in the glove similar to the hand position used in the stretch position. For this drill, he should keep his hands in that position as the weight shift is repeated.

He starts with his weight on the inside and the ball of the push-off foot. He keeps the push-off knee bent and pointing slightly toward the target. He transfers his weight by driving the push-off knee downward and toward the target, forcing his weight to the inside of the stride foot. He should make sure the stride-foot knee is bent and rides forward as his weight is brought over to it.

It is important to emphasize an inside-to-inside weight shift, from the inside of the push-off foot to the inside of the stride foot. While the bulk of the weight should be kept on the ball of the stride foot, the heel of that foot should be in contact with the ground and collect some of the weight.

The knee of the bent-stride leg should ride forward and move slightly to the throwing-arm side of the vertical mid-line. This action will create better balance and allow the throwing arm to be free of the stride knee and in front of it, while the pitcher gains maximum extension and moves from right to left (RHP).

STEP 26—From the stationary-stride position, the pitcher works with the hand separation. Earlier in the dry-run drill, the hand separation was introduced. At this point, it is time to refine this movement. The pitcher starts with his weight evenly distributed between the stride foot and the push-off foot, with his hands together, as in a stretch position. Simultaneously, he should move his weight to the inside of the push-off foot and quietly bounce his hands upward along the vertical mid-line of the body. The upward motion should not exceed six inches.

As his weight shifts against the inside of the push-off foot, the pitcher's hands should move down the vertical line of the body and separate when they reach the desired hand separation point. This action should be soft and relaxed, and the hands should be separated at the same place each time.

The pitcher should make sure this separation is done quickly, softly and in rhythm. This action is critical and is largely responsible for the throwing arm being in a proper throwing angle. This action is also relevant to the positioning and use of the front arm.

STEP 27—This phase involves following the procedures in step #26, plus incorporating the bottoming out of the hands after separation. After separating his hands, the pitcher should allow the hands to continue dropping down the vertical center line of the body until they reach full extension of both arms. This movement should be soft and relaxed, creating a natural and quick movement for both arms to be in a ready position for the throw. When the hands are dropped and allowed to bottom out, they will automatically travel away from each other and begin to move upward. This action makes the arm lift much easier.

As the pitching hand leaves the glove, the pitcher needs to make sure his fingertips point toward the ground. It will be necessary to rotate the thumb clockwise to the outside leg. The thumb rotation is slight, requiring no more than a quarter turn. While rotating the thumb, the pitcher should keep the fingertips pointing downward. They should remain in that position all the way up to the top of the arm lift.

The glove hand should remain relaxed as it breaks away from the pitching hand. The glove should be closed to the hitter with the fingers pointing downward. The fingers of the glove hand will level out as the arm is lifted, but it is recommended that the back of the glove presented to the hitter.

It is important to pay attention to the route of both arms. Each arm should break away and travel down, back and up in a direct path. The front arm should not be allowed to open or become inactive, and the throwing arm should not be permitted to wrap behind the back.

STEP 28—The procedures in step #27 are followed. Concentration should be on the arm lift of the throwing arm. As the throwing hand breaks from the glove, the finger tips should remain pointed toward the ground as the thumb rotates clockwise to the outside. At this point, the hand is beginning to move down and back and even starting to lift, provided relaxation and softness occurred at the separation point. The arm lift has begun. The pitcher needs to take over and direct the lift the rest of the way. He should keep reaching back until the throwing arm is extended to the arc of the throw. At this point, the pitcher should keep the finger pointing downward and he should lift his arm as though picking a ball off the batting "T." The lift continues until the hand and the ball are at the top of the arc of the throw. If the fingers remain pointing downward, the elbow will bend slightly during the lift. It is necessary to allow the arm to bend. Otherwise, the arm will feel tight, and the arm lift will be slowed. A straight arm also encourages the fingers to straighten, or the hand to rotate the fingertip upwards. The arm lift should raise the pitching hand to a position at least higher than the cap.

STEP 29—From the stationary stride position, the pitcher should place the weight on the inside of the push-off foot and place his arm at the top of the arm lift position. At this point, the fingers should still be pointing toward the ground. This action places the wrist in a position which is called a forward wrist. In other words, the wrist is still in a cocked or action position.

The position created by the movements discussed above should be a 90-degree angle (a right angle). That angle places the elbow at a position even with the throwing arm shoulder.

From this position, the pitcher should make a few imaginary throws and develop a feel for the proper angle and how the wrist automatically flops back as the elbow leads the throwing arm into the release point area. If the wrist is prematurely flopped back, the pitcher will have a feel of slinging the ball. This action will put undue stress on the elbow and shoulder area and will result in a loss of speed and direction.

STEP 30—The procedures in step #29 are followed, with special emphasis placed on concentrating on the pitcher being on top of the ball. The pitcher should have the feel of throwing downhill (i.e., he should visualize a downward flight of the ball). To throw in this manner, it is necessary for the pitcher to properly execute the separation of the hands and the arm lift.

As the throw is simulated from the stationary stride position, the pitcher should develop a feel of pushing-off the rubber. In addition, he should be able to extend his throwing arm toward the target and feel as though there is a continuing downward movement with the throwing hand throughout the entire throwing motion.

The fingers of the throwing hand should remain on top of the ball as the throwing action takes place. A proper separation of the hands and a correct arm lift will help to keep the fingers in this position.

STEP 31—From the stationary-stride position, the pitcher should execute the weight transfer, the separation of hands, the bottoming out, the arm lift, and the forward wrist, while continuing with the simulated throwing motion. His concentration should be on the extension and the route of the throwing arm as it moves in front of the body. From the beginning of the arm lift, the throwing arm should begin to make a circle. The throwing motion should complete that circle, making it as big as possible. This action will provide maximum leverage. If the circle is made shorter, or is bisected, leverage will be negatively affected.

To complete the circle, extension and direction are both important. To have proper extension, the pitcher should take his fingers to the target and make his arm follow the fingers. To move into the proper direction, the hand and arm extend fully toward the target and continue in a right-to-left motion (RHP). The throwing arm should finish on the glove side of the stride leg.

STEP 32—The procedures in step #31 are followed, with a particular concentration on the last part of the throwing arm action. To finish the circle, the pitcher's throwing arm should finish with the elbow of that arm touching the outside of the stride leg. In order to be in this position, his push-off foot heel should roll over.

STEP 33—To aid the finish of the arm action and to insure a complete follow through, the pitcher should concentrate on squeezing his stomach against the thigh of the stride leg as his arm extends toward the target. This action increases extension and adds impetus to the arm action, thereby taking pressure off the arm. The squeezing action further helps to properly align the body and frees the arm to extend and move from right to left.

Finishing with the stomach squeezing against his thigh will cause a pitcher's legs to do a lot of work. It will also help to force the front leg to ride in, thereby helping to disperse the weight properly on the stride leg. Because this action also aids the extension and right-to-left action of the throwing arm, it will provide a route for the throwing arm elbow to finish properly by touching the outside of stride leg thigh.

STEP 34—From the stationary-stride position, the pitcher should concentrate on refining the front-arm action. As the hands separate, the pitcher should make sure the glove hand is relaxed, soft and bottomed out. This action will allow the front arm to be taken into a functional position. When the front arm starts moving out and up, the pitcher should continue the front-arm lift until the glove hand reaches the approximate height of the chin. The front arm should be raised, but not higher than the chin. This movement should be relaxed and soft. The pitcher should think in terms of lifting, then take the glove hand out and extend it according to the direction and speed of the pitch.

As the front arm extends toward the target, the back of the glove should be kept toward the target. This action tends to keep the shoulders closed and prevents the front arm from opening too quickly.

After properly extending the arm, the pitcher should turn the glove over with the palm up, lift the heel of the glove slightly, and bring his arm back in to brush the inside of the elbow against the side of the rib cage. The elbow continues pulling until the glove hand is even with the pitcher's left breast.

When the front arm finishes with the glove hand near the left breast (RHP), it indicates that it is active and helping the throwing arm finish its motion. Lifting the heel of the glove after turning it over helps to keep the front arm at the proper height and creates better angles with the top half of the body. A good term for describing the action of the front arm is—take it out, thumb over, heel up and bring it in.

The extension of the front arm toward the target will vary from pitcher to pitcher. The front arm is the range finder and the meter for establishing rhythm, so it is very important to the delivery. Some pitchers will operate more effectively with a full extension, while other pitchers will be more efficient with less than full extension. It is important for each pitcher to establish the correct degree of extension.

STEP 35—Following the procedures in step #34, the pitcher should concentrate on the chest moving to the target. As the front arm is brought in toward the rib cage, the chest should be extended toward the target. This movement is called a barrel chest. During this action, the breast should be parallel to the ground and should be thrown toward the target.

This action will allow the throwing arm to gain maximum extension. In effect, it makes the lever long. The opposite of this action is a concave chest. A concave chest shortens the lever. The parallel breasts keep the shoulders level and help to keep the arm up and in its proper angle. Following these procedures will assure proper body alignment and propel the throwing arm directly to the target.

STEP 36—The procedures in steps #34 and #35 are followed, with particular concentration on the chin. As the chest is barreled and thrown toward the target, the bottom of the chin should be parallel to the ground. This action is called chin up. With the chin up and parallel to the ground, the chest will remain in the barreled position, which aids arm extension. This action also directs the body toward the target.

Many pitchers tilt their heads to the side. This movement will negatively affect arm angle and balance. Keeping the bottom of the chin parallel to the ground will enhance balance, direction, angle and arm extension.

STEP 37—The procedures in the last three steps are followed, with specific concentration on the eyes. With the chest barreled and the chin up, the pitcher should make sure his eyes are parallel to the ground and moving directly toward the target. This action keeps the head in proper alignment to the target and helps to keep the proper arm angle.

The last four drills are closely related. Often, working on any one of these drills will enhance the movements involved in the others. Therefore, selecting the drill that most fits the problem will save some time and eliminate unnecessary or redundant activities.

STEP 38—Following the procedures in step #37, the pitcher should concentrate on the push-off foot. To aid the finish of the throwing and the finish of the circle, the pitcher should turn the push-off heel over, moving the outside of the heel toward the ground. This action helps to extend the arm and allows it to complete the full range of motion.

The push-off foot is responsible for helping the initial push. As the arm reaches its full extension, the heel-over action is responsible for releasing the arm and aiding its continuation through the follow-through.

STEP 39—Beginning in the stationary-stride position, a simulated throw is executed. The pitcher does this by pushing his right knee downward, then lifting his push-off foot and bringing it over to finish the follow-through. The push-off foot will land in a position approximately even with, or slightly ahead of, the stride foot.

As the push-off foot is picked up, it should form a circle to the throwing arm side of the body before landing on the toe. After landing on the toe, the heel should be rotated over, as in the previous drill.

To illustrate this point, the pitcher should picture a small barrel in the area passed over by the push-off foot. Circling the imaginary barrel will give the proper lift and route for the push-off foot. Some pitchers will have a short, compact push-off action, while others will employ a higher lift of the push-off foot. The imaginary barrel should be the size necessary to accommodate the push-off of the individual pitcher.

The lift and circling of the push-off foot helps the chest, head and arm move into a forward and downward plane toward the target.

Summary

This chapter discussed dry-run drills. A dry-run drill is designed to improve pitching mechanics. By simulating the throwing motion, the pitcher can work on his delivery without the stress of throwing. The dry-run drill provides pitchers and pitching coaches an opportunity to explore an isolated part of the delivery, or to coordinate several parts of the motion. The repetition necessary to refine a skill is essential. Dry-run pitching offers such repetition.

By using the sequential steps, a checklist of fundamentals is developed. When these are repeated on a regular basis, the pitcher learns to feel and understand how the movements are connected. The pitcher begins to recognize the importance of each movement and is better able to see how they affect balance and rhythm. The sequential approach allows the pitcher or pitching coach to connect the series of movements as the pitcher learns the total pitching delivery.

Dry-run drills provide an excellent setting for reviewing movements, and encourages refinement of skills. By breaking down the delivery, the pitcher is able to move forward or backward through the sequences and repair a particular part of the delivery. This capability is extremely important during the course of the season. By having a system at hand which allows the pitcher to check each part of his delivery, a single review, followed by a few corrective measures, may solve (or prevent) what could be an even longer list of future problems.

By diligently tending to the skills involved in the dry-run process, injuries will be reduced to a minimum. Good balance, correct angles, freedom of movement, relaxation and rhythm are all important elements stressed in the dry-run process. Repeated work and emphasis on these drills will create a smooth and functional delivery, thereby helping decrease injuries.

Confidence is built by success. The pitcher with specific knowledge about each movement is fortified with the information needed to create success in the basics of pitching. Understanding how the body works and feels when throwing a pitch is extremely important to the total success of the pitcher. A pitcher who knows how to direct his body parts and how to land on a balanced stride foot and who develops a sense of feel for each movement is better equipped to compete at his maximum level.

Dry-run drills provide the pitching coach with a teaching station for a single pitcher or for the entire staff. This capability creates an environment in which repetition, exchange of ideas and the imparting of knowledge are magnified. Encouragement, corrections and improvement are the goals of this procedure.

It is important for coaches to note that any drill can also be practiced with live throwing. In fact, after the pitcher understands the particular movement, he will often get more out of the drill by actually throwing the baseball. Pitchers should throw when their arms are not put in jeopardy. It is important for them to throw with the same motion they normally use. If a pitcher simulates such a movement without the ball, he will gain almost as much from the drill as with the live throw.

Finally, dry-run drills will most benefit those who believe in them. These drills do not adequately service those who take them lightly. It is important for the pitcher and the pitching coach to encourage a serious approach to the process. When a pitching coach shows excitement and concern for the activity, the pitcher usually reciprocates with the same attitude. Focus, interest, concern and persistence will almost assure success in the development of sound pitching delivery.

7

Developing Pitches

Perhaps the first consideration in the development of any pitch is the grip. What is the proper grip? For the pitcher, it is the one that creates the most movement and the best control. Movement and control are sometimes in conflict. The pitcher may have exceptional movement with a particular grip but be unable to control the pitch. On the other hand, a pitcher may have excellent control with a grip that results in no movement. Therefore, the best grip must suit both control and movement.

The grip will not be the same for each pitcher. Each pitcher should work closely with his pitching coach. A pitcher should take into consideration the above factors, plus his own physical characteristics and the results he sees with the grip he uses.

A simple explanation of grips involves the description of the seams on the ball. The ball has narrow seams and wide seams. Gripping the ball across the wide seams will cause the ball to rotate evenly. In other words, every time the ball rotates a quarter of a turn, a seam will appear. This action will allow for a consistent spin. Gripping the ball across the narrow seams will promote greater side-to-side and downward movement. Gripping the ball across the narrow seams gives the same results as gripping with the seams. As the ball rotates, the narrow seams and the cross narrow seams will alternate on each rotation. This can easily be illustrated by having the pitcher grip the ball with two fingers along the narrow seams and asking him to rotate the ball slowly with the other hand. As the ball is turning, the seams will begin to widen until the completion of a half turn. At this point, two narrow seams will appear. Starting with the fingers across the narrow seams and rotating a half turn will find the fingers gripping the ball with the narrow seams. Consequently, on the four-seam spin, the ball tends to be faster and more consistent, with a possibility of a "hop" or a "rise" on the fastball. Whereas the two-seam rotation, or rotation along the seams, creates more lateral movement and a more inconsistent spin.

In developing the various pitches, the grip and the spin will be extremely important. A determination of the type of spin needed and the grip that enhances such spin will simplify and speed the learning process.

The pitcher should keep a baseball in his hand as often as possible. He should become familiar with the seams, the size, the weight, and the shape of the ball. He should squeeze, spin and roll the ball on his fingers, and become aware of the feel of the ball. The sense of feel is certainly one of the keys to throwing quality pitches.

The general throwing motion is similar on all pitches. The grip, the finger pressure and the angle of the wrist may vary with different pitches, and certainly will vary with different pitchers. Several different ways exist to throw a particular pitch. The pitcher and the coach should have a starting point which is based upon fundamental or standard procedures. Both should be open and willing to examine and explore various methods in order to arrive at what is most successful for each pitcher.

No two pitchers are built exactly the same, have exactly the same actions or even possess the same abilities. Even though there are basic fundamentals which should be followed in exploring these differences, there is no absolute correct way to throw any pitch. The way that is most effective and consistent for the pitcher is correct for that pitcher.

Attention to details quickens improvement. Noticing rotation, movement, control, and feel sets the stage for pitch development. When a pitch does something unusual, the pitcher should recall how it was thrown and try to repeat the same pitch. If the pitch can be repeated four or five times in succession, the pitcher may label this as a pitch to be considered for his "arsenal." In order for a pitch to be used regularly, it should be consistent and successful.

Fastball

There are two different kinds of fastballs—the across-the-seams fastball and the with-the-seams fastball. There are many variations of the grip for each type.

The across-the-seams grip is often called the four-seam fastball. This terminology means the index and middle fingers grip the ball across the wide seams. This grip creates a spin that allows all four seams to rotate evenly, causing pressure at the bottom of the ball to help fight the downward pull of gravity.

The four-seam grip is used by all position players because it offers control and consistent spin. As the ball leaves the fingers, the ball revolves in a backward rotation, resulting in an even and constant spin, with a seam appearing at each quarter turn. The even back spin helps control the ball. Generally, the movement on this type of fastball is of a vertical nature. When the ball is thrown with great force and quick spin, the ball will "hop" or appear to rise. As far as the pitcher is concerned, the even spin could be a plus or it could be a minus. Control is essential to the pitcher. It is also necessary for the ball to have movement. The four-seam rotation generally works well for the pitcher who throws extremely hard. When thrown hard, the ball will rise or result in what is called a "hopping fastball."

The with-the-seams or two-seam ,fastball is held with the index and middle fingers resting on and running parallel to the seams. The ball can also be gripped with the index finger and middle finger across the narrow seams. Holding the ball with the narrow seams, or across the narrow seams, will essentially give equal results. The grip causes an "uneven spin." Because of the manner in which the seams are sewn, the two-seam rotation causes a spin both across the seams and with the seams. This grip generally results in some type of lateral, or downward, movement. There are many other factors which affect the movement of the ball. One of these factors is finger pressure. If more pressure is placed on one finger than the other, the ball will probably move in the direction opposite the pressure. The pitcher should pay special attention to the grip and to how the ball is released.

The spread of the fingers also contributes to how the ball will move. Generally, fingers close together create movement and fingers apart help cut down movement. This, of course, is the case until the spread is exaggerated. An extreme spread turns into a forkball or split-finger fastball. A wider spread of the fingers usually results in the loss of speed.

Another element affecting the flight of the ball is the angle of the wrist as the ball is released. No two people have exactly the same wrist action. Wrist movement keeping the fingers to the outside of the ball causes the fingers to move across the top of and inside of the ball. This movement creates a sinker or screwball type action. The more extreme the movement, the more the pitch will relate to that movement.

The placement of the thumb is relevant to how the ball will react. A thumb held below and bisecting the index and middle fingers tends to help create a straight line of flight. Moving the thumb up and toward the inside of the ball will help create a sinker, or screwball type of spin. Moving the thumb further under and toward the outside of the ball tends to help the slider or sailing fastball rotation.

Having the arm up and keeping the fingers on top of the ball will greatly enhance the fastball. This position will allow the fingers to drive through the ball, thereby maximizing spin and velocity. Even a sidearm or three-quarter arm pitcher should have his arm up and his fingers on top of the ball. "Up" is not as high in either of these positions as the overhand thrower, but the fingers should be above the arm. The key is to raise the elbow approximately as high as the shoulder. The fingers should remain on top of the ball.

Arm extension and a proper and consistent release point are vital if maximum power and location are to be considered. Allowing the arm to freely extend creates a long lever and encourages the hand and the fingers to finish the pitch. Pitchers should think in terms of releasing the ball below the bill of the cap and in line with the left breast (RHP). This release point forces the action from right to left, shifting the weight over and through the stride foot.

A right-to-left arm action with full extension and a feel of release below the bill of the cap and at the left breast will add movement, control, and power to the fastball.

Many elements are involved in creating an effective fastball. A moving fastball with good location is difficult to hit. A pitcher who changes speed destroys the hitter's timing. Of course, the exceptional fastball is the master pitch. A pitcher should consider one or all of these elements in the use of a fastball. A wise pitcher matches his ability to the type of fastball he chooses.

The coach, pitcher and catcher should take note of both the usual and the unusual movement on all pitches. They should have a working plan. Each person involved should know how the ball is held and for what purpose. Often, a slight variation or adjustment will refine a certain pitch. It is easier to refine a pitch if it has a base, some substance and a background.

Not just one way exists to throw an effective fastball. There are basic starting points, but these are just points of reference. Each pitcher should be willing to listen, explore and experiment with information to develop his own fastball. Each pitcher has differences, both obvious and subtle, which make it necessary to adapt a pitch that suits his needs.

Adjustments and experimentation should be done in an educated and sound manner. Changes should not be based on a whim or a passing conversation. The type of exploration advocated is not an irresponsible, "fool around" activity, but rather an organized session designed to pay attention to detail and to evaluate the effects of adjustments. Decisions on change should be based on sound principles and careful consideration of these sessions.

The Curveball

Like the fastball, the curveball is also thrown many different ways. The curveball may be held across the seams or with the seams. The pitcher should start with one method and work to perfect the curveball. He should establish a base before exploring too freely. Adjustments are more meaningful if they develop from a foundation.

One basic starting point is the four-seam curveball. Gripping the ball with the index and middle fingers resting firmly on top of one of the wide seams, with the index finger held close to the middle finger, the thumb tucked and firmly pressing a wide opposite seam and with the ball pushed toward the palm will help create an even rotation. That means one of the four seams will appear as the ball spins forward a quarter turn. This spin will create a greater or sharper break downward.

In throwing the four-seam curveball, the pitcher should pull down with the middle finger and push up with the thumb. The pressure with the middle finger and thumb should be firm. The pressure with the index finger should be very light and should not create drag.

Another basic method is the two-seam curveball. Gripping across the wide seams firmly with the middle finger, lightly with the index finger and with the thumb tucked and firmly pressing one of the narrow seams will help create a tight-spinning curve ball with maximum velocity. Because the spin is uneven, the rotation will not be as great, which will cut down on the break. The amount of speed taken from the break is added to the forward speed, creating a faster curveball. The greater or bigger break on the curveball, the more reduction there will be on the speed of the pitch. Only the grip is different. This pitch is mechanically thrown in the same manner as the four-seam fastball. The pad of the middle finger will pull down toward a long seam, and the thumb will push up on a narrow seam.

Both of the methods just described are called a low-thumb curveball. This approach is probably the most acceptable procedure. Another procedure exists that works well for some pitchers called a high-thumb curveball.

Some pitchers have poor dexterity with their thumb. This situation occurs when the thumb appears to hang on the ball. Instead of helping the spin, the thumb actually causes drag and hampers the rotation. By moving the thumb up toward the index finger, it no longer pushes up; it is simply out of the way. The middle finger works in the same manner as the low-thumb curveball. The index finger, however, is now used to help the middle finger pull down.

The high-thumb curveball generally has a smaller break and greater speed than the low-thumb curveball. Some pitchers throw this pitch with a very sharp break. A pitcher should experiment with this curveball if his work with the more traditional method is unsuccessful.

Wrist curl dramatically affects the amount of break on the pitch. As a general rule, the greater the curl of the wrist, the bigger the curveball. By keeping the fingertip pads on top of the ball and by not curling or bending the wrist in toward the head, substantial speed and a sharp break may be attained.

Beginning "curve ballers" should start with the wrist straight, with only the fingers bent in toward the head. If he is unable to achieve satisfactory rotation after throwing several pitches with proper arm action, the pitcher should begin to make slight adjustments. He should start by bending the wrist a few degrees toward the head. If the results are unsatisfactory after throwing a few more pitches, the pitcher should continue to bend the wrist a few more degrees. He should continue this process until success is attained.

A successful curveball may be thrown with the wrist straight, with a completely bent wrist, or anywhere between these two points. A good curveball has a proper mixture of velocity and break. Each pitcher must work with the grip and wrist curl that produces the best mixture for him.

For years it has been quite common to hear the term "pull the shade down" when the pitcher makes a proper throwing motion. A reaction to this statement could be, "It depends on how far the pitcher stands from the shade." Arm extension is essential for both speed and break. Too short an arc will create a very slow pitch.

The proper arm action calls for a good, quick arm lift with the wrist in a position to throw a fastball until the hand is almost even with the head. The proper wrist curl should be executed with the hand held high. It should then begin to reach and move in a downward pattern. At full extension the elbow should bend slightly. As the hand makes its final pull downward and in, it should make a circle around the top of the ball with the middle finger. The arm action from the throwing arm side to the front arm side and should continue all the way until the throwing arm elbow is touching the outside thigh of the stride leg.

The release point is also extremely important. The pitcher should try to get the feel of releasing the curveball below the bill of the cap and in front of the front arm breast. Many pitchers stay "right" on the curveball. This action does not permit the fingers to pull down properly. The right-handed pitcher's throwing arm should go into a pattern from "right to left."

Having the arm at the proper height is one of the key ingredients to throwing an effective curveball. Relaxation at the point of hand separation helps to quicken the arm lift. Once the arm is at the proper height, the pitcher should feel as though he is throwing downhill. For the proper feel, he should imagine throwing over a wall just inches from the release point. He should visualize and feel the hand extending out and reaching just over the wall before quickly pulling down to force the ball to break down and into the target.

The stride leg also plays a major role in throwing a curveball. A stiff stride leg causes the body to recoil, thereby stopping the arm action. The stiff leg curve ball places tremendous pressure on the elbow joint. Bending the front knee allows the chest to reach out. This action frees the arm and assists in the final pulling action.

Arm speed is directly related to the effectiveness of the curveball. The pitcher should not mistake a hard action with the speed of the pitch. Often, in attempting to put more on the curveball, the pitcher forces the throw. This action generally leads to a pitch with little break and poor speed. The pitcher should relax, soften the arm and hands (particularly at separation) and think of hand-and-arm speed rather than power. Eliminating the necessity to over power the pitch creates a freedom of movement and allows the arm and hand to move at maximum efficiency.

The curveball is one of the best pitches in baseball. It requires good concentration and proper mechanics. This pitch needs maintenance and constant use. The pitcher should not put it on the shelf for two or three games and expect it to be effective.

There are many other ways to throw the curveball. All of these are derived from variations on the basic method. The pitcher should explore, examine, and experiment to arrive at the curveball that best suits him. He should incorporate a sound fundamental base and adopt only the pitch which improves on its predecessor.

Change-Up

One of the basic attacks the team in the field can use against the offense is the destruction of timing. A good change- up is one of the pitcher's best weapons to help in the war on timing. A change-up with a desired decrease in speed and an adequate level of movement thrown low is one of the most sound pitches in the game. If that pitch can be thrown to the outside part of the plate, it becomes even more effective. The speed should be related to the working speed of the fastball. The generally recommended decrease in speed for a change-up ranges from 11 to 15 mph.

There may be more ways to throw a change-up than any other pitch. Often pitchers call a palmball, knuckleball, split-finger or other specialty pitch a change-up. The change-up being discussed at this point is a standard change-up.

Deep-Grip Change-Up

Perhaps the original change-up is the deep-grip change. To throw this pitch, the ball is pushed toward the palm. Either a two- or three-finger grip is acceptable.

The throwing motion calls for a fastball action until slightly before release. At this point, the hand and arm pull down, with the fingers pulling down on the back half of the ball. The wrist does not break or snap; it remains relatively straight. Some refer to this pitch as the "stiff-wrist" change or the "pull-down" change.

Many pitchers experience difficulties in keeping this pitch low and in developing the pull-down" motion. Speed will be reduced using this method. Therefore, if control and movement can be achieved, this is a very acceptable change-up.

Three-Finger Change-Up

The three-finger change-up is perhaps the style most related, in grip and motion, to the regular fastball. The pitcher should simply add the ring finger to the index and middle finger, spread them, and move the thumb slightly toward the index finger. Moving the thumb will tend to add a sinker effect. Three fingers put more drag on the ball, resulting in a reduction of speed.

The arm action should not be slowed. The pitcher should simply make a mental command to throw the ball at a low-range working fastball speed. That is a speed approximately four miles an hour slower than that of the normal fastball.

To add more movement, the pitcher may put pressure on the inside of the ball. To slow the speed of the ball further, he can spread the fingers wider and move the ball slightly deeper in the hand.

Dead-Leg Change-Up

One of the easiest change-ups to throw is the dead-leg change-up. Every aspect of the throwing motion is virtually normal, except the push-off foot remains on the rubber. The push-off knee should drop down toward the ground. By restricting the push-off, speed should be considerable reduced.

From the batter's view, the arm, head and chest come through normally. This change-up is very difficult to detect. Using this motion with a three fingers or a deeper grip should give the pitcher an acceptable change-up.

Seaver Change-Up

Tom Seaver developed a change-up by forming a circle with the thumb and index finger, placing the circle to the inside of the ball and gripping with the other three fingers. Although unusual and rather difficult to control, the pitch has movement and cannot be thrown at full speed. When thrown properly, the ball sinks or moves downward.

Slip-Pitch Change-Up

The slip-pitch change-up is thrown by holding the ball with a looser-than-normal grip. The pitcher should apply just enough pressure to control the grip. As the ball is released, he should relax the wrist and fingers. The hand and arm speed should be normal. In fact, the faster the speed, the better. The pitcher should then allow the ball to slip out of the fingers, while applying enough pressure to control the pitch. When thrown properly, this pitch appears to back up.

Slider

Even though the slider has been around for a long time, it has been one of the reasons for lowering batting averages in recent years. A slider is very difficult to recognize. It does not break a great deal, but it breaks very late, making it appear to be a fastball until the last few feet or inches. This perception often causes the batter to either swing through the pitch or swing and hit the ball on the wrong part of the bat.

A batter who pulls his head or starts his swing early is easy prey for the slider. This batter will often hit into double-plays. A good slider-ball pitcher produces many ground balls.

This pitch is relatively easy to learn and is much easier to throw than a curveball. Controlling the slider is not quite as easy, however. To be effective, the slider must be thrown low. It is generally most successful when thrown outside to the right-handed batter, inside to the left-handed batter (RHP). The slider requires a great deal of concentration. When thrown in a careless manner, the result is often an extra-base hit.

Cut Fastball

Using the regular fastball grip, with the slight adjustment of moving the fingers to the outside of the ball, creates a quick, late movement. By holding the fingers off- center and cutting or driving toward the outside of the ball, both speed and movement of break are enhanced.

The wrist action is also slightly adjusted. The pitcher should roll the wrist a few degrees toward the outside as the ball is brought by the head. The wrist snap is a fastball movement. With the gentle roll and the off-center grip, the hand is already in place to go to the outside of the ball, therefore the final motion is a snap of the wrist rather than a turn. If the ball does not break enough, the pitcher can point the fingertips of the index and middle finger in toward the head. This adjustment should be made in small increments, progressively increasing the adjustment until the desired results are attained. The pitcher can continue using the fastball wrist motion with this grip.

If the cut fastball can be learned, it really offers the best in speed, provides a very deceptive break and is much easier on the arm than the traditional slider. By using the cut fastball, the pitcher is not in danger of hyperextending the elbow. Because of the fastball wrist snap, the throw is much easier on the arm.

Traditional Slider

The pitcher uses the fastball grip with the index and middle fingers very close to each other. He should keep the fingertips on the top of the ball as the throw is made. The motion is similar to a karate chop. The pitcher should place extra pressure on the middle finger, reach out, get good arm extension, make a small circle around the tip and outside half of the ball, and pull down firmly.

The traditional slider is sometimes referred to as a "nickel" curveball. It has a small break downward and a hooking action resembling a curve that does not complete its downward break. Too much downward action turns the slider into a curveball; therefore, the emphasis should be placed on sharp lateral movement.

For best results, the arm should gain height. The fingers should stay on top of the ball. The throwing arm should have full extension to the target. Finger pressure goes to the top and outside half of the ball. The right-to-left (RHP) pulling action in front should be loose and fast.

Knuckleball

The knuckleball is actually a pitch common to both "old-timers" and "newcomers." Its tantalizing, unpredictable movement makes the hitter's job difficult and the catcher's duties vigorous. Because the pitch has no discernible spin, it is very difficult to control. It is generally used by more experienced pitchers who, through hours of practice, manage to adequately control the pitch.

The fingernails of the index and middle fingers should be pressed into the middle of the seams. As the pitch is released, the two fingers are pushed toward the target, giving the ball a tumbling action. The greater the force produced by the fingers, the more the ball will move.

Generally speaking, the arm action used in throwing the knuckleball is less violent. There is no hard snap at the end of the extension. The pushing action with the fingers is much easier on the arm. A relaxed, quick arm throws a more lively knuckle ball than does an overpowering arm.

Using the knuckleball as the primary pitch will probably affect the speed of the fastball. Because most knuckleballs are more efficient when thrown at a slower speed and the wrist action is different, the pitcher may not be able to make the proper adjustment back to the fastball. The knuckleball is most effective when used as a primary pitch. The fastball is also a better pitch when used as a primary pitch. It is very unusual for a pitcher to have success throwing both pitches.

Forkball

The forkball has been around for years. The movement of this pitch varies. Sometimes it looks like a curveball; often, it appears to be a knuckleball; occasionally, it takes on a look of a slider; and at times, it even looks like a sailing fastball. Its movement is erratic and difficult to control. While it may be somewhat easier to control than the knuckleball, it is, nevertheless, a difficult pitch to master. Those who have mastered the pitch have truly found a great weapon.

The true forkball grip calls for the index and middle fingers to spread wide enough to hold the ball between them. Some experimentation with finding the best grip for each pitcher is necessary. Some individuals will find greater movement and control when gripping the ball between the seams.

Even though the break of the forkball is erratic, its direction can be somewhat guided by finger pressure. By applying pressure with the middle finger, the ball will take on a knuckle-slider or knuckle-curveball look. Pressure applied by the index finger will cause the ball to break similar to that of a sinker or a screwball with the knuckleball affect added.

Split-Finger Fastball

The split-finger fastball is everything from a forkball to a fastball with the fingers spread. The real distinction between a true split-finger pitch and a forkball is the grip. The fingers are spread less with the split-finger fastball. The difference in speed is dramatic. The split-finger is generally a much faster pitch than the forkball, and it does not break as much.

One method used in learning the proper grip is to slightly increase the distance between the index and middle fingers until the right speed and movement are established. The pitcher should throw a few pitches, checking the movement and speed of each pitch. He should continue widening the grip, throwing a few pitches and evaluating movement and speed until the best grip has been determined. By experimenting in this manner the pitcher will find a certain spread of the fingers to produce the best combination of feel, control, movement and speed.

The pitcher should work with finger pressure by applying pressure with the middle finger. He should record the results after throwing a few pitches. Next, he should follow this procedure with the index finger, adding extra movement to the ball. Equal finger pressure with a normal wrist snap will create a downward break of the fastball. Extra finger pressure on one side of the ball or the other will probably add another dimension to the pitch. Full extension, quick arm-speed and a forceful wrist snap will provide a good environment for the split-finger fastball.

Palmball

The palmball can be thrown relatively hard, or it can be used as a change-of-speed pitch. Because the ball is held back in the hand, the speed will be slower than a normal fastball. If thrown with good extension and a forceful wrist action, the pitch may behave with an exceptional break. The break may resemble a curveball or a split-finger pitch.

Several kinds of grips can be used with the palmball. Generally, the thumb is higher on the ball on this pitch. It will be moved up the ball toward the index finger. The thumb and third finger are the primary pressure points on one style of grip for a palmball. The thumb, index finger, middle finger and third finger are the points of pressure with still another style of grip.

To maximize speed and movement on the palmball, the pitcher should place emphasis on arm speed and extension. He should drive the fingers through the ball with a forceful wrist snap.

If the major objective for the pitch is a change of speed, the pitcher should pull down at extension with the fingers dragging hard at the back of the ball. The wrist action is not a snap but a dead-wrist movement.

As with all pitches, educated experimentation is important. This factor is exceptionally true of unusual or hard to control pitches. The palmball certainly fits this category.

Screwball

The screwball is still used by modern day pitchers, but it was even more popular in the early days of baseball. Its unusual movement is responsible for its popularity. The pitch moves in a manner similar to a curveball, only it moves in the opposite direction.

When thrown hard, the result of the screwball is a lot of ground balls and strikeouts. When thrown at slow speeds, ground balls are very common.

The grip is similar to that of the fastball with the fingers together. Generally, more success is attained when the ball is held off center, with the index and middle fingers more to the inside of the ball. Added pressure to the inside of the ball with one of these fingers will help to create the proper movements.

There is a very violent movement across the top of the ball with the fingers. This movement continues over the top of the ball. It takes on a slicing action to the inside half of the ball and finishes with extreme inward rotation.

During the recommended exploration period, the pitcher may discover that an adjustment with the fingers held toward the outside half of the ball may produce a better break. Starting at the outside and cutting across the top of the ball sometimes appears to offer more surface to work with.

Gaining arm height, keeping the fingers on top of the ball through release, cutting through the inside half of the ball and good arm extension with complete follow-through will be important ingredients for an effective screwball.

The pitcher must be very diligent with mechanics when throwing this pitch. Even when thrown with care, the screwball puts a great deal of strain on the arm. When thrown without consideration of mechanics, there is a very good chance of injury.

Summary

This chapter discussed the fact that developing pitches can be an exciting undertaking for the pitcher. Any one of a number of factors (e.g., learning to create better spin on the pitch, adding more speed or developing a new pitch) can provide meaningful incentives to the pitcher. Any of these aspects could improve the pitcher's chance to win. Both the pitcher and the pitching coach should keep in mind, however, that it takes time to perfect a pitch. A new grip may appear to help for a few pitches, but it can suddenly become ineffective.

When experimenting with new grips and finger pressure, the coach and the pitcher should make sure there is a purpose or goal in mind. If more movement is the goal, then the pitcher can apply different finger pressure to gain the desired results. He should try slightly different grips to accomplish this end, and carefully make mental notes on what has been tried. He should decide what works and doesn't work and discard the things that don't work and move on with the grips and pressure points that result in a better pitch. Developing pitches should be a very organized endeavor, and not a haphazard venture. While this process can be very enjoyable, it should not turn into a "fool around" session.

Both the pitcher and the coach should keep an open mind and evaluate each throw carefully. The pitcher should be willing to listen and learn and remember there is no absolute correct grip for each pitch. Each pitcher is unique. A slight difference in grip or finger pressure could make a difference for one pitcher and work to the detriment of another.

The pitcher should not work on developing pitches before learning the mechanics of pitching. Sound mechanics will make the development of pitches easier. Good balance, proper angles and correct arm position are important in throwing any pitch.

8

Teaching Tools

The minds of the coach and the pitcher are the most important tools for learning. If properly used, no radar guns, pitching screens, or pitching targets are needed. A pitcher with a proper understanding, a commitment to doing things properly and good visualization skills can make any correction necessary, without gimmicks or added stimulus.

The situation in the above paragraph calls for a perfect coach and a perfect pitcher. Most of us fall somewhere short of perfection; therefore, extra props or special equipment may be necessary to reach the goal. There are many products on the market which serve as good teaching aids. Video cassettes, film, photography, lighter and heavier balls, physical fitness equipment and strike zone targets are just a few examples. When used properly, each product has value.

Often, valuable teaching tools are available at no cost. A paper cup, a piece of rope or a string, a broom handle, a stick, a piece of old rug or rubber mat, a chair, or even a batting "T" can be used to illustrate a point or to create a worthwhile drill.

Before turning to props, the pitcher is encouraged to use his mind and creativity in solving problems and making corrections. Often, overuse of gimmicks creates a new problem—dependency. Hopefully the pitcher will aggressively pursue a self-reliant path to learning. This path leads to confidence, self-discipline, and creativity.

Some rough spots may occur during the course of learning about pitching. When the coach is unable to explain or illustrate his point, or the pitcher is unable to comprehend the lesson through regular means, the use of an extra teaching tool should be explored. The following are a few examples of devices that can help smooth the road to understanding.

Pitching Screen

This device is a large protective screen (6' x 8' or 8' x 8' preferably). The frame should be filled with netting. The net protects the ball and acts as a built-in retrieval system. The screen can be of great help to a pitcher who is working on fundamentals. A regular or specific part of the throwing motion can be practiced and can be repeated as often as necessary to gain results.

One of the greatest features of the pitching screen is that it does not talk. It does not say, as the catcher often does, "Get the ball over". The screen affords the pitcher the opportunity to work on specifics in relation to mechanics without concern for control. This capability is extremely important when correcting or refining a difficult or poorly understood movement.

Encouraging the pitcher to work independently on the screen will improve his self-reliance. The drill entails throwing to the screen, which is an individual endeavor. This situation gives the pitcher the opportunity to repeat a movement or series of movements enough times to obtain a sense of feel. Because he is only 15 to 20 feet from the screen and is not required to throw at top speed, he is able to make many throws without placing undue strain on his arm.

A pitching coach is also able to station himself on the opposite side of the screen, giving him a front view of the pitcher. At this short range and in this favorable position, the coach is better able to evaluate and instruct.

Rubber Pad or Rug

Placing a thin rubber pad just outside the area where the stride foot lands will act as a reminder to the pitcher who opens up too soon. It can also help alert the pitcher who overstrides. Landing on the pad or rug indicates an incorrect stride. Placing the pad just to the inside area in which the stride foot lands will signal the pitcher when his stride crosses over.

Crossing over, overstriding, and opening the stride too soon will create problems, and may also result in an injury to the pitcher.

Coaches should be very careful not to use thick, hard, or slippery material for the warning pad. A hard surface does not allow the cushioning of dirt. An extremely thick material elevates the stride foot, which could hamper rhythm, balance, and angles. A slippery material is extremely dangerous.

Chair

The pitcher may find several uses for a chair. One is to help him move his heel over and have the proper height with the push-off leg. By placing the push-off foot on the chair with the toe and the arch touching the seat, and with the stride leg and foot in a proper stride position toward the target, the pitcher is able to practice the heel over or follow-through position of the push-off. Almost any part of the pitching motion can be practiced from this position.

Using the chair as a marker for height and position of the stride leg is very effective. By placing the chair in front of the pitcher at a distance which allows for his stride toe to brush against it as he begins the stride forward with the hip serves as a marker for the front leg position. Placed in a position in front of and the proper distance away from the pitcher's stride toe, the chair gives tangible reminders of height and distance away from the body of the stride foot as it pivots and starts to follow the front hip to stride. The toe should gently brush this marker at the start of the push-off.

This drill is particularly beneficial to the pitcher who tightens and bunches too severely during the pivot. When the pitcher brings his stride leg heel back in toward his push-off leg, the result is usually tenseness and tightness throughout the body. A tight arm does not throw well. A tight push-off leg does not drive well. Tightness slows arm action and causes breaks in rhythm.

Touching the marker and holding the foot back until the front hip starts the drive helps the pitcher learn to deactivate the bottom of the stride leg. The holding pattern for the lift foot is a slight pause, not a complete stop. It should be held just long enough to allow the front hip to start the push-off. Deactivating the bottom half of the stride leg helps the pitcher stay closed longer and creates greater force with the push-off. Staying closed maximizes power and direction.

The side of the chair may serve as a marker. A tall plastic bucket, a batting "T" or a pylon may also be used as a marker for the extension, relaxation and positioning of the front leg.

Chair or Bench Uses

A bench or a chair is a good tool for helping the pitcher to get the feel of a right-to-left action (RHP) and to feel the extension with the arm, head and chest. This action enables the pitcher to develop balance. The chair also helps to get the push-off foot elevated, giving the pitcher the feel of circling with his push-off foot. It is also another method of drilling the heel-over action.

The Chair and Its Many Uses

The chair can be used to measure the height of the leg lift and the reach of the lift-leg foot. The chair can also be used as a guide for the toe of the lift leg and can serve as a reminder, as in the front foot fence drill, for the pitcher to keep the bottom half of the lead leg up and back as long as possible.

The chair can be used to measure the height of the leg lift and the reach of the lift leg foot.

The Broomstick

A simple broomstick may aid the pitcher in throwing a curve ball or any other pitch that is not being thrown with proper arm height. One of the essential fundamentals involved in throwing a good curveball is getting the arm up and a hand on top of the ball. By standing approximately 10 feet in front of and slightly to the side of the pitcher, with the broom stick held parallel to the ground and at a height which forces the pitcher to throw over it, the coach may use this reference point to improve the arm lift. As the ball is released, the coach should simply lower the broom stick.

This broomstick may also be used to help achieve better hand height for the fastball. The stick is lightweight, very portable and can be used to adjust the height of the arm lift at the direction of the coach. Gradual increments may be the answer for some pitchers, while exaggerated increments may work for others. A rope or string, strung in front of the pitcher, may be substituted for the broom.

Broomstick or Bat to Help with Mechanics on the Curveball

A coach or fellow pitcher should position himself approximately 10 feet in front of the pitcher and a foot or so outside the throwing arm side of the pitcher who is throwing. The coach or fellow pitcher should extend a bat or broomstick in front of the pitcher, approximately 12 to 15 inches above the thrower's head. For safety reasons, the bat should be lowered slightly as the ball is released. This target, or point of emphasis, encourages the pitcher to get his arm up and to have the feel of throwing downhill.

Paper Cup

Placing a paper cup on the ground in the spot where the hand should pass during the follow-through should serve as a target for the arm direction.

In addition to serving as a direction marker, the paper cup may also serve as a reminder for the pitcher to finish with his chest out and down. By picking up the paper cup after completely finishing the throw, the pitcher will be able to measure this part of the throwing motion.

A paper cup may also be used to help in the push-off. The knee should drive toward the ground. A paper cup, placed in the spot where the knee would land if the driving action continued all the way to the ground, may provide a physical and visual reminder for the push-off knee.

Often, when the knee drives downward for a few inches, the push-off foot follows and makes a circular motion toward the outside. This motion is sometimes described as "circling a barrel." Placing a paper cup in the area of the imaginary circle should help the pitcher who is a foot "dragger," or a pitcher who has a lazy or inverted type of push-off. Getting the foot over the cup will give the pitcher the basic feel of the proper push-off and the lift action of the push-off foot.

Using a Paper Cup to Help the Push-Off Action

A paper cup should be placed at a position directly below the push-off knee at extension. This placement will give the pitcher a target, or point of emphasis, for the push-off knee. The front hip should start and lead the push-off action. This action is then followed by a downward push of the push-off knee and a simultaneous drive off the rubber with the ball of the push-off foot.

Almost touching the cup, or at least driving down in that direction with the push-off knee, is the object of the drill. It will help to improve the push-off action.

Paper Cup to Help Throwing Arm and Follow-Through Direction

The paper cup should become a target for the hand at follow-through. When the pitcher's throwing hand is in the area of the cup at follow-through, it means he has extended properly and has bent his back and his stride leg to complete the right-to-left action with the throwing arm (RHP).

Paper Cup Used to Discourage an Incorrect Push-Off

For the pitcher who executes the push-off by directing the push-off foot toward the glove hand side of the body, the coach should place the paper cup approximately eight inches toward home plate and in line with the back heel of the push-off foot.

The backward dragging action with the push-off foot restricts the push-off and hinders the follow-through. Initially, the push-off foot should push, then lift and then form a circle to the throwing-arm side of the pitcher's body. The circle is followed by the foot contacting the ground with the toe. The heel should then continue to roll over. This action allows the arm to continue its full range of motion.

Among its many uses, the paper cup can be used to discourage an incorrect push-off.

Paper Cup Used to Discourage Excessive Dragging of the Push-Off Foot

For the pitcher who drags his push-off foot in an extreme manner, a paper cup should be placed a distance approximately 8 to 12 inches from the rubber toward home plate, and in alignment with the toe of the push-off foot.

Pushing-off and lifting the push-off foot over the paper cup eliminates the dragging action and provides a more powerful push-off. It also produces better angles with the top part of the body.

The paper cup is also helpful in preventing the pitcher from excessively dragging his push-off foot.

Plastic Bucket

A plastic bucket is also a very useful teaching tool. It is lightweight and portable, and its use presents no hazards to the user. The bucket can be used as a small hurdle that the push-off foot must lift above. The pitcher should concentrate on pushing-off the rubber. He should then lift the push-off foot and form a circle over the bucket. This action helps to force the top part of his body toward and downward at the target. The bucket should be placed on the ground to the pitching-arm side of the pitcher and toward the plate, approximately half the distance of the pitcher's stride. The bucket should not interfere with the lead-leg lift.

The bucket may also be used as a hurdle for the lead-leg lift. If used for this purpose, the coach should simply place the bucket in front of the stride foot when the pitcher is in his stretch position. The coach should require the lead leg to clear the bucket during the stride. For the pitcher who has the habit of slinging or lowering the lead leg too quickly, the bucket will be a physical reminder of his poor habits.

Use of Pictures and Photographs

The use of action photographs of a pitcher also serves as a good teaching tool. Because most people like to see themselves, photographs can act as a motivator. Pictures are very helpful in showing the proper mechanics. To be able to actually see what has been described is a great asset. Taking pictures of the stride, the push-off foot, the follow-through position, or any other phase of the delivery will illustrate a desired point to that pitcher and to the other pitchers on the staff.

Using pictures of established pitchers to illustrate a particular part of the delivery is also extremely effective. Showing a sound fundamental used by Major League pitchers will offer concrete evidence of correct mechanics. On the other hand, showing established pitchers with a flaw will demonstrate that a need exists for improvement at all levels. Pictures also create debate and elicit questions and answers.

Shoestring

A shoestring can be used to indicate the direction of the stride. As a general rule, the pitcher should align the arch of the push-off foot with the target. The stride foot should land slightly to the glove-hand side of the outstretched shoestring. If the pitcher needs to open the stride even more, he should align the shoestring with the heel of the push-off foot to the target. The stride foot should land to the glove-hand side of the shoestring. If the pitcher has plenty of twisting action with the upper body and needs to be as closed as possible at the stride position, he should align the shoestring with the toe or the push-off foot to the target. Again, the stride foot should land along the parallel line and slightly to the glove-hand side of the shoestring.

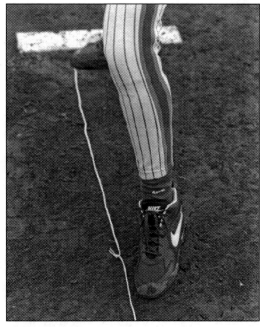

A shoestring helps indicate the direction of the pitcher's stride.

Videotapes

In recent years, the camcorder and videotapes have become a relatively inexpensive and very functional tool. Whether viewing a lesson on videotape or taping the pitcher on a regular basis, the videotape provides a wide range of benefits.

The versatility of video machines is unparalleled. The viewer is able to repeat, stop at any point, slow down or go one frame at a time. This capability allows the delivery to be scrutinized and analyzed. Many flaws, or correct movements, that might otherwise take hours to detect with the naked eye may be found very quickly.

Since flaws are often able to be quickly observed on videotape, a great deal of discretion should be used in identifying them to the pitcher. In slow motion, the flaw is often highlighted or exaggerated. Sometimes what is seen in slow motion is not as bad as it looks. The coach should make sure viewing a videotape does not turn into a negative or harmful session. At this point, the coach should establish an itemized list of priorities. Making this list will pay dividends and allow the pitcher and the pitching coach to focus on only one or two things at the top of the priority list.

Batting "T" Used to Help Arm Lift

If the pitcher has problems placing his arm at the proper height, or if he experiences difficulties with the first phases of the arm lift, the batting "T" may serve as an excellent teaching aid.

The coach should place the batting "T" behind the pitcher and on the throwing-arm side. To locate the proper distance, the pitcher should simulate a throwing motion. After separating the hands, the throwing hand should drop, move back and start to lift. The spot where the lift begins is the correct placement. Using a stretch position to have the proper perspective of the correct position, the batting "T" should be in line with the back pocket of the push-off leg. It should be far enough behind the pitcher to cause an extended throwing arm to reach it. The height of the "T" should be adjusted to suit the size of the pitcher.

The coach should place a ball on the "T," and have the pitcher pick the ball up with the fingertips pointing toward the ground. The pitcher should keep the fingertips pointing down as the arm lifts to its maximum height. The pitcher should then proceed with the throw. Repeating this drill several times will help to illustrate the proper position of the hand and wrist during the arm lift. It will also demonstrate the correct pattern of the throwing arm after the separation of the hands.

Utilizing a batting "T" helps a pitcher learn proper arm height and arm lift.

Summary

This chapter discussed the fact that the mind and its imagination are the best teaching tools. The pitcher and the coach should rely on the imagination to correct and refine problems. When a pitcher's mind is blocked and needs a temporary aid, then and only then, should a coach and the pitcher rely on any gimmick or drill which breaks through the temporary struggle. These drills should be creative. Often, the act of thinking of a particular tool to use in solving a problem will help clarify some of the causes of the problem.

9

Velocity

The best, and most used, pitch in baseball is the fastball. From little league pitchers to Major League pitchers, the basic pitch is the fastball. For a few pitchers, the fastball is overpowering. For others, the fastball is the primary pitch, but it must be spotted to be effective. Some pitchers must rely on changing speeds and cleverly using other pitches to complement their fastball. Others attain success by creating movement for the fastball. An average-speed fastball with movement is often harder to hit than a hard, straight fastball. There are many ways the speed of a pitch can be used to enhance its effectiveness.

The key to good pitching is to destroy the timing of the hitter. Overpowering pitchers destroy timing by simply throwing the ball past the hitter. The hitter's timing is disrupted because he is unable to get the bat in the hitting zone in time to make good contact with the ball. This kind of pitcher simplifies the game. Because of his strength, he does not need to place the pitch in particular spots of the strike zone. An overpowering pitch that connects with any part of the strike zone will usually be successful. Unfortunately, very few pitchers are blessed with this kind of ability. Most pitchers need to supplement the fastball with variations in speed, placement of the pitch, or movement.

Each pitcher should assess his own abilities and figure out his strengths and weaknesses. He will then be equipped with the proper information. If his fastball lacks speed, he can choose to improve that speed or to specialize in control, guile or movement. The pitcher should capitalize on his strengths.

In an earlier chapter, the working fastball was discussed. That is the fastball each pitcher must use. The working fastball is simply the best speed, combined with the best control and/or the best movement. Most pitchers can throw the ball at a higher rate of speed than the working speed. By throwing at a lesser speed, the pitcher should find that he can control each pitch better.

Once the working speed is established, the pitcher will have a watermark to guide him toward improvement. Increasing the working speed usually adds to the pitcher's effectiveness. Knowledge of speeds allows the pitcher to maximize his ability. With this knowledge, he can develop a plan to improve his fastball.

Every pitcher would like to have a better fastball. This objective can be accomplished through hard work and careful planning. To improve the speed of the fastball, the pitcher must throw some of his pitches with a maximum effort during most workouts. During a heavy- or medium-throwing workout, he should throw 10 to 15 pitches as hard as possible. To do this, he must be in good shape and injury-free. Hard-throwing is best done at the end of the workout.

The grip and rotation on the ball are extremely important. Gripping the ball across the wide seams will create an even, or equal, spin. Gripping with the wide seams, or across the narrow seams, will create an uneven rotation. This rotation will cause the ball to sink or to move to the side and downward. If the goal is to increase the speed of the fastball, then the ball should be gripped across the seams. Working to improve the speed of the fastball will pay great dividends. The pitcher will develop arm strength and durability. He will develop a better understanding about grip and rotation. His work habits will improve. He will have an evaluation system. From these benefits, he will have the proper information to intelligently select the fastball that best suits his abilities.

Any pitcher can improve the speed of his fastball. When he improves the speed of his best pitch, he will also improve his working speed. If the top speed of 90 mph is improved to 92 mph, the average speed should also improve at a similar rate. For example, if the working speed is 85 mph, an 87 mph working speed fastball should result.

Most pitchers are interested in how hard they throw. When the radar gun is brought to the practice field, pitchers become motivated. Regardless of how hard they throw, the radar gun creates enthusiasm. Although the speed of the pitch does not guarantee success, it does provide a starting point. This starting point can be used to suggest what fastball the pitcher should adopt. If the speed of his pitch is fast enough to dominate or overpower the hitter, then control and movement are secondary. However, should the pitcher possess only average speed, then location, movement, variation in speed or a combination of these factors will become significant.

Control of the fastball is a necessity for some pitchers. Pitchers who throw their best fastballs, and get poor results, need to choose another alternative. That alternative may be to throw the pitch with less speed. By taking speed off the pitch and placing it in a more difficult area to hit, the pitcher takes command. Keeping the ball in on some hitters, for example, negates the hitters' strength. Spotting the ball on the outside part of the plate will create problems for the pull hitter. By moving the ball around in the strike zone, the pitcher becomes the aggressor and the planner. The hitter cannot rely on the pitcher to serve the pitch in a favorable area. This factor creates doubt in the hitter's mind and allows the pitcher to attack the hitter by using location as a weapon.

A well-placed fastball can be very effective. It can create a ground ball, a double-play, a pop fly or a ball hit to a pre-planned area. A pitcher who controls his fastball enables his teammates to excel. He can defuse an explosive hitter's power, lessen the effectiveness of a contact hitter and coordinate his defensive players with the pitch. A pitcher without great speed can still be very effective.

Throwing at different speeds is another way to use the fastball. An average or a below-average fastball can be very tough to hit if it is thrown at different speeds. Changing speeds disrupts the hitter's timing. Power hitters are particularly vulnerable to a change of speeds. This style of pitching is very frustrating for most hitters.

The pitcher needs to understand his abilities. It will require a great deal of patience. He will need to decide the speed at which he has the best control. He must work within that zone. This approach shows the hitter a particular speed. The pitcher should vary the speeds. By throwing at speeds of one-to-five mph slower on various pitches, he can maintain control and simultaneously destroy the hitter's timing. Occasionally, the pitcher can throw a pitch harder than working speed. This aspect will cause additional timing problems for the hitter.

By throwing pitches at manageable speeds, with an occasional pitch thrown harder, the pitcher presents a very unpredictable picture for the hitter. This approach will give the pitcher approximately six different speeds to use with the fastball. Five of those speeds are manageable. The very hard pitches, which are beyond the manageable range, should be used sparingly. These pitches can be used when the pitcher is in control or when the pitcher needs to gain control of a particular situation.

The speed of a pitch can be used in different ways. If the speed overmatches the ability of the hitter, then that is a successful fastball. If the speed is not overpowering, the pitcher should choose another type of fastball. Throwing pitches at different speeds can be almost as effective for some pitchers. When throwing harder is not the answer, then the pitcher should throw slower.

There are a variety of fastballs. A dominating pitch born from speed is hard to beat. Most pitchers are not gifted with this ability, so they must adapt the skills to the fastball that gets the best results. How speed is used depends upon the skill level of the pitcher. There are four major categories from which to choose when developing this pitch: power, control, movement and changing speeds. Most pitchers throw a fastball that combines two or more of these. A straight, average fastball can be improved by adding some movement or by placing it in strategic locations. It can also be improved by changing the speed of each pitch.

Power Fastball

The power fastball is usually thrown by gripping the ball across the seams. This grip creates consistent spin and helps to work against gravity. This fastball will either be straight and hard or it will appear to rise. For the ball to rise, very tight spin is required, and the release should feel well out in front. Good back spin is required, and the ball should leave the index and middle fingers at approximately the same time. Uneven rotation will cause the ball to move to the left or the right. This uneven rotation also creates movement toward gravity. In effect, uneven spin takes some speed off the pitch.

The position of the arm is critical. It should be lifted in order to maximize the speed of the fastball. The finger should be on top of the ball. When a delay occurs in getting the arm up, the fingers get below the ball as the ball is released, thereby decreasing the spin and slowing the arm action.

The speed necessary to cause the ball to rise will probably be more than 88 mph. For the pitch to overcome the force of gravity, great velocity is required. The spin of the pitch and power toward the target are both extremely important factors in developing a power fastball.

Finger pressure is also very important. The ball should be released evenly off the first pads of the fingers. The ball should be gripped with the first pads of the fingers. A ball held in this way allows the pitcher to maintain a balanced grip on the ball. When the ball is held too far toward the tips of the fingers, balance and control are affected. If the ball is placed back in the hand, speed will be affected. This grip creates drag, or causes more parts of the hand and fingers to contact the ball as it comes out of the hand. This factor will cause the ball to lose speed or to move left or right.

A power fastball does not necessarily need a rise to be effective. If the pitch destroys the timing of the hitter, it is a successful pitch. If the batter has trouble getting the bat around on an 82 mph fastball, a straight fastball at that speed will get the job done.

A true power fastball is held across the seams. Pitchers throw a power fastball in order to throw the ball by the hitter. It does not necessarily mean the ball needs to be missed. A pop-up, a weak ground ball and a simple fly ball are all the results of a power fastball. This pitch is used to create timing problems for the hitter. It causes the hitter to start his swing early, meaning the hitter is unable to adjust to the various areas of the strike zone. The power fastball also makes the hitter susceptible to other pitches.

Changing Speed on the Fastball

Each pitcher should decide whether he can overpower the hitters with his fastball. Most pitchers are not overpowering. They should use the fastball in a different way. Throwing the fastball at different speeds can be very effective. If the pitcher is throwing a fastball at one speed, and the results are hard hit balls or consistent base hits, he should explore the practice of changing speeds.

The first step is to find out a pitcher's working speed. This step is done by having him throw for several days in different settings and evaluating each workout. His working speed is simply the best speed at which he can effectively and consistently throw strikes. Once that speed is learned, he can use that as his base. He will also have the same success with pitches four to five m.p.h. slower. He can use a fastball that is faster than his working speed if he selects situations where control is not a premium.

The following chart illustrates how the variation of speeds can be used.

Pitch 1	78 mph
Pitch 2	77 mph
Pitch 3	76 mph
Pitch 4	75 mph
Pitch 5	74 mph
Pitch 6	84 mph

In the previous illustration, the pitcher's working speed is 78 mph, and his top speed is 84 mph. The following is an example of how the variations in speed could work on a given batter:

Batter #1	
Pitch one	78 mph strike
Pitch two	75 mph ball
Pitch three	77 mph ball
Pitch four	74 mph strike
Pitch five	76 mph strike
Batter #2	
Pitch one	77 mph strike
Pitch two	78 mph strike
Pitch three	84 mph ball

Spotting the Fastball

If movement and speed are missing from the fastball, then placing it in specific locations in different situations will also prove to be successful. The pitcher will increase his effectiveness. If the pitcher can hit a precise target, he makes the job of the hitter more difficult. A well-placed pitch to a hitter's weakness, or a pitch in an unsuspected spot to the hitter, destroys the hitter's timing.

Most hitters look for a location, a certain pitch or a certain speed. When the pitcher uses location as a weapon, he is often effective. Throwing several pitches to the outside part of the strike zone, he sets up the opportunity to throw effectively to the inside part of the plate.

A power pitcher can use location. He is not required to be as fine as the pitcher with less speed. The power pitcher can work from the middle out or the middle in of the plate. He can also work the middle up and the middle down of the plate. By spotting the ball in these general locations, he enhances his ability to use power more effectively.

The control pitcher must pitch to specific spots. His success is dependent upon his ability to hit the smaller targets. Often, the pitcher who uses the fastball in this manner is more consistent than the power pitcher. The power pitcher may dominate on a given day. The pitcher who spots his fastball can also be very successful.

Spotting the fastball can also be aided by using movement and by varying the speeds on the fastball. If done properly, the pitcher who spots the ball may be over-powering on occasion. He simply sets the hitter up for a certain pitch in a certain location, and then throws the fastball to that location. If the hitter is not prepared for that pitch, the pitch will appear to overpower him.

Movement on the Fastball

A pitcher who does not possess an overpowering fastball may need to use movement to disrupt the timing of the hitter. Movement itself can be overpowering, especially when high speeds and movement are combined. Although movement reduces the speed of the pitch, sometimes the movement more than makes up for the loss of speed. To make the ball slide or sink will probably take four to eight mph off the pitch. A curveball or a change-up will reduce the speed even more.

By applying the proper finger pressure and releasing the ball in the proper manner, movement will take place. Generally, when the pitcher wants to add sinker or slider spin, he should hold the index and the middle fingers together and with the seams.

Greater movement is enhanced by the narrower contact point. Widening the grip straightens the flight of the ball. However, if the grip is exceptionally wide, greater movement and less speed will result. Split-finger fastballs and change-ups are often thrown with wider grips.

Good movement on the fastball makes it difficult to hit solidly. A hitter may get a piece of the ball, but that is exactly what the pitcher is trying to force him to do. The pitcher's objective is to show a pitch, make the hitter think it is a normal pitch in a desirable location, and then have the pitch dip or move. This method induces the hitter to hit the pitch, but not successfully.

Movement creates ground balls, pop flies, fly balls and an occasional strikeout. High speeds with movement can make the pitcher as dominating as the power pitcher. Using movement as a tool will help the pitcher in many ways. His defense will be tuned in to the game. Ground balls and fly balls create activity. Movement on the pitches creates ineffective contact by the batters.

As a rule, movement will help reduce the number of pitches thrown because it creates poor contact. Many balls are not hit well and will result in a ball put in play. Throwing a ball in on the hands is done to get the hitter to hit the ball on the handle of the bat. A ball on the outside corner with movement is thrown to induce a ground ball. Pitchers with movement also throw more double-play balls.

A sinking fastball can be thrown by holding the index and middle fingers together and by moving the thumb up toward the index finger. The hand action should go to the inside part of the ball. Greater finger pressure applied to the inside part of the ball will create greater movement on the pitch. The pitcher should not try to turn the wrist over. Too much internal rotation of the wrist will dramatically reduce the speed of the pitch, causing the pitch to act as a screwball. A good sinking fastball has two elements— speed and movement.

It is also important to have the throwing arm up for a good sinker to occur. Good arm extension is essential. The fingers should be on top of the ball as it is brought up into throwing position, and they should be on top of the ball at the release point.

Each pitcher should develop a sense of touch and feel with each pitch. A few pitches in the bullpen will tell the pitcher what kind of finger pressure gives him the best results. Some pitchers will get better results by pressing to the inside part of the ball with the inside pad of the middle finger. Others will get better results by using the middle or outside pad of the middle finger. Occasionally, a pitcher may find that the index finger supplies the greatest pressure. Pitchers should not be afraid to experiment in a sensible manner.

Another important factor for the pitcher when he throws a good sinking fastball is to make sure the hand finishes the throw. This factor requires a fully-extended throwing arm and hand. The hand should feel as though it is being thrown through the ball directly to the target.

To make the ball sail, or to achieve a slider-type spin, the grip and release are both important. The ball should be gripped by placing the index and middle fingers close together. The pitcher should grip the ball with the seams, and pressure should be applied to the outside part of the ball. The inside pad of the middle finger is normally dominant. However, the middle of the pad or the middle finger may serve other pitchers better. Again, the index finger may be a better source of pressure for some pitchers.

Movement is developed by those pitchers who pay attention to the spin and the rotation of the pitch. Learning how to improve the movement on a pitch is simple if the pitcher notices how the ball rotates during each throw. Even when playing catch, the pitcher should notice the spin of each thrown ball.

In simple terms, if a pitcher or player can make the ball spin in such a way to make it go straight, that same pitcher or player can also make the throw have movement. The pitchers should apply pressure to the ball, and as the ball is released, the pitcher should pull down on the back of the ball. This action will cause the ball to rotate backwards. If the ball is gripped across the seams, and the release from the middle and index fingers is even, the ball will tend to rotate consistently backward to the target. Provided the arm angle and wrist action are correct, the throw will be straight.

Pressure to the outside part of the ball will cause it to move in a right-to-left direction, and it will take a downward plane. Pressure to the inside part of the ball will have the opposite effect. The amount of pressure, wrist-and-arm angle, and the force with which the ball is thrown will also affect the spin and rotation.

Pitchers should spend a lot of time playing catch with each other. During these sessions, careful attention should be paid to rotation, finger pressure, release and angles. They should talk to each other about these factors. They should try to tighten the spin on the fastball and to experiment on taking the hand to the inside part of the ball. They should evaluate the results. Next, they should throw a few pitches and apply pressure to the outside part of the ball, and again evaluate the results. They should notice the spin on each pitch. After a few sessions like this, pitchers should be able to read rotation and produce spin in the direction they choose.

Combination

Most pitchers are not in the "overpower" class. A player who is gifted with a great fastball should use it. He should make pitching very simple. He should throw the ball hard, get it over the plate and not worry about much strategy. If power beats the hitter, then why use anything else? But since these kinds of pitchers are rare, a combination of power, movement, control and change of speeds is probably the best weapon for most pitchers.

By changing speeds on the fastball, the pitcher makes it difficult for the hitter to time the pitch. By working all areas of the strike zone and wisely selecting the zones, the pitcher does not allow the hitter to become fixed on one area. By adding movement to the fastball, the pitcher further disrupts the hitter's ability to wait for a certain pitch. Wise use of all elements discussed will serve the pitcher well and will even make an average speed fastball look faster.

It is important for each pitcher to know his own strengths and weaknesses. He should use the strengths and make sure they are the elements that are honed and sharpened on a daily basis. He should cover the weaknesses by cleverly drawing from the available resources that have been discussed.

Pitchers should strive to improve the speed of the fastball. Maximum speed does not have to be used on every pitch, but it can be a tremendous asset in crucial situations. Pitchers who register increases in maximum speeds also improve their working speed. The ability to throw most pitches at higher speeds will pay dividends.

How to Improve Speed

Many ways exist to improve pitching speed. Sound mechanics, long toss, straight-line long toss, throwing with maximum effort, developing durability, flippers exercises, and developing arm strength are factors to consider. When placed in the hands of a committed pitcher, the pitcher will see results.

Sound mechanics provide the pitcher with a base. Good balance, proper grip, good rotation and freedom of movement are the ingredients of sound mechanics. A pitcher can throw hard without good mechanics provided he is gifted. That same gifted pitcher can throw harder and longer with good mechanics.

The spin, or rotation, of the baseball is a very important factor in both speed and distance. The proper grip will help the pitcher create correct rotation. The grip used should correlate with the type of fastball to be used. Lateral and downward movement will negatively affect the speed of the throw. True backspin will provide the best rotation to fight gravity and keep the ball in flight longer.

To gain the most distance out of a throw, good back spin is required. Lateral or downward action will decrease the speed of the throw. In throwing to achieve the best in distance and the best in speed, the pitcher should grip the ball across the wide seams and create backspin.

Balance is also extremely important. Good balance provides stability and direction. Many pitchers throw the ball with great force only to have some of that force negated by poor balance. This situation creates very bad angles, which, in turn, steals power and causes control problems. Good angles are created by directing all movement toward the target. When the pitcher can throw from a balanced push-off foot to a balanced stride foot, he establishes proper angles. Whether throwing for distance or for speed, good balance is essential.

Strengthening the arm is another important factor in developing a better fastball. A sound strength program will help to develop speed and durability. It will also help to prevent some arm injuries. In addition, a higher level of strength will enhance a pitcher's level of confidence and durability.

A strength training program for pitchers should include the entire body, with particular emphasis on the triceps, forearms, wrists, hands and fingers. The shoulder is also extremely important. It can be adequately exercised with a three-pound weight or a tennis-ball can filled with sand. These exercises will develop and strengthen the rotator cuff area.

The fingers play a major role in the act of throwing. Strong fingers provide greater spin and supply greater force to the baseball. Finger strength also adds movement to the fastball and distance to the throw. Squeezing a tennis ball, spinning a baseball, and using a baseball to do isometric exercises and specific throwing drills will help to strengthen the fingers. Strengthening the fingers will produce a better pitch, by adding bite to the curveball and speed and movement to the other pitches.

The wrist of the pitcher should be both strong and flexible. Stretching exercises and a drill called "flippers" will increase the range of motion and add strength. A stiff wrist does not allow a complete range of motion. The throwing action is restricted at both the beginning and the ending of the throw. A supple and strong wrist action will greatly improve the throw.

Wrist curls will develop a pitcher's forearms. These curls will also improve finger and hand strength. Another way to gain strength in the fingers, hand, wrist and forearm is by winding up a rope tied to a weight. A light weight of three to five pounds tied to a rope that is attached to a cut off handle of a bat or an eighteen-inch piece of broom stick makes an excellent strengthening devise. Standing straight with his back unbowed, the pitcher should simply hold the handle, or broom stick, about chest high with the arms outstretched and palms facing upward. He should begin winding the rope around the handle with a series of wrist curls. He should complete the curls by unwinding the rope by reversing the curls. The drill can also be executed with the palms toward the ground.

Special Throwing Program

Any player can improve his throwing. Not only accuracy, but the speed and distance of the throw, can be improved. Long-toss or throwing for distance, if done properly, will help the player to develop the ability to throw the ball farther and harder. Straight line long-throwing will add distance and speed to the throw. Developing flexibility with the wrist through "flipper" and stretching exercises will allow the pitcher to maximize his ability. Organizing and measuring the results of these activities provides a road map for the pitcher's development.

This program needs careful supervision. It should only be undertaken by those who are very serious about improving the distance and speed of their throws. If not followed regularly, it will be of little or no value. If the pitcher is not in good condition or is not conscientious, the program may be harmful to him. The program requires a maximum effort on several throws. Only the pitcher who is properly focused and conditioned should be allowed to take part in this program.

If this program is followed for four weeks, improvements of up to 15 to 20 feet and speeds of up to four mph may be added to the player's throw.

Improved Throwing Program

The following steps are designed to improve throwing. Properly done, they should improve both a pitcher's throwing speed and his throwing distance. This program should be performed every other day (three times per week) for four weeks. Using a chart similar to the "Improved Throwing Chart" presented later in this chapter will give the pitcher or the coach a method for recording relevant information from the pitcher's participation in the suggested throwing improvement program and for assessing the effectiveness of the pitcher's efforts.

Step 1: Flipper Exercise
- 30 seconds of exercises with 30-second rest periods.
- Pitchers start the exercise with their arms hanging to the sides, fully-extended.
- The exercise is then done with the arms fully extended in front of the body at chest level.
- This exercise should be continued for 15 minutes, with the pitchers alternating positions, activity and rest.

Step 2: Wrist Stretchers
- The pitcher should hold his arm out in front and bend the wrist forward as far as possible. He should hold for a for count of 10. (4 sets)
- With arm outstretched, the pitcher should then bend the wrist back as far as possible and hold for a count of 10. (4 sets)
- . With arm outstretched, the pitcher should bend the wrist back and use his other hand to pull back and increase the level of flexibility of his wrist, pulling it back as far as he can. He should hold to a count of 10. (4 sets)

Step 3: Measuring Speed
- After the player is fully warmed up, the coach should measure his pitching speed with the radar gun.
- The coach should either measure off 60 feet 6 inches or have the pitcher throw from the mound. The coach should use the mound for pitchers and flat ground for other players.
- The coach should record the best speed of five throws.
- The coach should then record the date and speed of the best throw.

Step 4: Long Toss (Straight Line)
- The players should play catch by throwing the ball in a straight line (no arc). They should take approximately 10 throws.
- They should then move back in increments until the maximum throwing distance is identified.
- The coach should record the best throw and the date.

Step 5: Long Toss (Distance With Arc)
- The players should take 10 throws and stretch out. They should not try to get maximum distance (These are throws designed to stretch and loosen).
- After getting fully loose, they should take five throws for distance.
- The coach should record the best throw and the date.

Step 6: Maximum Effort
- After warming up fully, the players should make 10 throws with an all-out effort—60 feet, 6 inches for pitchers; 90 feet for position players.

Use of the Radar Gun

The radar gun is a very useful tool. It helps the pitcher understand his abilities. Some say it discourages the pitcher who is not a hard thrower. Others think it puts too much

Name _____

Position _____

Improved Throwing Chart

Beginning Speed _____ Beginning Distance _____

Final Speed _____ Final Distance_____

Date										
1. Flippers										
2. Wrist Stretchers										
3. Measuring Speed										
4. Long Toss (Str. Line)										
5. Long Toss (Arc)										
6. Maximum Effort										

emphasis on throwing every pitch with an all-out effort. It really depends on how it is used and what emphasis is placed on the measurements.

The radar gun has many uses. Measuring the top speed of the pitch is only one. It can also be used to measure the speed differences of the various pitches. This practice teaches the pitcher that only slight mental adjustments are needed to change the speed of a pitch.

Measuring speed gives the pitcher a starting point. It tells him where he is and where he needs to go. Evaluation is essential to learning and teaching. The radar gun gives quick and precise evaluations. Proper use of the radar gun can motivate. The learning process is aided by the meaningful feedback. Development of pitches is enhanced by its use. The radar guns helps to teach how speed can be used.

If the radar gun is only used occasionally, pitchers will probably be concerned only with how hard they are throwing. Therefore, regular use of the radar gun is much more effective. Using it to figure out each pitcher's working speed and measuring the speed differences of various pitches will be much more fruitful. Each pitcher will become more aware of his own skills and how he can best use the skills.

Each pitcher should know the difference in the speed of his fastball and his curve, change, slider or other pitches. No absolute speed differential exists for all pitchers. The following table shows what can be considered to be normal speed differences:

Speed Differences		
Best speed Fastball	Working Fastball	4 mph less
Working speed Fastball	Curveball	12 mph less
Working speed Fastball	Change up	12 mph less
Working speed Fastball	Slider	6 mph less

These speed differences are only approximations. Each pitcher is different. The working speed for some pitchers may be less than four mph off their top speed. On the other hand, the difference may be as much as eight mph. Either way, the working speed is simply the best speed at which a pitcher has control.

Some pitchers will throw the curveball with greater velocity and tighter spin than others. If so, their speed differences may be only 10 mph less. The key is results. If the

Name_____

Radar Gun Chart

	FB	CU	CH	SL	Other Pitches		FB	CU	CH	SL
1						41				
2						42				
3						43				
4						44				
5						45				
6						46				
7						47				
8						48				
9						49				
10						50				
11						51				
12						52				
13						53				
14						54				
15						55				
16						56				
17						57				
18						58				
19						59				
20						60				
21						61				
22						62				
23						63				
24						64				
25						65				
26						66				
27						67				
28						68				
29						69				
30						70				
31						71				
32						72				
33						73				
34						74				
35						75				
36						76				
37						77				
38						78				
39						79				
40						80				

Key:
FB = Fastball   CH = Changeup
CU= Curveball   SL = Slider

	FB	CU	CH	SL	Other Pitches		FB	CU	CH	SL
81						121				
82						122				
83						123				
84						124				
85						125				
86						126				
87						127				
88						128				
89						129				
90						130				
91						131				
92						132				
93						133				
94						134				
95						135				
96						136				
97						137				
98						138				
99						139				
100						140				
101						141				
102						142				
103						143				
104						144				
105						145				
106						146				
107						147				
108						148				
109						149				
110						150				
111										
112										
113										
114										
115										
116										
117										
118										
119										
120										

SUMMARY: Did he vary speeds well?

Best Speed: Workable Speed:

FB ____   FB ____

CU ____   CU ____

CH ____   CH ____

SL ____   SL ____

Range:

FB ____   CU ____

CH ____   SL ____

curveball is sharp and has enough break to destroy the hitter's timing, it will deliver the desired results.

The change-up can be effective from speeds of 10 to 12 mph less. When the speed is much slower than this range, the change-up is usually not as effective. The exception would be a change-up that has outstanding movement. The movement becomes a bigger factor than the speed difference. Some speed difference is still important, however.

A great slider is one that has both good speed and good movement. If the slider has too much break, it will not have good speed. If it is thrown too hard it will probably not have enough break. Tight spin is the key. A small sharp break is usually the most effective slider.

Information from using the radar gun should be recorded and evaluated on a regular basis. The results of his efforts should be shared with the pitcher. The "Radar Gun Chart" in this chapter is only a guide. A good pitching coach always leaves room for exceptions. The speed differences in the chart merely act as starting point. Common sense and good judgement should override the chart.

Summary

This chapter discussed the fact that the fastball is an important pitch that can be used in many ways. An overpowering fastball can dominate hitters. However, cleverly changing the speed that a pitch is thrown can also be effective. Each pitcher should understand his own abilities. This understanding will help him decide how to use best his fastball.

Some pitchers are blessed with the ability to throw hard. Others must work extremely hard to develop a fastball. In either case, to keep the fastball, it must be used often. In each bullpen workout, the pitcher should throw the last few pitches at full speed.

Several ways exist to improve the speed at which a pitcher can throw a ball, including conditioning, weight training, and a well-organized throwing program.

10

Control

The pitcher must develop a high degree of control in order to be successful. The level of competition will affect the definition of "control." For the little leaguer, control means throwing strikes. It simply means the pitcher has enough skill to throw the ball into or near the strike zone. As the pitcher moves up in competition, control entails throwing to more specific and smaller portions of the strike zone. Control is always very important. If the pitcher has an outstanding fastball, great movement or another redeeming pitching quality, control may become less of a factor. This factor is especially true at the lower levels of baseball. Even with superior speed and stuff at higher levels of play, control will increasingly become more important. Advanced hitters have enough experience and discipline to lay off the pitches that are not in the strike zone. Umpires are also more strict with the strike zone at higher levels of play.

Control also includes the strategy and situations of each game. Good control calls for the pitcher to be able to effectively pitch in many different competitive situations. As the pitcher moves up the competitive ladder, his duties and responsibilities grow. Added to the need to throw the ball into the strike zone is the necessity to deal successfully with each game situation. The game situation may call for a ground ball in one instance, or a fly ball in another situation. In other words, the pitcher must be ready and capable to pitch in many different settings. Control is one of his best tools.

A Plan

Good control and throwing with accuracy requires a plan. The pitcher who sees a need for consistency and has a desire to pitch with consistency is a pitcher with a plan. Control comes to those pitchers who are in control of themselves. It does not come to those who simply throw without paying attention to mechanics or the proper target.

Most notably, the pitcher who cares only about striking out the hitter is a candidate for poor control. The pitcher who focuses on making the hitter look bad on a single pitch, instead of getting an out, is also susceptible to wildness. Conversely, the pitcher who truly enjoys strategy and pitching to win each game is a good control candidate.

In every plan, the pitcher should include a thoroughly thought-out and quality warm-up. Each throw should have a particular target in mind. Even when playing catch, the pitcher should throw to hit a very specific target. His target should be a body part of the receiver. Throwing to hit the receiver in the shoulder, the knee, the waist or the neck is a sensible activity. No ball should leave the hand of a pitcher without a definite location intended for that thrown ball. This action is the basic, and first, step in developing the necessary concentration required to throw a baseball and hit the target.

An example would be for the pitcher to designate six areas of the body as different targets. The targets could include the following: (1) Right shoulder of receiver, (2) right hip of the receiver, (3) right knee of the receiver (4) left shoulder of receiver (5) left hip of receiver and (6) the left knee of the receiver. Each player should throw five throws to each target and mentally record the number of times he hits the target. A warm-up of this type takes about three to five minutes and gives each player 30 throws. This method provides a setting to allow each player to measure his accuracy and to evaluate himself each day.

Sloppy habits, careless routines and failure to address the importance of consistent control will prevent the pitcher from developing control skills. Developing goals, designing a purpose for each thrown ball, and competing for a successful outcome will help the pitcher to make steady improvement in the area of control.

Each Throw Has a Purpose

The pitcher should never throw a ball without having an exact destination in mind. Generally, it can be said that pitchers who have a clearly designed plan for each pitch are pitchers who have good control. Whether throwing to a catcher or throwing to strings, the pitcher should sight the exact spot in his mind and then commit to that target on each pitch. The same advice should be followed when he throws to a stationary target or to a partner playing catch. It is extremely important for the pitcher to make this a habit.

The mind is a computer, and the body, if trained, will do what the computer tells it to do. Without proper material in the computer, the read-out will give inconsistent and meaningless data. The way to train the body is to take it through very specific and repetitive routines. The pitcher should have a definite objective for each pitch and trust his body to execute the command.

Conditioning

Some pitchers can concentrate and physically execute well for a few pitches, but then they suddenly lose their effectiveness. Often, this loss is simply the result of poor conditioning. Throwing a baseball with accuracy requires a great deal of both physical and mental stamina. Each pitcher should follow a steady regimen of organized running, stretching, weight training and throwing to fully utilize his abilities. Failure to follow such a regimen causes a loss of control and may lead to severe and lasting injuries.

A sound conditioning program will keep the arm and body in shape. When the body is weak or poorly conditioned, it is more susceptible to stress and pressure. A tired arm and body are unable to respond to the needs of a winning effort. Touch and feel disappear with a lack of conditioning. All skills will diminish when the body is weak or fatigued.

Mental conditioning is equally as important as physical conditioning. Mental preparation and conditioning need the same organized training that is found on the physical side. Steady, planned and goal-oriented routines of a mental nature are necessary to develop the concentration for good control. Organizing each day's practice, planning each workout with care, and establishing daily and long-term goals are absolute necessities if proper development and growth are important.

Repetition

To develop skills, repetition is essential. Repeating a skill properly and refining that skill require persistence and commitment. Many hours of work are required in order to develop physical skills. Learning about the release point requires repetition. To develop good control, the pitcher must be willing to drill on a consistent basis. Good practice habits will result in improvement. Just going through the motions will not produce positive gains. Drills done poorly often produce negative results.

Dry-run pitching, bullpen work, visualization periods, intrasquad games, batting practice, situation pitching, team drills, and other throwing drills are all important. These should never be done without a reason or without a sound purpose. Coaches should follow each activity with a careful evaluation. The pitcher does not necessarily need to have the coach's input at every turn, although the input should be welcomed and should provide help. It is the pitcher, himself, who needs to take control of his own destiny and motivate himself.

Mechanics

Sound mechanics play a major role in developing and maintaining control. Of course, exceptions exist at any level of play, most notably at the Major League level. There are several Major League pitchers who are among the most gifted athletes on earth, but even the most successful and gifted athletes would be better at their trade if they pitched with sound mechanics.

Sound mechanics enhance balance, create freedom of motion, improve rhythm, improve the proper use of energy, minimize injuries, increase leverage, and create proper angles. While control is possible without good mechanics, control is more easily attained when sound pitching techniques are used.

Centering

Another word for centering is concentration, but the word concentration often confuses some athletes. An athlete may be "concentrating" on many different things simultaneously. Concentration is meaningful and profitable to the athlete when he can concentrate on exactly what is needed, at the exact time it is needed. Centering, according to visual expert Bill Harrison, is a word that fits the needs of the pitcher.

To throw a baseball, hit the target, put movement on the ball, disrupt the timing of the hitter and get the desired results requires both physical and mental exercise. Successful results depend upon the method that is employed. The pitcher should analyze the situation, visualize the desired results, center on only those things that he wishes to accomplish with that pitch and then execute the plan. Dr. Bill Harrison's system has four steps: (1) analyze, (2) visualize, (3) center and (4) execute. The key to the plan is to see what is needed and focus on only that aspect, while keeping all other matters in the background.

Analyzing

Prior to each workout, each drill, or each situation, the pitcher should carefully analyze what needs to be done to be successful. If the objective is to throw the ball down the middle and at the knees, he should let that be his only goal for the moment. He should not add any other baggage for the trip. That is the job, and that is the only thing that matters at the time.

The pitcher should learn to analyze in segments, in situations or in pitches, and concentrate on one part at a time. This approach will give him a specific objective to perform. Each task will be simplified and made easier to accomplish.

Visualization

Visualization is a word commonly used by eye experts. Whatever the activity, athletic or non-athletic, if it requires concentration, then the practice of visualizing that activity before it is attempted is extremely helpful. Simply playing a quick motion picture in the mind of what exactly is wanted will add to planning and executing of that activity. Perhaps the athlete who most dramatically brought attention to this exercise was Michael Jordan in an NBA basketball game. The scene shows him shooting a free throw with his eyes closed. This scene is a good example of the ultimate effort in visualization.

Executing

It is important for the pitcher to know exactly what he wants to do. He should work in the present, discard clutter and center on only those things that will cause the desired result. If, for instance, the pitcher wishes to induce a ground ball, he needs to throw a low pitch. He should see a clear picture of the results before throwing the ball. No negative scenes or extra data should be put into the mental picture.

Pitchers who experience inconsistency with control are pitchers who see too many details at a time. For example, they often know what they want to do but instead of executing, they add clutter. Crowd noise is magnified in the mind. The possibility of failure is brought to the forefront. The dugout of the opposing team catches the pitcher's eyes and ears. Tension draws the pitcher's attention. Distractions get in the way and cause detours. All negative data must be discarded if success is to become a consistent possibility.

A pitcher should fortify himself with the right tools to get each job done. Too many tools, or the wrong type of tools, often interfere with a successful outcome. He should evaluate the job, select the right tool and know what to do with the tool. He should trust his judgement and set out to succeed.

Setting Priorities

It is extremely difficult for a pitcher to concentrate on throwing to a specific target while simultaneously concentrating on the mechanics of pitching. The mechanics should have been taken care of in practice.

During practice, all things that help the pitcher attain control should be carefully and methodically developed. These things should be ranked and organized. They should be added to the list of offensive weapons for each pitcher. These things should enhance the pitcher's control. The pitcher should not allow any of these details to become negative baggage. In a game situation, he can isolate the exact detail that brings winning results.

Control requires great concentration and freedom to create the movements that accomplish the prescribed goal. Thinking too much about mechanics, past perform-ances, future performances, or things that interfere with the job is not productive.

A pitcher's goal, of course, is to win each game. To win the game, he must win several battles. Lack of proper attention to each battle could result in failure to complete the final goal. The pitcher should know the situation, evaluate it, plan for it and carefully carry out the plan. He should take responsibility for the outcome, and be ready to repeat this process as often as is necessary to succeed. Purposeful and well-organized throwing is essential. Throwing to targets, such as strings, tires, and canvas, helps to develop control. Throwing batting practice with a purpose is helpful. Throwing in the bullpen and in a game or game-like situations are all control enhancers. Control may be dramatically improved in any of these settings if the pitcher is responsible.

Throwing to Have Control

Baseball goes through cycles of pitching philosophies. Many coaches advocate protecting the arm by limiting throwing, while others are proponents of throwing every day. Pitchers in Japan, for instance, throw every day, and they throw many pitches during each workout. Japanese pitchers are known for having good control. There are, however, excesses at both ends of the spectrum.

Sensible throwing is the answer. Not every workout should include full-speed throwing on every pitch. Throwing workouts should fluctuate from light throwing days (25 to 50 pitches) to heavy throwing days (75 to 100 pitches). When the season starts, the same routine can be followed, but common sense is a necessary ingredient. Pitchers who work on a three-day rest program should throw once between starts. A medium or heavy workout is suggested on that throwing day. On a four-day rest program, the pitcher should throw twice between starts. One should be a heavy workout, and one should be a medium workout (35 to 50 pitches).

During these workouts, pitchers should throw at half- to three-quarter speed. The last 10 to 20 pitches should be thrown at full-speed, or 10 to 20 of the total pitches should thrown be at full-speed. All pitches in the pitcher's repertoire should be used and should be thrown with good control in mind.

Again, control is attained by throwing a baseball at a target and executing enough times to establish touch and feel. This action is always done with concern for the pitcher's arm. Each bullpen workout that has control as part of the plan should include the charting process. This process will give the pitcher a concrete standard and allow him to see the results of the workout.

Throwing batting practice with a prescribed goal in mind is also very productive. Making hitters hit the ball on the ground creates a game-like setting. Counting the number of strikes thrown during each pitcher's batting practice stint will also serve as a standard. Measuring and evaluating performance develops incentive. Drills like this give the pitcher a goal or a plan.

Situation hitting is another control pitching challenge for the pitcher. In this instance, a pitcher's goal is to throw strikes and prevent the hitter from successfully executing the offensive situation. For instance, if a runner is on third base with no outs, the ball must not be hit in the air. If a runner is on second base with no outs, the batter should be prevented from hitting the ball to the right side of the infield. By setting up these situations in practice, the pitcher can practice in gamelike situations. This approach helps to improve concentration. In many of these situations, good control by the pitcher can be measured.

Setting up imaginary situations in the bullpen is a good method to create competitiveness and goal-oriented outcomes. The coach should develop the situation, and the pitcher should be challenged to throw certain pitches to designated areas. Success is measured by the pitcher's ability to throw pitches to the phantom hitter's weakness. The coach is the judge and can create as much or as little pressure as needed for each pitcher.

Control is relative to the skill level of the pitcher. The pitcher who has great stuff and a great fastball should not be too concerned about hitting corners of the plate. This kind of pitcher should let his stuff and speed work for him. By throwing more to the middle of the plate, the pitcher can maximize his potential.

If a pitcher is not gifted with great stuff or with great velocity, he must rely on good control and changing speeds. This type of pitcher should throw to specific spots. His success will depend on his ability to hit these spots. Many pitchers who have average stuff win because they can throw to specific locations. Pitches in the low part of the strike zone are usually hit on the ground. Placing the ball in an area six inches below and six inches above the knees will further improve the odds. Throwing the ball down and inside or down and outside helps direct where the ball will be hit. Keeping the ball on the corners will place control of the game in the pitcher's hands. Good control allows him to throw up and in to the hitter. This action forces the hitter off the plate. It also sets up a plan for throwing to the outside of the plate. The pitcher should not throw to the middle of the plate.

Controlling more than one pitch is also extremely important for the pitcher. It is even more important to the pitcher who lacks a good fastball or a pitcher who lacks great stuff. Controlling at least two pitches during the game is a necessary ingredient to winning. A pitcher who has good control of only one pitch will make the hitter's job easier. A different look or a different speed serves to upset the timing of the hitter. As the level of competition increases, control becomes much more critical.

At the top levels of competition, the need for hitting exact spots is essential. The pitcher should think of the out zone as an "L" shape. The good areas for the pitcher to throw are down and away, down and in, and up and in.

Strategy

Knowledge of strategy is helpful in developing control. The ability to force the hitter to hit a ground ball improves the chances of getting an out. Successfully dealing with various situations, by controlling the location of the pitch, is beneficial to the pitcher. By inducing ground balls and learning to control situations with his ability to control each pitch, the pitcher should become more convinced that control is his ally.

A plan for improving the ability to throw the ball in precise areas should be built into each workout. A pitch inside may keep the batter from advancing the runner from second to third base. Low pitches create ground balls. Pitches low and away reduce the chances of a ball being pulled. Getting ahead of the hitter will increase the pitcher's chance of success. A good plan and proper location of pitches are a winning combination.

Sharing the Plan with the Catcher

Sharing the plan with the catcher confirms the pitcher's commitment because two people are now working toward the same goal. This sharing will improve interest and create a more vigilant and helpful catcher. An interested, alert person sees more details than one who is not interested and alert.

Throwing to the catcher, with the catcher setting a target in a particular area, is also a competitive and focused drill. Acting as the coach in this situation, the catcher assumes the role of judge. This role places the catcher in a positive position and in a leadership role. He can encourage, push, help, remind and motivate the pitcher. In this situation, specific goals and outcomes exist.

Anything which highlights hitting a target is better than throwing with no real purpose in mind. Success and failure create a competitive environment. Both the pitcher and the catcher will be encouraged to step up to a higher competitive level. The result will be a purposeful workout.

Constructive criticism is a part of any learning process. It shows interest and creates enthusiasm. When the pitcher loses focus, an interested catcher can help him get back on track. Daily routines often need special attention to be effective. The catcher can offer such attention.

Encouragement is also important. An enthusiastic catcher motivates by pointing out positive gains made by the pitcher. A well-thrown pitch or a good effort should draw praise. Consistency should be rewarded. A well-executed plan should draw the most attention. A caring catcher encourages, criticizes, evaluates, praises, reminds, leads, listens and guides the pitcher. Stationary targets are inanimate objects. They merely offer a target. The catcher, on the other hand offers a target, and gives advice.

The mitt of the catcher is the best of all targets. It provides the same picture for the pitcher that is used in the game. The catcher also provides an incentive for the pitcher. His actions and comments are valuable assets. A catcher who uses both of these assets can get the most out of the pitcher.

The catcher shows interest when he encourages the pitcher to hit spots. Good body language and positive actions by the catcher will create an environment that enhances better control. Giving a good target, challenging the pitcher to hit it, and giving the pitcher credit for success helps the pitcher's power of concentration. The activity becomes enjoyable and purposeful.

Strings, tires or stationary targets do not talk back. They neither encourage nor discourage the pitcher. The catcher reacts. He encourages, challenges, persuades and even disciplines the pitcher. It is very important for the pitcher to establish a good working relationship with each of his catchers. The pitcher should share his plan with the catcher before and during each workout.

Trusting the Body

Touch is a word used to describe the connection between the mind and the body. Touch is the sense of contact between the fingers and the baseball and the sense of control through the throwing motion. It relates to the hand, the fingers and the arm.

Feel is similar to touch, but it includes the entire body. Feel has to do with the sense of movement and the control of each part of the delivery. A pitcher with good touch and good feel is a pitcher who has good control.

Holding, gripping, spinning and squeezing the baseball will help to improve the sense of touch. A pitcher should take part in these practices daily because they breed familiarity and improve the senses. By keeping a ball in his hand as often as possible, the pitcher will become familiar with its weight and size. Holding or carrying the ball for a few minutes each day will enable the pitcher to develop a sense of weight and how that weight relates to the grip and the throwing motion.

The practice of gripping the ball for a few minutes each day is very productive. The pitcher should practice gripping each pitch. This action will help to decide the degree of finger pressure. The pitcher should become more familiar with where the ball is held to produce the best results. Contact points on the ball are very important. The simple procedure of griping the ball creates opportunities to learn more about contact points.

Spinning the ball is another great exercise to help develop touch and feel. The pitcher should use the curveball grip (low-thumb grip) to spin the ball. He should hold the ball out in front of his chest and spin the ball up in the air by pulling down with the middle finger and pushing up with the thumb. After a few practices, the pitcher can tell which pressure points produce the best results. The best pressure points will create tighter spin and greater height.

Squeezing the baseball is an isometric exercise that not only develops strength, but also offers a training ground for learning more about the sense of touch. By taking a few minutes a day to repeat this isometric exercise, the pitcher will develop stronger fingers and improve his touch and feel. During the exercise, he should pay attention to the texture of the ball, the height and feel of the seams, the position of the ball in the hand and the weight of the ball.

Pitchers should carry a ball around during practice and practice these drills. Every practice should include these drills. These exercises can and should be repeated while watching television, listening to the radio or during other available times.

Making Control A Priority

A pitcher with great stuff and poor control can win. A pitcher with poor stuff and great control may also win. Great stuff and great control produce a championship-level pitcher. Because good control makes any pitcher better, it should be a top priority.

Pitchers who suffer from poor control usually have poor practice habits. They only concern themselves with control at key times. During these key times they try to elevate their focus, but often fail because they are not fully prepared. Poor practice habits leave them ill-equipped to do the job. In other words, they don't care enough to make necessary changes during the practice setting. They may become concerned and embarrassed when failure rears its ugly head, but that concern is not lasting.

Methodical, persistent and well-organized practices are necessary. Any pitcher can improve his control if he has enough desire. Control is not accomplished overnight. Commitment is required, and persistence is essential. The pitcher needs patience for this goal to be accomplished.

Many requirements must be met to attain good control. It is easy to see why some pitchers are wild. Wild pitchers are impatient and are not persistent, They are not totally committed. They do not have a plan for developing control. They are aware that control is a troublesome issue. They are aware that control comes and goes. In other words, they just are not able to come to grips with how and what to do about control.

Target Areas

The pitcher should divide the strike zone into target areas. The target for beginners is the entire strike zone. As the pitcher improves, he should advance to a smaller and more specific target. The target ranges from a large general area to a very small target. The following chart illustrates six examples of various targets.

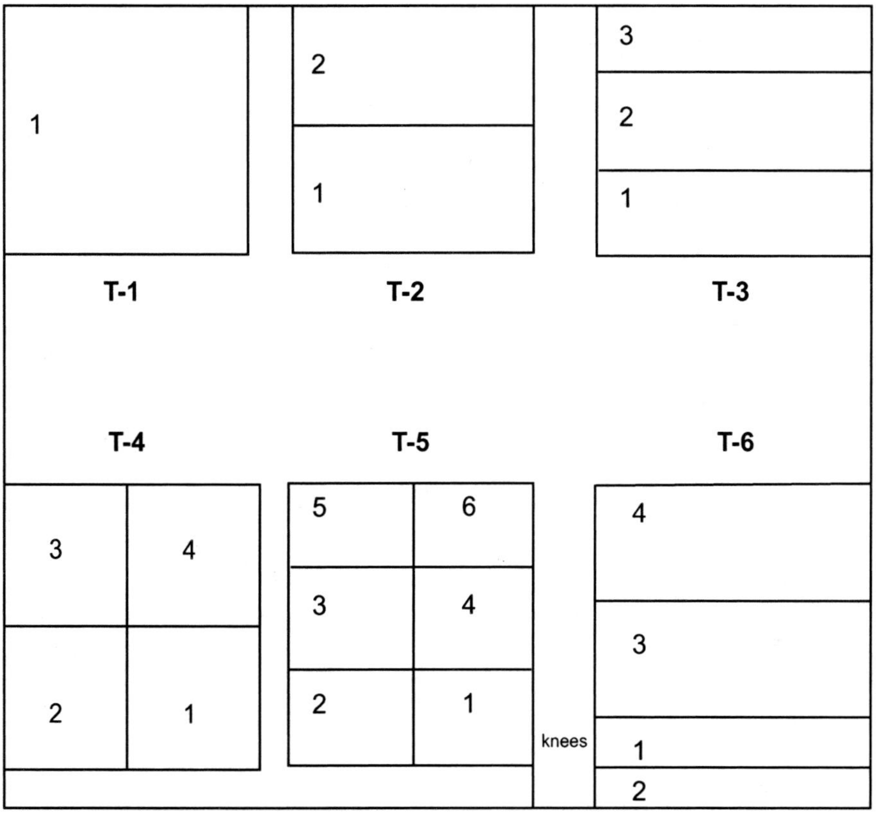

T-1	T-2	T-3
T-4	T-5	T-6

By paying attention, control can be improved. The pitcher should make control a priority and evaluate his progress on a daily basis. One means of evaluation is that of counting and charting the pitches. The coach should count the number of strikes thrown during each workout. This action will provide a watermark for the next workout. If one more strike is thrown in the next workout, then improvement has been made.

The strike zone can be broken down into sections. The whole strike zone can be used for beginners or for those pitchers who are extremely wild. Above and below the waist are the zones for the next level. An area over the plate and at the knees can represent a third area for the pitcher with higher goals. Other areas can be developed for those pitchers who are more advanced, such as the outside corner of the plate and the knees.

To add incentive, imaginary games can be played by having the pitcher face imaginary hitters during his workout. The pitcher should be given the situation for each at-bat, with control as his major objective. His results should be evaluated and recorded. This drill challenges the pitcher and helps him learn to focus on short-term goals. Success with these short-term goals will lead to successful long-term goals. Short, monitored workouts teach the pitcher how to develop persistence and patience.

Knowing Your Working Speed

Working speed is a combination of velocity and control. Often the reason for poor control is a pitcher who tries to throw too hard. Other pitchers have not developed an ability to judge the speed of each pitch. Many pitchers fear they will experience more control problems if they take some speed off the pitch. Any pitcher can develop and understand his working speed.

The coach should use a radar gun to chart each pitch, charting the balls and strikes. The coach should have the pitcher evaluate the chart after each performance. During the game or workout, the pitcher should throw at least ten pitches at maximum speed, and vary the speed of the remaining pitches. He should throw from one to ten miles an hour slower than the maximum effort. The coach should tabulate the number of pitches thrown at each speed for strikes and identify the speed at which the highest percent of strikes were thrown. That speed will become the pitcher's working speed. Once the working speed is established, the pitcher will have a better understanding of the relationship between accuracy and velocity. He should have a foundation that will become his starting point and enable him to know the speed at which he can throw to get the best results. Working at a manageable speed allows the pitcher to take control of his abilities. He can throw more strikes, and the change in speeds will disrupt the hitter's timing.

Purposeful Bullpen Workouts

Many different workouts can be created to help the pitcher. These can be both challenging and motivating. Each drill should suit the needs of the pitcher. A bullpen workout should also vary according to the ability of the pitcher. The workout for beginning or low-skilled pitchers should be simple. Higher standards can be set for those pitchers with higher skills.

Summary

This chapter discussed the fact that, in order to develop control over his pitches, the pitcher must first gain control over himself. Organization and discipline are essential ingredients in developing good control. The pitcher should have a plan for each practice and each game.

Pitchers Bullpen Chart

Name Date	Num. Pitches	Num. Strikes	FB		CU		CH		SL		Other		Percent Strikes	
			B	S	B	S	B	S	B	S	B	S	B	S

Making the best out of the present is important. A pitcher who focuses on the job at hand, and gives that job his undivided attention, is usually successful. He avoids clutter. He decides what is important and what is not important. This focus and attention allow him to concentrate on the important factors.

Control can be attained by even the wildest of pitchers. The pitcher needs to want to achieve control and be willing to work for it. Planning, organization, commitment, and persistence can pave the way toward the development of control, while daily evaluations keep the pitcher on course.

11

Gamesmanship

A competitive, aggressive pitcher is tough to beat. Some pitchers are known as "gamers." These pitchers are at their best in the toughest of game situations. The game itself seems to motivate these competitors. The gamer enjoys the excitement and the thrill of testing his skills against the opposition. Gamesmanship can make up for a deficiency in velocity, stuff, control or mechanics.

A pitcher who possesses great mechanics, but is not a good competitor, will find the winning path difficult to reach. A great fastball pitcher who is unwilling to battle in tough situations will also end on the losing side more often than necessary. Good control alone will not be enough to make the pitcher a consistent winner. The best breaking ball or sinker ball pitcher often falters when he loses his competitive spirit.

Competitive people are usually those people who can motivate themselves. At the base of their motivation is the desire to win. The exhilaration and feeling of fulfillment from winning are fuel enough. The anguish caused by losing bites and gnaws at the inner fiber of the competitive athlete. He has a choice. He can sink his teeth into the game and resolve to be successful, or he can give less of himself and only occasionally find success. There are steps that a pitcher can take to become better at gamesmanship. Preparation is a starting point. Developing good practice habits and accepting responsibility are both important, as well.

Pitching takes a great deal of effort. Some activities involving the pitcher's workout are isolated from other team activities. This situation is an opportunity to take a responsible approach, or it offers many chances to slack-off. There are many pieces that need to be put together to make up a complete package for the pitcher. Any extra time or unsupervised time is best spent by refining one or more of the various pitching skills.

The pitcher should ask, "Will this activity improve any of my skills?" If the answer is yes, then he should go on with it. If the answer is no, his skill improvement is being put on hold. The wisest use of time is measured by the performance in game situations.

A concerted effort by the pitcher during each practice session will pay great dividends. Even if only slight improvement occurs, there is movement toward the goal of success. Sloppy, foolish activities lead to loss of control, poor mechanics, and many other negative results.

A pitcher who takes it upon himself to improve his skills is a pitcher who stands out in the crowd. Waiting for someone else to direct and control the learning environment is not advised. If a pitcher's control is lacking, he alone is responsible for correcting the inadequacy. Mechanics, velocity, stuff and gamesmanship are the pitcher's responsibility. He may seek help and advice, but his actions are the ultimate cause of gains in improvement or the cause for any setbacks.

Preparation

Preparation is the oil that makes the pitcher's motor run. Without proper preparation, the pitcher is not fully equipped to bring out his best. Both mental and physical preparation is necessary. Readiness to play does not just happen, it requires thought, planning and effort.

To compete at a championship level, physical conditioning plays a major role. A well-conditioned athlete is willing to endure. He does not falter because of fatigue. He does not give in when extra effort is needed. Fatigue has a way of making people less courageous. It also invites shortcuts and encourages bad habits.

Commitment to hard work and a willingness to give a maximum effort in practice situations, not only help physically, but also strengthen a pitcher's mental approach. The pitcher should learn to complete each assignment with a full effort. This effort pays dividends in the late innings and during the toughest moments of a game.

Preparation is continuous. Some situations are common, since they occur regularly in each game. A vigilant effort to develop the skills necessary to successfully deal with these situations should be a part of the pitcher's daily workout. Working from the stretch position, backing up bases and covering first base are examples of these situations. Getting ahead of the hitter, throwing strikes and fielding bunts and come-back hits are other examples. Daily practice sessions should include working on the skills related to these situations.

Mental preparation includes dealing with the moods that are common to athletes and people in general. Generally speaking, there are three different kinds of moods— (l) just right, (2) slightly off, and (3) really off. In the "just right" mood, the pitcher is motivated, eager and ready to play. No change is necessary. In the "slightly off" mood, the pitcher is not quite ready to play. His energy level may be low or he may be a little too nervous. To play at his best, his mood needs to be improved.

In the "really off" mood, the pitcher is dramatically unprepared to play. His motivation may be lacking. He may be extremely nervous. To compete with success, a great deal of work must be done.

Each pitcher must take inventory of his physical and mental skills and make sure these skills are honed and fully prepared for the rigors of the game. The pitcher should not wait for a blast of energy or a windfall of luck to come his way.

Developing Confidence

Good competitors are confident. They believe in themselves and their abilities. They also believe that they deserve to beat their opponent. Some of them start with more confidence than others, but confidence can be learned. It is learned in stages. It starts with mastering the fundamentals. Refining those fundamental skills is the next step. The final step is applying those fundamental skills to the game itself.

Most pitchers (all baseball players in general) find the first two steps toward developing confidence to be less exciting than playing in the actual game. These players essentially attempt to skip the most important part of the learning process. The development and refinement of fundamentals should not be taken for granted. These two important steps truly set the stage for developing lasting and meaningful confidence.

Confidence is found by becoming familiar with each part of pitching. Mechanics, control, velocity, stuff and gamesmanship are the parts of pitching that each pitcher needs to learn. Confidence grows as the basic skill improves. In other words, in the areas that have been neglected, the pitcher will display a lack of confidence. Familiarity breeds confidence.

A pitcher should develop control playing catch before going to the bullpen. He should develop control in the bullpen before pitching in a game situation. If the pitcher's control is good in the bullpen, the game control will usually be better as well. A sudden loss of control in the game is a clear sign that better work is needed in the bullpen.

If the mechanics of the pitcher are poor in the game, they will not be improved by pitching in another game. Basic work in drills and in the bullpen is needed for the pitcher to gain confidence in his mechanics. The game highlights the results. It also highlights what is being done properly and what is being done poorly. It is true that some corrections can be made in a game, but the best time to make corrections is before the game.

Confidence comes from experience. If a pitcher has experienced a given situation several times successfully, his confidence will grow. Therefore, practice can develop confidence, or it can lead to a lack of it. By repeating things correctly, the pitcher proves to himself that certain aspects of the game can be done properly.

Repetition

The development of confidence requires repetition. A competitive athlete learns to enjoy repetition. He realizes that by repeating certain situations and drills, his confidence is bolstered. Perfecting the skills required to accomplish success in these activities provides positive tools for the game situation. Fortified with knowledge, the pitcher has personally placed himself in each of the potential game situations. Knowledge and experience breed confidence.

Paying Attention to Details

The championship athlete takes nothing for granted. He pays attention to details. Good gamesmanship requires attention to details by the competitor. Those who consistently win are ever vigilant in looking for their opponent's strengths and weaknesses.

Obvious information, such as the score, the number of outs and the count on the batter, is necessary to formulate a plan. The good game player wants much more. His plan calls for an all-out attack, with winning as the final goal. To achieve this goal, specific information is needed. The pitcher who has winning as a purpose remembers the last few at-bats of the hitter he faces. He collects information on swings and the make-up of these hitters. The base-running skills of each hitter are recorded. He is aware of strategies used by the opposition and is prepared for the attacks of his opponents. In other words, he is totally tuned into the activity.

A game can be watched in many different ways. Some people watch the game in a casual manner, selecting only parts of it for viewing. They don't pay much attention to the rest of the game. Competitive pitchers cannot afford to watch a game in this manner. A hard-fought game may be won because one opponent lost sight of his goal for only one play or only one pitch. Winners are aware that an oversight on any detail may lead to a loss.

A pitcher who has trouble remembering hitters also has trouble remembering other important details. If his memory is short, a pen and notebook will serve him well. He should write down all the information gathered on each hitter and each team, and file that information to use on each succeeding encounter with the opposition.

A good exercise to help the pitcher retain details is to practice recapping each inning. The pitcher should add as much detailed information as possible. When this is done satisfactorily, he should do two innings at a time. As the ability to gather information improves, the number of innings recapped at a time should be increased. Some pitchers get good enough to give a detailed account of an entire nine-inning game.

Sizing-Up Opponents

Gamers size-up their opponents. They want to know who can beat them. An opponent with some special talent should be scrutinized. The good competitor is aware that any opponent can be formidable. He merely wants to know as much about each opponent as possible. This information is helpful in pitching strategy.

Offensive players have certain tendencies. They have certain routines and patterns that are incorporated into their play. Some players have predictable habits, while some do not. It is important for the pitcher to have such information. Body language is a great source for gathering data. Most runners do something differently when stealing a base. The same is true of bunters. Even hitters give away part of their plans with positioning, stances and demeanor. A competitive pitcher diligently gathers these clues. Any one of them may give him a competitive edge.

Learning to Feel the Game

Great players are not only more observant, but they also have a feel for the game. It appears that they can anticipate the future. They can prepare for things that will happen. Only through great concentration can this kind of anticipation occur.

The value of getting a feel for the game is obvious. A pitcher with this finely-honed skill has a distinct advantage. He can look at the game without being distracted. Players who have no feel for the game are distracted by the pressure of the game, the outside elements and their own inability to focus.

Pitchers who suddenly have control problems, give up hits in crucial situations or appear to blow-up in some games are guilty of ignoring the game. These pitchers often work hard. They show concern when faced with problems, but appear to make no improvements. Becoming more familiar with the details of the game will put them in touch with the game.

It is very important for the pitcher to focus on only the things that can make a difference in the outcome of the game. The pitcher should concern himself with the things he can control. If the bases are loaded, for example, concern for getting ahead of the hitter should be the focal point. This situation can be difficult. The difficulty should be noted, but should not become the focal point. Solving the problem is the issue that should be addressed.

Pitchers who are known for their ability to pitch under pressure can see the game as it unfolds. They can get into the flow of the game. They recognize important moments and react in a positive way to each moment. By staying tuned-in to each pitch and each play, they are aware of what has happened, what is happening and what could happen. This careful assessment gives pitchers a better chance to control the events.

It is important for the pitcher to become a part of the game. By gathering and evaluating detailed information, familiarity with the game itself is enhanced. For the pitcher to truly feel the game, he must recognize and remember details.

Playing in the Now

Successful people have a way of seizing the moment. The importance of each moment is recognized. They understand that success is the result of putting the pieces together. Some parts are more important than others. Each person has a role to play. The most useful time is the present.

The past has already been used. It can help or it can be harmful. Stewing over past errors or mistakes will only make matters worse. Living in the past while neglecting the present is a foolish endeavor. Recalling good performances and using those mental pictures to prepare for the present is a positive exercise. Experiences can be used in very positive ways. Setting watermarks, evaluating growth, developing confidence or creating enthusiasm are good examples of how to make the past useful.

The future has not yet arrived. It does hold great promise. It also holds mystery, anticipation and puzzlement. For the pitcher to spend extraordinary amounts of time in the future can be disastrous. The future can be great but it depends upon the past and the present. Adjustments are made in the present. If the past has been filled with mistakes, corrections can occur in the present. The future is where the past and the present are going.

A game in which the pitcher is pitching should be the most important game he has ever pitched. What he does with each pitch will decide the outcome of the game. Good results are created by spending quality time with each pitch.

Working in the now has other positives. Often pitchers record wins before the last out is made. They may have only three more outs left in the game. Suddenly, the opposition creates a rally and snatches the victory. The pitcher began living in the future and did not take care of the present. The pitch being thrown at this moment is the most important. Getting the next out is important, and giving quality thought and work to the present job is how success is made.

Staying busy with each immediate situation helps to eliminate nervousness for the pitcher. Staying busy steers the ship toward its destination. Thinking about things that have not yet happened, or staking a claim on something not yet earned, disrupts the journey.

Pressure and tension are relieved when plans and effort are started. A pitcher should pitch the game one pitch at a time. He should discard the past quickly and work in the present. This approach to the game will build a good future.

Recognizing Skill Levels

For a pitcher to throw each pitch with consistency, coordination, rhythm and balance, good concentration is necessary. The levels of these skills fluctuate with each game. Over the course of a season, some of these skills change slightly or dramatically. The pitcher can correct, fix or adjust to such changes. A drop in speed may warrant a new strategy. Changing speeds and using a greater variety of pitches should be considered. If the curveball does not have the normal sharp break or is lacking in control, the pitcher must use other pitches to compensate.

A pitcher should not completely give up on any pitch. With diligent effort and good concentration, the pitch may become effective later in the game, requiring readjustment in strategy. The pitcher should not panic when there is a slight drop in the efficiency of one pitch. The pitcher has many tools to accomplish his goal. He should simply evaluate the skill level on that day and use the tools that best fit the work.

A pitcher should understand that each game is special and has its own special challenges. Some games are high-scoring affairs that challenge the pitcher to pitch with a big lead or with a big deficit. Other games are low-scoring events that allow no room for bad pitches or mistakes. A good pitcher adjusts to these situations and pitches accordingly.

Pitchers do not show up at the ball park with the same finely-tuned skills every day. They also do not show up at the park with the same emotional state every day. Each pitcher should realize these factors and should evaluate both his mental and physical status. Emotional adjustments may be more important than physical adjustments, although both are essential.

Focus

"He was in the zone" is a term to describe a pitcher who has thrown an outstanding game. "The zone" is a mystical mental state. It means the pitcher could focus clearly on each situation as it appeared. All distractions were put on hold. Only the things that were pertinent to the situation were dealt with by the pitcher.

High competitive levels require an intense focus. A pitcher should examine each game and all of its parts. He should decide which parts require the most attention. Pressure and tension ebb and flow. Some pressure is self-induced. Some pressure is caused by the situation, while some is caused by factors not directly involved in the actual playing of the game.

Many things can be controlled by the pitcher. Control of his decisions, demeanor, commitment and actions is his responsibility. He is in control of his competitive level and his skills.

The pitcher has no control of what fans say, how the other team behaves, the weather, an error by a teammate or the decisions of the umpires. Even though the pitcher has no control over these factors and similar situations and conditions, he does have control over how he will react to them.

Good concentration is critical. There are a multitude of things that attract attention. The pitcher is obliged to make clear choices about these attention grabbers. For the pitcher to properly focus, the right choices must be made. He should decide what is important, screen the list quickly and center on the things that truly make a difference in the present situation. For example, in a crucial situation, the defense may have made a critical error to load the bases and put the pitcher in a winning or a losing situation. The pitcher must make a choice. He can choose to fret over the mistake and complain about the difficult situation. A better decision would be for him to size up the situation and center on how he can successfully deal with it.

If the pitcher has developed the proper tools, he will find each situation to be an exciting challenge. He should think of himself as a tool chest. He should find the proper tool, figure out how to use it and show how it works.

Positive Approach

Winners are possibility thinkers. Possibilities of succeeding dominate their thoughts. They do not allow themselves to fall prey to negative thinking. They give little thought to failure. Their motive is to find a way to win.

A pitcher who finds himself in a situation with the bases loaded should become a possibility thinker. Striking out the first batter and getting the next batter to hit into a double play is one method to get out of the jam. There are always many solutions to any problem. The pitcher should explore these solutions. Instead of thinking about the negative possibilities, he should concentrate on positive strategies. Pop ups, fly balls, ground balls and strikeouts are possible conclusions. There are several other possibilities for success in this situation. The pitcher should only think in the positive manner.

After deciding that success is possible, the next step is for the pitcher to apply the effort and concentration to get the job done. This process virtually eliminates negative thoughts. The pitcher becomes so busy with the positive that he has no time for the negatives.

A pitcher brings his personality on the field. Some personalities tend to be positive, while others tend to be negative. Pitchers with positive attitudes have a distinct advantage. Those who have negative attitudes should learn to take a positive attitude to the pitching mound. Looking at the game through positive eyes will help to change attitudes. Self-evaluation, positive self-talk, and allowing coaches and teammates to help in the evaluation process will also help the pitcher develop a positive outlook.

Pitchers who look at even the toughest of situations with determination and enthusiasm will receive many side benefits. Defensive players play better for these pitchers. The pitcher's attitude is projected on his teammates. A positive attitude on the mound creates motivation and develops team attitude.

Demeanor

Body language is extremely important for the pitcher. His demeanor is a mirror of what he thinks and feels. In tight situations, a pitcher who looks worried, or shows a lack of confidence, is easy prey for an aggressive hitter or base runner. A pitcher should learn to carry himself with confidence and poise .

Temper tantrums and signs of disappointment reveal weaknesses. Negative reactions to events or decisions also send undesirable messages. They show that the pitcher is not in control of himself. These reactions send a message to the opposition. They display weakness and imply that the pitcher has lost his competitive edge.

Mental Toughness

Pitchers are faced with a variety of challenges. Each pitch is critical. Only one bad pitch or one miscue could result in a loss in some games. In other games, an error or an undesirable pitch may not make a difference in the outcome. The mystery facing the pitcher is constant during each game. Pressure and tension are therefore constant. They may rise and lower, but they are built into the pitcher's game.

Solving a mystery requires persistence and endurance. Pitchers who give in to the pressure of the moment are not tough competitors. Mental toughness is the ability to stay poised in all situations. When the toughest challenges appear, the pitcher's inner strength is tested.

Each time the pitcher fights through a difficult challenge he grows stronger. Each challenge should be approached as a test. To score well on the test, the pitcher should be prepared and committed to succeed. For a high score at the end of the grade period, high marks on several tests are needed. Many challenges must be met during the season for the pitcher to claim success.

Mental toughness can be strengthened. A measure of growth is in the approach. Running toward a challenge is better than running away from one. A mentally tough pitcher invites the challenge. He looks forward to the competition and is motivated by that challenge. It lifts his game to a higher level. It gives him a chance to play at his best. He should use the positive approach in practice sessions and develop routines that include only positive actions. He should look for situations that challenge in practice and run toward those with an eagerness to show his skill. Positive self-talk should greet each situation. Unwillingness and lack of eagerness to face an issue often form the biggest hurdles. Enthusiasm toward facing issues makes the task less difficult.

A person looking for something to do is more likely to succeed than a person who shuns the work. A pitcher should get busy on a plan to achieve the goal and make the necessary adjustments. If the plan doesn't work, he should design a new plan and keep planning and working until the job is done.

Work habits that pursue excellence develop a path toward mental toughness. Doing each drill right, and at game speed, creates the proper background for improvement. Situations are pursued with a high regard for workmanship. Mental toughness results from a strong work ethic and a willingness to meet a challenge.

Dealing with Disappointments

An athlete's life is filled with highs and lows. Disappointments come in all sizes. There are big ones and small ones. The ultimate success of an athlete depends upon how he handles failure. Batting slumps are very common for hitters. Pitching slumps are equally frustrating. Although pitching slumps are not widely publicized, they do occur. When a pitcher experiences a major drop in performance, the team is more dramatically affected than when a batter is in a hitting slump.

A pitching slump creates a major dilemma. The procedure each pitcher uses to correct his problem is critical, because confidence is lacking. Slumps create a great deal of confusion. Proper steps are needed for skills to be retained. If the pitcher is in a state of panic, the difficulties will usually increase. On the other hand, if logic, patience and persistence are applied, he will reestablish his effectiveness. Knowledge of his craft and good work habits help prevent slumps and aid in recovery if one occurs.

Setbacks are inevitable for all athletes. Pitchers are not exceptions. An unintended hanging curveball often creates a setback or a disappointment. A poorly-located pitch can be equally damaging. These setbacks will happen to even the best pitcher. How he responds is the important issue. Recovery from a disappointment often dictates the outcome of the total performance.

Sometimes failure is necessary in order for the pitcher to discover how to create a win. Until the game is finished, there is neither a loss nor a win. This reality is also true with a pitching performance. Pitchers win games by giving up several hits, a few walks and a few errors. If the hits, walks and errors do not result in runs being scored, then the pitcher has been successful. Each hit, walk and error was a disappointment. The pitching performance following these disappointments decides whether any of them will affect the outcome of the total pitching performance.

Dealing with Success

Winning breeds confidence and brings joy. It is fulfilling and motivating. Winning shows that a degree of success has been attained. Some players make great gains in the winning environment, while others develop bad habits.

Success is rewarding and brings positive rewards. Success also travels with high expectations and high standards. A great deal more is expected from a successful pitcher than from one who is unsuccessful. This expectation creates greater demands. Some pitchers are attracted to the higher demands. Many seem to feed off the success. They grow and mature in this setting. Great enjoyment and satisfaction come from the accomplishments. The tension and pressure ignite their competitive fires.

For some pitchers, however, success is seen as a permanent state. They become confident and take for granted the reason for their success. A pitcher who has difficulty with success often finds it difficult to concentrate on proper priorities. He often shows signs of just going through the motions. His competitive edge is often missing. He assumes that the success he has enjoyed will automatically reappear at his beck and call. Normal routines and precise execution are carried out only periodically.

Pitchers who fall prey to this malady are often those pitchers with the best natural ability. In the past, they could excel without fully competing. Initially, they work hard enough to establish superiority, then they begin to coast, or lay back, and rely on their natural talent.

To avoid these kinds of setbacks, the pitcher should begin by establishing goals that relate to his ability level. These goals should be evaluated regularly by both the pitcher and the pitching coach. Both long-term and short-term goals should be set. Periodic adjustments should be made with these goals. Accountability lies with the pitcher. The pitching coach should guide the pitcher and hold him to his commitments.

Success should never be viewed as permanent. Proper maintenance and continued growth are necessary ingredients to create successful results. When one goal is met, a new one should take its place. Reaching and climbing builds higher standards. Expecting yesterday's achievements to carry today's performance results in losing efforts.

Setting Standards

Mentally tough people are willing to endure. They fight hard in the heat of battle. Their immediate goal is to win. Short-term goals are easily defined. This mind-set is the first step in setting standards. The desire to accomplish is a prerequisite to the setting of standards.

The goal should be defined, and a clear picture should be made in the pitcher's mind. A final destination is extremely important. To get to that point, the pitcher should draw a map of how to get there. Short-term goals keep him on course. For the pitcher to reach the desired destination, he should include restraints. The game is the period it takes to play a complete game. The season is his time limitation for that particular year. His career is the final limit.

Both the season and the career definitely involve long-term goals. Accordingly, the pitcher should start with a single season to set standards and establish goals. "What do I want to accomplish this season" is the primary question. "How do I do these things" is the second question. In answering these questions, the pitcher first establishes what he expects of himself. Next, he sets out to learn how to reach those expectations.

The goals should be more than just idle dreams. They should be high enough to make the pitcher reach within the realm of possibility. He should clearly define the goal and make it come alive. He should draw detailed mental pictures and recall them often. The clearer the picture, the more attainable the goal will be.

Standards are set by establishing goals. If the goals are high, the standards must be high. Once a commitment to the goals and standards is noted, the trip has begun.

At this point, through sweat and tears, the pitcher must have a firm resolve. High standards will assure completion of the goal.

By a complete commitment to each short-term goal, the pitcher moves toward his long-term goal. Developing good work habits and exhibiting a tough mental approach are the proper tools for maintaining standards and reaching goals. This objective includes the pitcher connecting each workout with the desired result. An open mind that is willing to seek helpful information is necessary to fulfill a dream.

Success is usually the result of many successful accomplishments. It is not the result of a single accomplishment. These accomplishments should not be ignored or overlooked. A game, for instance, is won by carefully taking care of each situation in that game. This situation is where the sweat and tears should be applied. Some pitchers are guilty of only fretting and worrying about the long-term goal. To reach it, the everyday chores must be done first. Repetitious drills should be done with enthusiasm and commitment. Persistence should be developed.

Anything with value has a price. High goals and standards are expensive. They are worth the effort. Mentally tough people are willing to pay the bill.

Being a Finisher

The final phase of the mental-toughness test is how the pitcher finishes. A good pitcher is a good finisher. He realizes that to win there is a beginning, a middle, and an end to the game. Some pitchers are good until they encounter problems. Others are good through the first phase of problems, but are unable to complete the job. The good pitcher seems to get better as the game goes along and is particularly tough when the competitive level is elevated.

A finisher practices finishing. Every wind sprint is completed. Practice is finished with good effort. Each situation is completed with a full effort. The pitcher should develop a routine that calls for good finishes.

Short-cuts change routines. They often destroy the rhythm of the activity and soften the approach, beginning a downward spiral toward mediocrity. The season is long and presents many challenges. Each game also has its disappointments. The pitcher should face those challenges and disappointments. Despite the difficulties presented with each, the finisher endures and overcomes.

Summary

This chapter discussed the fact that competitiveness is both inherited and learned. Some pitchers are extremely competitive by nature. Others must work to improve in this area. A careful analysis of the situation and a sound evaluation of the pitcher's approach are helpful in improving the competitiveness of the pitcher.

A pitcher who learns to block out distractions and focus on only those things that make a difference is usually on the winning side. This pitcher is able to look at each situation clearly. He is able to decide what is important and what is not. This insight enables him to put his best foot forward.

Any pitcher can upgrade his gamesmanship. Commitment and discipline are necessary elements of success. By disciplining himself, the pitcher plans and works with a purpose. Commitment keeps the goal in sight.

12

Fit to Pitch

A pitcher should be the best conditioned athlete on the field. A well-conditioned pitcher is better prepared to compete. He is more intense. A pitcher's arm is his greatest weapon. It can be protected and preserved if it and the rest of his body is in proper physical shape.

Many activities can be performed to help the pitcher get his body into peak physical condition. In choosing from this long list of activities, it is important to develop some programs that are both interesting and productive. A productive one should include as many activities involving baseball-related skills as possible.

One of the best conditioning activities for a pitcher is running. If a pitcher runs enough, he may eventually get in good aerobic shape. A running program alone, however, will not address all of the conditioning aspects and primary components of fitness. Proper throwing routines, stretching, weight training, adequate rest, and a sound diet should be included.

A sound running program should be made up of at least four different kinds of running drills: long-distance running, wind sprints, agility drills, and baseball-related drills. Careful selection of drills from each group will create a conditioning program that challenges, motivates, and produces the desired results.

Long-Distance Running

Long-distance running helps to develop endurance (stamina) and to foster a high degree of personal discipline. Some pitchers do not like distance running at the outset. Although this type of running may not be at the top of their list, it does not mean that it should be avoided. By running long distances, the pitcher learns to push himself through mental barriers. He maps out a specific distance and completes the journey. Such an achievement gives him a feeling of fulfillment. Keeping a record of the distance covered and the time it took adds a challenge. Completing the distance and improving the time improves incentive.

- *Specific distances.* It is important to develop a variety of long-distance running drills. Courses of varying distances (e.g., one, two, three or four miles) should be charted. The course that is selected to be run on any given day should be one that fits the rest of the practice schedule. Overtime, different courses should be run in order to break up the routine and make the activity as interesting as possible.
- *Timing the run.* Time should be used to assess the level of conditioning. Time can also be used as a challenge or an incentive. Competitive people like to be challenged. A 6-minute mile, for example, indicates that the pitcher is in reasonably good aerobic condition. For some, it is a challenge. The time, of course, can be also used to establish minimal requirements. If the purpose of the run is to maintain a conditioning level, setting a minimum time requirement may be all that is necessary. If a higher level of conditioning is the goal, then the run should either be performed at a faster pace or for a greater distance.
- *Foul line runs.* Another excellent distance running drill involves running from one foul line to another. For example running eighteen foul lines are approximately one and three quarter miles. This run is psychologically more difficult because of the turn arounds involved. To run this in 13 minutes would be similar to running a normal 2-mile course. Running the foul-line to foul-line course has value when run at a steady, continuous pace, without a time limit.
- *Use variety.* Long-distance running can be enhanced by running a variety of courses. If there are hills, steady inclines, or other special features on the courses, the run can become more interesting or more challenging. Changes in procedure often make the activity more interesting.
- *Running laps.* Running laps around a running track or around baseball drills can also be an effective method of conditioning. This type of running can easily become monotonous if run regularly, however. One of the primary advantages of this form of running is the fact that both time and distance can be readily measured.
- *Train drill.* The train drill is primarily a distance running activity but it does include some sprinting. The drill emphasizes endurance. In this drill, the pitchers form a line and the coach establishes a course for them to run. Each pitcher begins to jog. The pitcher at the back of the line sprints to the front of the line. All other pitchers continue at a jogging pace around the course. The last pitcher in line sprints to the front of the line; this sequence is repeated until the drill is finished. Six to eight laps around the playing field or around a track provides a good work out.
- *Pick up and recovery.* This drill is a good exercise. It can also be run competitively. In this drill, the coach divides the pitchers into small groups. A line is formed with each

group. Six baseballs are placed at the front of each group. Six gloves are positioned ten yards apart in front of each group. The pitcher at the front of the line picks up a baseball and sprints to the first glove and places the ball in it. He then races back to pick up another ball and sprints to the second glove and places the ball in it. This procedure should be followed until he has placed a ball in each glove and returned to the starting point. At this point, the second pitcher in each line sprints to the first glove. The ball is picked up and returned to the starting point, where he lays the ball down. He then sprints to the second glove, picks up the ball and returns it to the starting point. He completes his assignment by picking up the remainder of the balls, one at a time, and returning each to the starting point. The drill is repeated in this fashion until each pitcher in each group has run the course. One complete repetition through the drill covers 420 yards, which is a good workout. Running it twice provides an excellent conditioning routine.

- *Egg rolls or pick-ups*. This frill is designed to develop both endurance and stamina. Stretching and bending are also by-products of this drill. The drill involves dividing the pitchers into pairs. Standing about ten feet apart, the partners face each other. One of the pitchers acts as a feeder by rolling a ball to his teammate who serves as a "receiver." The feeder is responsible for counting. The drill begins by having the receiver shuffle from side to side and travel about five to six steps in each direction. The feeder rolls him the ball. He should field the ball with both hands and toss it back to the feeder. No glove is needed. The feeder should be in a position of good balance to catch and return the ball quickly. The feeder should roll the ball in a consistent manner. If the pitcher is in good physical condition, he should do about 100 of these daily. At the start of the season, twenty-five is a sufficient number.

- *Left and rights*. This drill is similar to the egg roll drill. No ball is used, however. The condition results are similar. The pitchers form a straight line facing the coach. The drill is started by having the line of pitchers shuffle sideways in the same direction. They travel a distance of fifteen to twenty-five feet and touch the ground with both hands. The pitchers then shuffle back to the starting point and touch the ground with both hands. The normal width (i.e., 20-25 feet) of a warning track is ideal. The coach should place a diligent pitcher at the front of the line and suggest that the other pitchers keep up with his pace. Shuffling over and back should count as one trip. Twenty repetitions (trips) will provide a good workout.

Sprints

Sprints offer a different type of conditioning. For those who are already in reasonable shape, sprints provide an opportunity to improve running mechanics, and to use the explosive skills needed for the game. If enough sprints are run, the pitcher can get an excellent anaerobic (i.e. short bursts of energy) workout. Similar to other forms of training, running sprints can be used either to maintain existing fitness levels or to enhance conditioning levels.

- *Short sprints*. The best results come from running relatively short sprints run at full speed. This type of training requires that the pitcher be in good condition. If his conditioning level is inadequate, he will tire quickly and be unable to run at full speed. Fifty to sixty yards are ideal distances for wind sprints. Eight of these sprints run at full speed are more productive than ten or more sprints run at a slower speed.
- *Competitive sprints*. Competitive sprints add to the challenge of training. Running the required number of sprints while competing against another pitcher will benefit both pitchers. Competing against more than one pitcher often further motivates those involved. Running against the clock is also another way of challenging and motivating the pitcher. As with running distances, adding variety upgrades the level of participation. Short relay races can identify how to accomplish the same purpose while providing a change of pace. The coach should simply decide how much conditioning is needed and identify how to accomplish that end with one of the many sprint-related activities. The drill should be made competitive when a high level of conditioning is required. Another approach to raising the conditioning benefits of a drill is to make the drill more difficult (i.e., increase the number of sprints or the distance sprinted). The number of sprints should be reduced if the primary purpose of this drill is maintenance.
- *Rabbit drill*. This drill involves quick bursts of speed and helps develop a degree of endurance. It also enhances and encourages competitiveness. This drill involves using the base paths as a running course. Eight pitchers are stationed forty-five feet apart around the bases. One pitcher will be at each base, while another will be at a spot halfway between each base and between home plate and both first and third base. On a signal, the pitchers begin to sprint around the bases. Each pitcher should touch each base. He should try to catch the pitcher in front of him. If he tags the runner in front of him, he drops out of the drill, leaving a bigger space for the pitcher behind him to cover. As the successful pitchers in this drill eliminate themselves, they create a greater challenge for those remaining in the drill. Common sense should be used. If only two or three pitchers remain and the distance separating them is great, the drill should be stopped. This drill should be performed quickly and run with maximum effort. It should not be used to punish or embarrass a pitcher.

Agility

Agility drills are designed to improve agility, to increase endurance, and to help general conditioning. The bending and twisting involved in these exercises will help to condition the back, stomach, and legs. These kinds of drills should help to improve balance. In addition, they may enhance quickness and even help hand-eye coordination.

One of the most effective forms of training to enhance a pitcher's level of agility involves the use of dry-run drills.

The following drills, taken from the dry-run series, are designed to develop agility. Many of these drills strengthen and stretch the various muscle groups. An important point to remember is that any activities that improve quickness and balance could be used to create an agility drill.

- *Balance drill.* (Refer to any of the 39 steps in Chapter 6 on dry-run drills.)
- *Form running.* Form running is made up of several different maneuvers, including high knees, Polish skip, heel to buttocks, bounding, relaxed chin and arm pumping.
- *Backward sprinting.* In this drill, the pitchers perform short sprints but run them with their backs facing the finishing line. This practice encourages high knees and helps improve body balance and coordination.
- *Relays with the ball.* In this drill, pitchers work in pairs and sprint fifty to sixty yards while playing catch. They should be approximately fifteen feet apart and maintain that spacing as they run the race. They sprint the distance and return. When both finish the return trip, the ball is tossed to the next two competitors, and the drill is repeated until all competitors have taken part. If several pitchers are involved, they can be divided into teams with two pairs, three pairs, or four pairs. The best approach is to keep the teams small in order to make the drill more competitive and to allow the drill to be conducted much quicker. As a result, greater interest in the drill will be created.
- *Relays with ground balls.* This drill is similar to the previous drill, except that the ball is kept on the ground. Instead of playing catch, the pitchers throw ground balls to each other while running the race. Much more bending and twisting is done with this procedure.
- *Jump, stride, and clap drill.* The pitchers form lines facing the coach. Four or five lines with two players in each line are ideal. There should be enough space for each player to move freely. Each pitcher starts in a stride position. He then jumps and lands with his feet changing places and clapping his hands underneath his lead knee. This sequence is repeated several times. Each player should rest and repeat this drill for several sets. Balance, stretching, and conditioning are all involved in this drill. Enhancing the ability to coordinate the legs and arms while maintaining balance will be helpful to the pitcher. These movements are related to some parts of his delivery.
- *Direction drill.* This drill involves having the pitchers form lines similar to the previous drill. The coach points down for forward movement and up for movement backward. He points to the pitchers' left for movement in that direction and to their right for movement in that direction. Four to five steps in the direction pointed is the normal distance to cover. If the movement is forward, the pitchers take regular running steps in that direction. If the movement is in any other direction, the pitchers should take crossover steps. The change of direction should be done quickly and smoothly. Three to four minutes of this activity is adequate. It should be done regularly. This drill is designed to enhance both agility and conditioning.

Baseball-Related Running Drills

The most productive way to reach a well-conditioned state is through baseball-related running drills. Not only do these provide a source of physical conditioning, they also serve to add to the skill level of the pitcher. A drill that calls for the pitcher to cover first base, for example, requires running, technique, and timing. Running in this instance is directly connected to the pitcher's game responsibility. Many different drills of this type exist. Repeated fielding of bunts, ground balls, or fly balls will develop conditioning and skills. A few additional examples of baseball-related drills would include the following:

- *Pitchers around the infield.* This drill takes approximately 45 minutes to complete. It is usually done with the entire pitching staff. It includes bunt and base coverage between the first baseman and the pitcher, ground balls, communication, and base coverage among the second baseman, first baseman, and the pitcher. Double plays from the first baseman to the short stop to the pitcher who covers first base. Bunt communication between the pitcher and the third baseman is practiced. The pitchers work on backing up third base on throws from the outfield to third base. The final part of this drill is the pitcher covering home plate on a wild pitch or passed ball.

- *Baserunning.* An excellent conditioning drill can evolve from using the pitchers as base runners on short alignments and long alignments. This type of drill will enhance both a pitcher's baserunning skills and his level of endurance.

- *Back-up drills.* Many drills address multiple aspects of training. One of these is the back-up drill, which is designed to enhance both conditioning and techniques. During the alignment drills for outfielders and infielders, the pitchers can be incorporated into the drill by backing up bases. This practice not only gives the pitcher a good physical workout but teaches him the proper way to cover the base. The pitcher is required to cover the proper base, get to the coverage area quickly and make sure his alignment is correct.

- *Fielding ground balls.* Pitchers can get an excellent workout by fielding ground balls. A good fielding pitcher is an asset to his team. By fielding ground balls as an infielder, the pitcher becomes better skilled as a defensive player. The coach can divide the pitchers into small groups (two to three players in each group) and fungo to each group. Each pitcher should field twenty-five to fifty ground balls.

- *Fielding at the mound.* Pitchers should also be required to field ground balls when they are on the mound. A variety of ground balls should be hit. It is best to begin the drill with slow- or medium-speed ground balls. The degree of difficulty should match the skill level of the pitcher. As the pitcher improves his skills, the degree of challenge should be increased. During this drill, the pitcher should simulate a throw (or actually throw) to the catcher. He should follow through properly. In an attempt to create a game-like situation the coach hits the ball back to the pitcher. Proper practice in this instance will develop fielding skills, improve conditioning, and help the pitcher develop confidence. It will also reduce the fear of getting hit with the ball.

- *Fielding fly balls.* Running is the prime method to attain a well-conditioned state. How that running is done by the athlete determines his physical condition. A well-defined reason for running and a purpose for the activity create a better environment. Running to catch a ball is challenging; it increases interest and makes the running more enjoyable. The pitchers can be divided into groups. The groups should be kept small. Groups of not more than three are ideal. The coach can hit fly balls to the pitchers in the manner he hits fly balls to the outfielders. Three to five minutes with each group will produce an excellent conditioning exercise. Skill is developed during the process.
- *Lead drill.* Usually, all pitchers are included in this drill. The pitchers form a line near the coach with a fungo. Each pitcher should have a baseball. The first pitcher tosses the ball to the coach and then runs a prearranged route. The coach fungoes the fly ball to that pitcher. The fly ball should be in front of the pitcher and should provide a challenge. After the first ball is hit, the next pitcher in line tosses a baseball to the coach and proceeds to run the same route as the previous pitcher. The drill is repeated until the workout is finished. Each pitcher returns to the end of the line after retrieving his fly ball and waits his turn to run again. It will take some experimentation with each group to get the proper timing. The types of routes run can vary. Each pitcher in the line can run a route to the right and then alternate by runing to his left on the next turn. Skill with the fungo will greatly enhance the benefits achieved by the drill. If the coach is skilled enough to make each fly ball a challenge, the drill will be exciting and worthwhile. The same drill can be done without the use of a fungo bat. The coach can throw the ball instead of hitting it. He simply throws the fly ball and leads the pitcher to it.

Summary

This chapter discussed the fact that the best running drills are those that have some connection to the game. Covering and backing up bases, fielding ground balls or fly balls or running the bases can benefit each pitcher in several ways, including improving his defensive skills and techniques and enhancing his level of conditioning.

Distance running builds endurance. This helps the pitcher to be a better finisher. Sprints help with the explosiveness necessary for throwing and fielding. Baseball-related drills often include sprints and distance running. Such drills can also address agility and competitiveness. A variety of drills should be used to make conditioning challenging and enjoyable.

13

Care and Conditioning of the Arm

Plain old common sense is the best guide to follow in caring for the pitching arm. On one hand, too much activity is dangerous, on the other hand, too little activity is equally dangerous. The arm will send the message, the pitcher needs to listen to these messages.

Overuse of the arm may create an injury. That injury may be temporary, or it could become career ending. Throbbing or dull pain is not normal. Such pain is an alarm signal for the pitcher and the pitching coach. Common sense should tell the pitcher that he should proceed with caution. If pain results when the arm is raised, lowered, or extended, another alarm has been sounded. Throwing should be stopped and the pitcher should seek diagnosis from a qualified physician. A physician who specializes in athletic injuries is recommended; one who specializes in arm injuries is best. Normally, the pitcher will know if the arm is damaged. However, if there is any doubt, he should always seek the advice of the physician.

It is common practice to blame arm injuries on overactivity. This situation should be a concern of the pitcher and the pitching coach. It should not be the only one, however. A pitcher may injure his arm because he has not thrown enough pitches to prepare the arm for throwing. He should throw in the bullpen between starts. Often, the pitcher who fails to do this develops arm injuries. In his attempt to save his arm, he gets the opposite results.

Lack of conditioning is another reason for arm injuries. The muscles of the legs, back and stomach must be in good condition to withstand the rigors of pitching. Fatigue in these areas places extra stress on the arm.

Poor mechanics are probably the number-one cause of arm injuries. Common sense should tell us that throwing from an unbalanced position to an unbalanced position will place undue stress on the arm and other body parts. That same common sense should also tell us that all parts of the body should be coordinated and in rhythm to get the best results. The best use of energy and force is applied when they are coordinated and directed to the target.

The arm and body should be protected before, during, and after activities. Diet, rest, conditioning, and the use of proper clothing are important factors in this regard.

A sound diet that supplies energy is essential. Food supplements may be used, but normal meals should be sufficient. Regular meals consumed on a regular schedule will be adequate. Avoid crash diets and junk foods should be avoided. Pitchers who need more information on what constitutes a sound diet should consult a trainer or physician for assistance.

Often overlooked is the proper amount of rest. It is extremely important to develop a regular routine that provides the body and mind an adequate time to rest. Some people require more sleep than others; it is important to determine the number of hours required for the best results. Erratic sleep patterns create non-productive and inconsistent results. It is easy to fall into bad habits. Broken sleep patterns often cause the pitcher to tire easily and to lose his focus.

Chapter 12 discussed different running drills and ways to reach peak condition. The important point to remember is to use common sense. Too much of anything is bad, while too little of anything is also bad. Overzealous running programs that leave the pitcher with no energy for the game performance are unsound. Too much rest or the failure to maintain the well-conditioned state is equally illogical.

The pitcher should learn about his body. He should know what it can do and what it cannot do. Careful attention to throwing techniques will help develop knowledge about the body. An adequate amount of rest is crucial. A pitcher must organize his schedule so that adequate rest is provided.

Identifying Injuries

An important job for the coach and the pitcher is to identify injuries. The coach cannot accomplish this goal without the help of the pitcher. By the same token, the pitcher needs the coach's understanding and counsel when injuries are reported.

Throwing a baseball repeatedly will cause soreness. This activity is not unlike running in that regard. Moderate throwing or running normally has no ill effects. When the activity is increased, some soreness may be noticed. If the activity is dramatically increased, the soreness may become more severe. By the same token, an irregular running program followed by strenuous wind sprints or heavy running activities, usually results in a great deal of soreness or even muscle strains, pulls or other damage. Irregular throwing activities, followed by extended workouts or heavy-duty throwing drills, may give the same results. Soreness is a natural and normal result of working out. It is a warning, however. Soreness is caused by the activity. What the pitcher and coach need to know is the degree of the soreness and if the soreness is the kind normally associated with the particular activity. Often, it is simply an indication of the phase or state of conditioning. For example, on the day following the first bullpen workout, the pitcher's arm will probably be stiff and sore. The muscles of the shoulder, forearm and back are the most susceptible. He may even experience some soreness in the back muscles on his pitching arm side. This discomfort is normal unless the soreness is more extensive. Soreness to the touch is normal.

If, after that first workout, the pitcher reports both soreness and pain, an important alarm has been sounded. This is not normal. Further diagnosis should follow. A trip to the trainer followed by a trip to a physician is the most prudent action to take. At the least, a rest period with no throwing is advised. This procedure should be followed each time the pitcher reports his condition to be more than normal soreness.

After each game, the pitcher will have soreness. He should not have pain. Stretching, running and light throwing will help to get rid of the soreness. He should not throw in the bullpen or do any other extended throwing activities after he has thrown in a full game. The number of pitches and the number of innings are important. The situations and difficulties in the game should be evaluated. The pitcher's level of conditioning and his mechanics should draw attention. The weather conditions should also be considered. Each of these factors is important. None should be overlooked.

If the pitcher pitched a complete game he should not throw the next day. Throwing for the purposes of stretching, loosening, and getting rid of waste products in the arm and body is all right. A pitcher who only threw 40 to 50 pitches but labored through two to three innings should be treated as though he threw nine innings. If the pitcher threw in extremely hot weather, and reached a state of fatigue after a few innings, that pitcher should be treated as though he threw a complete game. If, on the other hand he threw three innings, using only nine pitches, he probably could throw in the bullpen on the following day.

A pitcher with good mechanics puts less stress on his arm than a pitcher with poor mechanics. Three or four innings thrown with poor mechanics will put more strain on the arm than a pitcher with good mechanics throwing a full ball game.

The difference between soreness and pain is monumental. Soreness can usually be worked through. Pain is an entirely different circumstance. The pitching coach and the pitcher should be able decide the difference. Pain requires treatment and rest. One particular treatment or one full day of rest may be enough to get the pitcher back on track. Trying to play through pain may result in greater damage and a longer recuperation period.

The coach is not a physician. He should not give a diagnosis. His experience and knowledge may provide him with some clues, but neither of these is enough to diagnose or treat an injury. Sending the pitcher to a qualified trainer or physician is his best alternative. Some problems are very simple to solve. When the injury is severe enough to prevent the pitcher from throwing, it is an easy call. That pitcher needs a doctor's care. A sudden drop in velocity may also provide an easy clue. A dramatic change in the pitcher's delivery is another telltale sign that something is wrong. Throbbing or piercing pain are other indicators of an emergency. If the pitcher reports pain when he takes his arm through a full range of motion, the coach should listen. These are just a few of the most obvious ways to decide that the problem is more severe than just normal soreness.

Pitchers are not always honest. I once had someone tell me that to listen to a pitcher was not very wise. Pitchers, he said, want to win. They will tell the coach what they feel the coach wants to hear. He said the pitcher would never reveal an injury for fear of being removed from the game or missing a turn to pitch. The solution to that particular type of philosophy is simple—don't ask. The coach should draw conclusions by using other data.

A good coach knows his pitcher. If the pitcher has a history of saying only what the coach wants to hear, there is no need to ask that pitcher about his arm. It is obvious what he will say. He will not give factual data. Somewhere in the early stages of coaching, the pitching coach should strive to develop rapport with his pitching staff. Good rapport means trust has been established.

Without trust, the learning process is extremely difficult. Information from the coach is necessary; input from the pitcher is equally important. If either has a reluctance to talk to the other, suspicion and doubt interfere with the learning process. A pitcher needs to be able to say how he feels, what he is thinking, what he understands and what he does not understand. The coach needs to be able to rely on the information he receives from the pitcher. If the pitcher experiences pain after throwing a certain pitch, he should feel free to discuss that with the coach. If a drill, pitch, or method of throwing causes pain, the pitcher should provide the coach with this important information.

Keep the Arm Covered

Young pitchers are often careless; they neglect to protect their arms. A jacket or sweatshirt should be worn between innings and after breaking a heavy sweat. The reason for covering the arm is to keep it warm. Allowing the arm to cool down may result in stiffness. If the arm is inactive for an extended period and cools down, extra time is needed to get it ready for activity. Returning to action with a stiff or tight arm may lead to an injury.

Long sleeves are recommended. Some pitchers develop the notion that sleeves restrict and bind. This idea can be remedied by wearing an undershirt that properly fits. The next step is to get accustomed to wearing the sleeves. The benefits will outweigh the short-term discomfort. A long sleeved shirt will keep the arm warm and allow the pitcher to return to activity ready to compete.

After the game or practice, the pitcher should wear a jacket or sweatshirt. The jacket or sweatshirt can be of a weight that matches the climate. Extremely cold weather warrants a heavy covering. Milder weather may only require a lighter weight garment. A heavy workout should be followed by a slow cooling-down period. Cold air hitting warm muscles cause stiffness and tightness. Wearing warm clothing to cover warm muscles will prevent injuries. It preserves the muscles for further activity.

Proper Warm Up

It is important to warm up properly. The pitcher should jog and run enough to break a sweat before any throwing takes place. He should also take the time to stretch and loosen the muscles before throwing. He should then start the throwing warm up by playing catch at short range. Initially, he should take a few throws at a distance of 30 to 40 feet and then work back to the sixty-feet, six-inch distances. When the pitcher is fully warmed up at this distance, he should finish by making a few throws at a greater distance. In incremental increases in distance of five to ten feet, the pitcher should make an additional ten throws. His final throw should be between 90 and 120 feet. The exact distance of the throw should be determined by the ability and conditioning level of the pitcher.

The warm up for pitching in the game should include the aforementioned routine followed by a bullpen workout. The bullpen workout consists of a quick review of mechanics, control, stuff, velocity and gamesmanship. At this point, the pitcher is getting ready to compete. He is preparing to open the game with his best stuff. This warmup should include preparation for all potential situations that will confront him in the game. This time is not a casual loosening-up period.

All game pitches should be used in this warm up. To be ready for the game, the pitcher should be ready to throw his best fastball on the first pitch of the game. His curve ball, slider, change or other pitches should be equally prepared. The early innings of the game should not be used to prepare. Preparation should take place before the game.

Concentration is extremely important. Centering on specific details will pay dividends. Developing a bullpen plan economizes the work load. Before entering the bullpen, the pitcher should have stretched and loosened the muscles involved in throwing. Each pitch in the bullpen should have a purpose. It should be thrown with a target in mind. It should be thrown with a certain speed in mind. The sharpness of spin on the breaking ball should be assessed. Movement and location of the change-up should be evaluated. Concentration on these specific things will help prepare the pitcher for the game.

When the pitcher leaves the bullpen, he should be mentally and physically ready to enter the game. He should throw enough pitches to be ready for action, but not so many that a few are left in the bullpen. He should avoid throwing extra pitches to get rid of anxiety or nervousness. Other routines can take care of these feelings. Doing stretching exercises, a few short wind sprints, reviewing the game plan, or reevaluating the hitting charts of his opponents are a few examples of how he can diminish his anxiety.

The number of pitches will vary with each pitcher. The number will depend on several factors, including the body type of the pitcher, his level of condition, the weather conditions, and his ability to focus. Some pitchers can get ready with 35 to 50 pitches. Other pitchers may need more. Not all of these pitches are thrown at full speed.

Often pitchers use time as a measuring tool for warming up. Fifteen to twenty minutes is considered normal. Others need more time. This difference would have something to do with each pitcher's tempo. Some pitchers work at a fast pace. Others work at a slow pace. A slow-working pitcher needs more time to warm up.

The Double Workout

The double workout is helpful for some pitchers. If a pitcher has a history of struggling in the first inning of his games, the double workout is worth trying. His problem may stem from poor preparation. Proper attention to details may be overlooked because of nervousness or anxiety. As a result, a pitcher's control may be below par to start the game. The speed of his pitches may be less in the first inning than in any other part of the game, or his rhythm may be out of sync. He simply struggles in the first inning.

Some measurable signs for this problem exist. Over several games, his pitch count is greater in the first inning than in any of the other innings. He gives up more base hits in that inning than in other innings. He appears nervous in that stage of the game. There is a noticeable difference in his mechanics in the initial inning. If a pitcher is plagued by any or all of these regularly, the double workout may be helpful.

Normally, the starting pitcher warms up about 20 minutes before the start of his first inning. Each pitcher will develop his own routine. Some start this process earlier. Others require less time. The routine should fit the physical and mental makeup of each pitcher.

When the double workout is used, the pitcher should go to the bullpen approximately 45 minutes before his first inning. He should then complete his approximately 20-minute pre-game throwing routine. He should warm up as though he were going into the game to pitch. He then should return to the dugout or dressing room. At this point, he should develop a routine that fits his own particular needs. This routine may consist of mental preparation. A review of the opposing hitters will get his mind on the parts of the game he can control. He may want to review his assignment on bunt defenses, first-and-third situations or other aspects of his defensive responsibilities. A review of mechanics may be helpful to him.

The routine may be more physical than mental. A period of meditation may be helpful. If the early-inning problems are caused by lack of concentration, the routine should be developed to create mental pictures of specific activities being done successfully. If the problems are a result of poor mechanics, the routine could include a dry-run session. At this point, the pitcher could simulate the pitching delivery, placing emphasis on the troublesome areas. Creativity is required. A series of steps should be developed for each pitcher that will get his mind and body ready to compete. A simple rest period may be routine for some.

Approximately 10 to 15 minutes before his first inning, the pitcher should start the second warmup period in the bullpen. Since he has thrown earlier, the second session should not require as much time as the first session.

This system gives the pitcher a chance to shave off the rough edges. The first trip may get rid of some nervous energy and rid him of anxiety. The extra preparation allows him to get a better feel for pitching. A routine between workouts provides a game-readiness stage. He is mentally touching the game and it parts. This routine enables a pitcher to perform before the game starts.

Most people are more productive when they are kept busy. The double workout gives the pitcher a specific assignment. It keeps him busy. Instead of waiting nervously to start the game, he is working. This approach fills a void for some and works to their benefit.

The Arm Needs to be Used

Several different schools of thought exist on how the pitcher should use his arm. Some believe that pitchers throw too many pitches. Some believe that pitchers do not throw enough pitches. Still others think that each pitcher should be monitored by limiting the number of pitches. The number of innings pitched is another measuring tool.

An ongoing debate among baseball people exists about the number of rest days between starting assignments. Some proclaim that pitchers should not throw in the bullpen between starts. Others believe that the bullpen workouts are necessary between starts. Some coaches measure the workload in the bullpen by time. Others measure the work by number of pitches thrown. One coach may require that the pitchers throw batting practice. Another may firmly and staunchly disagree.

Frankly, there is an endless debate about almost all aspects of pitching. For example, mechanics may be diligently taught by some coaches and be of secondary concern to others. Most believe that mechanics are important, but some feel that pitchers throw the way they throw and any change may negatively affect performance.

Arm injuries can be caused by any number of things. Throwing a single pitch improperly may injure the arm. Throwing too many pitches may be harmful. Not throwing enough may be harmful. Throwing too often may cause damage to the arm. Poor condition may be another factor. The list goes on.

Hanging one's hat on a single source is a dangerous and foolish endeavor. Using pitch limitation does not necessarily prevent injuries. In fact, it may be a factor in causing injuries. For example, pitcher "A" is limited to 100 pitches per start. In his first start, he throws 35 pitches before being replaced because of ineffectiveness. In his second start he throws 50 pitches before his removal. His third start is even less productive. He is replaced after throwing 25 pitches. His fourth starting assignment is more productive. He has a shutout through 100 pitches. His limit is 100. In this example, the pitcher's previous performances did not prepare him for that many pitches.

The rule limiting the number of innings can be deceptive. If the maximum number of innings allowed is three, the pitcher may make 100 pitches to accomplish the task. Another pitcher may throw nine pitches to accomplish the same task. The pitcher who threw 100 pitches in three innings probably threw too much. The pitcher who threw nine pitches could safely throw more innings. In the hypothetical example, however, the limit is three innings.

Strict limits on days of rest do little to prevent injuries. A pitcher with tight muscles normally requires more recuperation time than a pitcher with loose, long muscles. Failure to recognize this and other differences and factors is illogical. Three days of rest between starts may be ideal for one pitcher. Another may require four days between starts. A pitcher who has labored in his previous start may need extra time to recuperate.

Weather conditions should also be considered. An extremely hot day, for instance, may sap the energy from a pitcher before he reaches a prearranged limit. Humid days may cause the same problem.

Pitchers recovering from an injury should not be measured with the same criteria as healthy pitchers. Safety cannot be measured with number of innings pitched or by the number of pitches thrown. Other factors must be included if intelligent safeguards are established.

There are many reasons for arm injuries. A coach, a school system, or an organization cannot prevent injuries by establishing rules based on a single factor. The number of innings and the number of pitches should be evaluated. The length of rest periods is important. The pitcher's mechanics should be reviewed. His physical state and the weather conditions must be considered. The number of game appearances will also play a role. His mental state and the number of pressure situations he last faced should also be considered. To select only one of these and declare it to be the fail-safe answer to the prevention of arm injuries makes no sense. In fact, it is irresponsible. Experience and knowledge are important factors. Common sense is also very important. Without these, limitations are useless.

Youth leagues and school leagues often establish rules that are not based on common sense. The bureaucratic approach is to establish limitations that fail to deal with the real problem. In these situations, reason is often overruled by cosmetic limitations. In some areas, a ten-to-twelve-year old is limited to six innings of pitching per week. Since he is limited to six innings, he will probably pitch six innings each week. Under this rule, a pitcher may labor through six innings by throwing 200 pitches. In this example, the rule obviously did not protect the young pitcher's arm.

The same kind of scenario could be shown for the number of pitch limitations. If a youth league sets a limit of 75 pitches per game, this rule alone will not solve any problem. In fact, it may create some. A youngster who is extremely wild may throw 75 pitches in two innings. He is not violating the rule. However, common sense and experience would not have allowed him to throw that many pitches in only two innings. It is obvious that he labored through the performance.

The number of pitches thrown in a game or a workout is obviously one important factor in the total scheme of pitching. Pitch number is not the only factor, however. It is probably not even the most important one. How were the pitches thrown? What types of pitches were thrown? Were the pitches thrown properly? What was the purpose of the throwing activity? How much rest was taken after workouts and games? What was the setting in which the pitches were thrown? What was the competitive level during the activity? Did the level of conditioning match the number and type of pitches thrown? These are important questions that need answers. The answers will provide the kind of information needed to prevent arm injuries.

Resting the Arm

The arm requires rest after heavy throwing activities. A heavy bullpen workout should be followed with a day of rest. The length of the rest period will be dependent upon the type and length of the throwing activity. Three to four days of rest are necessary for the pitcher who has pitched a complete game. This guideline is also true for the pitcher who has thrown several innings or several pitches.

During the days of rest, the pitcher can throw in the bullpen. If he is working on a three-day rest period between starting assignments, he should get one workout in the bullpen. If he is working on a four-day rest period between assignments, two bullpen workouts are recommended.

The pitcher should not throw in the bullpen on the day following a heavy workout. This point includes games, heavy bullpen workouts and situation drills in practice. On this rest day, he should play catch. The throws should be easy. A few long throws to loosen and stretch the arm are acceptable.

A simple rule of thumb is one day on and one day off. One day on means he is throwing in the bullpen or in another activity that taxes the arm. On the day off, he should do little throwing. The arm should not be taxed. It should be allowed to recuperate.

Bullpen workouts are different from throwing in the game. If the bullpen workout is moderate or light, the pitcher probably could throw the following day. He definitely should not throw on the day following a heavy workout in the bullpen. Occasional, a pitcher's arm may require two days of rest after a heavy bullpen workout.

Experience shows us that three or four days of rest is needed after making several pitches in a game. Unfortunately, no data is yet available that scientifically validates an exact formula. Some pitchers will pitch effectively with four days of rest. Others will pitch much better with three days of rest. Most will be less effective with more than four days of rest.

Baseball goes through cycles. Years ago, pitchers worked with three days of rest. In those days, major league teams operated during the season with a four-man rotation. Starting pitchers had three days of rest between starts. A fifth pitcher was used as a spot starter; he was called a swing man. This fifth starter could fill in for a tired arm. He was also used to give the four starters an extra day's rest as needed during the season.

Several years ago, the "five-man rotation" became popular. This plan gave each starting pitcher four days of rest between starting assignments. Those who supported the extra-day rest period claimed it saved the pitcher's arm.

The debate will always be a part of baseball. Some baseball people argue that there are only so many pitches in each pitcher's arm. Others argue that extra rest and overcautious protection of the arm will result in loss of control and poor conditioning. The answer is undoubtedly somewhere in the middle.

The arm should be kept in shape. Sensible throwing between starts will keep the arm in sound physical condition. By throwing between starts, the pitcher can maintain the feel and the touch that allow him to compete at his highest level. Too much throwing will deaden the arm. This practice may cause injury to the arm. Even if it does not result in an injury, it will be counterproductive.

Only the pitcher and the pitching coach have the information to make sound judgments. Injuries are found at both ends of the spectrum. Pitchers who throw too much develop arm injuries. Pitchers who throw too little also develop arm injuries. It is important to establish some guidelines. The guidelines should be developed from all the available data. Number of innings, number of pitches, strength of the pitcher, mechanics of the pitcher, previous workload, and how the pitcher's arm feels are some vital pieces of the puzzle.

The most important source of information comes from the pitcher. One of the most critical lesson that the pitcher can learn is to listen to the messages from his arm. The pitching coach should be astute enough to qualify the information he receives from the pitcher. If the pitcher is not reliable, the coach should use other data to arrive at a sound decision.

The guidelines can be used in several ways. For example, early in the season is a critical time for pitchers. How much should he throw? How many innings should he pitch? These are questions that each pitching coach faces. A simple solution to this dilemma is to set a safe limit. This limit should be based on experience and judgment.

Setting up safe guidelines is critical. The pitching coach is sure that 50 pitches or four innings are safe numbers for the pitching assignment. A safe limit would be 35 pitches or three innings. To be safe, however, the coach should set the limits lower. By taking off 15 pitches or one inning from what the pitcher is capable of throwing for a particular assignment, the pitching arm is protected. The coach should merely use the numbers as a guide. If three innings are completed before 35 pitches are thrown, the pitcher is finished. If 35 pitches are thrown before three innings are completed, the pitcher is removed. In other words, the coach is working in a safe limit environment. An extra inning may be pitched or a few more pitches may be thrown if the pitcher is in the safety limit. Along with considering these numerical limits, the coach should evaluate the pitcher's mechanics. In other words, the coach should collect and examine all available data before deciding when a pitcher has thrown enough on a given day. With this information and the input from the pitcher, the arm of the pitcher is protected.

Treatment with Ice

Icing the arm after heavy throwing workouts has become a standard treatment. It stops bleeding and helps the recovery process. Throwing a baseball causes small micro tears. This process results in bleeding and swelling. The ice is used to stop the bleeding and lessen the swelling. The recommended treatment time is 15 to 20 minutes.

During the treatment time, the pitcher should be cautioned. He should be aware of some warning signs that the ice should be removed from the arm, including tingling and numbness in the arm. If either happens, he should stop the treatment. The tingling or numbness occurs because the ice is affecting a nerve.

Ice is an effective treatment, but it can be overused. It is not necessary to use an ice pack after a light-throwing activity unless the pitcher is recovering from a previous injury. Ice should not be used as a pacifier or to satisfy a ritualistic need.

More is not always better; fifteen to 20 minutes of icing is usually sufficient. Ice does not have the same effect on all pitchers. A twenty-minute treatment for one pitcher may be sufficient. Others may recuperate faster with less icing time. The ice should not be kept on the arm any longer than 20 minutes.

The day following the pitching assignment, the arm should be exercised. Swimming is a very effective activity. The water affords some resistance but does not place great stress on the arm. A fifteen-minute swim helps the arm get rid of the waste products caused by the micro tears. In addition, recovery time is hastened.
Early Season Workout for Pitchers

A pitcher should have at least five weeks of practice before he throws in a game against outside competition. A sample five-week throwing program would include he following:

First Week
- Play catch the first three days for about 5-10 minutes at a distance of 40-60 feet. This is to stretch the arms and legs. Throw at half speed.
- The last two days, throw 15 pitches to a catcher. Balls should be thrown half-speed

and half of the pitches should be thrown from the stretch. Of the 15 pitches, five should be curves.

Second Week
- Start with 15 pitches and build up to 25 the first three days.
- The last two days throw 35 pitches.
- Pitches should be thrown half-speed half from the stretch. All types of the pitches should be thrown. This action will prepare the arm for breaking pitches, as well as fastballs.

Third Week
- First three days throw 35 pitches half-speed and then 10 pitches three-quarter speed.
- Throw 50 pitches the last two days, 25 at three-quarter speed.
- During the third week, alternate the workouts, throwing heavy one day and light the next day. On the light-throwing days, heavy running should be done.

Example:	Monday —	35 pitches
	Tuesday —	heavy running
	Wednesday —	35 pitches
	Thursday —	light throwing
	Friday —	50 pitches, intersquad game on Friday. Have each pitcher go one inning. In the next intrasquad game the pitcher should throw two innings.

Fourth Week
- Throw 50-75 pitches, alternating heavy and light. Throw half at three-quarter speed. The last day, 10-15 pitches should be thrown hard..
- A good pitcher should have at least three pitches—fastball, curveball, and a change up.

Fifth Week
- Throw 75-100 pitches at game speed. The pitcher should now be ready to throw a 9-inning game. However, the number of pitches should be limited to 75 in his first start after this five-week program. The second start should be limited to 100 pitches. This recommendation is in keeping with the other safety measures suggested in this chapter.

Intrasquad Innings

During the five-week throwing period, each pitcher should get in at least 20 innings of intrasquad competition, or have 20 innings equivalent to intrasquad competition. A competitive inning could be done by performing a simulated inning in the bullpen. Three outs pitched in various situations can also be counted as an inning of competition. This procedure prepares the pitcher for game competition. The pitches to be thrown in the bullpen should be those that the pitcher would throws in game situations. Make sure that each pitcher is adequately rested after he competes (i.e., before he throws again).

FSU Baseball Pitcher's Off-Season Workout

Organize your off-season workout time with conditioning and arm readiness as a major priority. This goal can be accomplished by utilizing a small block of time each day for physical activities.

It is essential that every pitcher report to the January practice session in good physical condition. This level of fitness will allow him to refine the skills necessary to attain success. Because we do not have a great deal of time before our first game, a pitcher's off-season conditioning efforts will pay dividends.

Mental preparation is equally important. Preparation and planning are important. Both short-term and long-term goals should be set. Short-term goals to be accomplished during the off-season period should be established. Plans to accomplish these goals should be developed. Pitchers must be advised of the necessity to carry out these plans. Following this procedure will help them mentally prepare for the coming season. In turn, this preparation will provide them with the discipline to carry out long-term goals.

Three Sample Off-Season Workout Plans

Simple Work Plan
- Run wind sprints (15 @ 50 yards) every other day with 30 seconds rest between sprints.
- Run for distance every other day (from two to five miles), choose from a, b, or c*:
  a. 2-mile run—normal run 15 minutes
  b. 2-mile run—test run 13 minutes (perform this run at least twice during the break)
  c. 5-mile run—under 37 minutes
- Throw a minimum of three times per week. Alternate days to allow a rest day after throwing. This practice will permit the arm to recover. Follow one of the suggested two programs.

Throwing Program Plan #1
Throwing program I is for the pitcher who has not retained an adequate level of throwing condition from the winter league.
- Start with 25 pitches—1/2 speed
- Second workout 25 pitches—1/2 speed last 10 pitches 3/4 speed
- Third workout 35 pitches—3/4 speed
- Fourth workout 35 pitches—3/4 speed
- Fifth workout 50 pitches—3/4 speed last 15 full speed
- Sixth workout 50 pitches—3/4 speed last 15 full speed
- Seventh workout 65 pitches—3/4 speed last 20 full speed
- Eighth workout 65 pitches—3/4 speed last 20 full speed
- Ninth workout 75 pitches—Full speed
- Tenth workout 75 pitches—Full speed
- After the 10th workout, each throwing day should consist of 100 pitches

In throwing program plan #1, half of the pitches should be thrown from the stretch. The pitcher should change speeds, and work for control. He should find a reliable catcher. If it is not possible to have a catcher everyday, the pitcher should substitute the screen for the catcher. The screen can be used at least once per week. This option will give the pitcher an opportunity to work on his delivery. Twenty minutes should be set aside every other day to do the dry-run drills. These drills should be done on the running days.

*This option will prepare a pitcher to successfully complete the 6-minute mile requirement. The pitcher should time himself using a stop watch. Every pitcher should make sure the 6-minute mile at least twice before reporting for the first day of practice.

Throwing Program Plan #2
This program is for the pitcher who has retained an adequate level of arm and leg conditioning from the winter league to the present time.
- Start with 75 pitches
- Second workout 75 pitches
- After second workout, throw 100 pitches on each throwing date.

The pitcher should make sure he throws from the stretch at least 50 percent of the time. In addition, the pitcher should vary his speeds and work for control while throwing. He should also find a reliable catcher. When a catcher cannot be located, the pitcher should use the screen. In fact, using the screen once per week is suggested. This practice will provide the setting for good mechanical recall and repetition. At least

20 minutes every other day should be set aside to do dry-run drills. These drills are best done on the running days.

> *Every Pitcher Must Be Mentally and Physically Ready for a Winning Season!*

Summary

This chapter discussed the fact that the pitcher's arm is not only a valuable tool for the pitcher, but is also an important defensive weapon for his team. The pitcher and the pitching coach should pay careful attention to it. The pitching arm should be used properly. It should be worked enough to handle the wear and tear. Precautions should be taken to insure that it is not overused.

It is important to know the difference between soreness and pain. Soreness and stiffness are the result of heavy physical activity. Pain is the result of an injury. If there is any doubt, a physician should be consulted.

All available data should be used in order to protect the pitcher's arm, including innings pitched, number of pitches, stressful situations, mechanics, weather and any other pertinent information that is available. Each factor is important. A wise, experienced coach, using this kind of data, along with honest feedback from the pitcher, will provide a sound safety net for the pitcher's arm.

To be successful, the pitcher needs to throw between starts. His arm should be well conditioned. Injuries occur on both sides of the throwing spectrum. A pitcher can injury his arm by failing to throw enough to keep it in shape. On the other hand, he can injury his arm from overuse.

14

Closed-Eyes Training Drills

Everyone learns from experience. Through trial and error, new ideas emerge and better ways of teaching are learned, and through both successes and hard knocks, coaches develop better ways to present material. Each drill and each game is full of suggestions. You just need to be vigilant and receptive. For example, a drill that results in player improvement, team unity, and overall enthusiasm should be noted and carefully dissected, meticulously recording the factors that created such a successful outcome. On the other hand, a drill that nets negative results should be examined in the same manner. Improvements and changes should result. So, each game and each practice supplies you with an abundance of teaching material.

The learning process is relatively easy for some and very difficult for others. How the material is presented and how it is received becomes extremely important. Information is received in three ways: audio, visual, and kinesthetic. Considering how each pitcher receives information is an important step in transmitting ideas and fundamentals.

The auditory pitcher, or player, needs to *hear* the information. Use statements such as, "Did you hear what I just said?" "Listen carefully to the following steps," and "Repeat back to me the information." A tape-recorded lesson is very valuable for this type of learner. It is also important to develop an audio vocabulary that has many different ways to say the same thing. Of course, that is true of teaching in general.

The visual learner needs to see the delivery, the arm action, the stride, and the way each is being executed. His method of learning could be considered "mimicking." He may not understand the nuances of the activity, but he is able to ape the physical part of it. Visual terminology should be developed for the visual learner. Use statements such as, "Let me show you how to land on the inside of your stride foot," "Notice how your pitching teammate keeps his knee inside his stride foot," or "Show me how he did that."

For the kinesthetic learner, doing, or *feeling*, the activity is his vehicle for receiving information. He needs to feel the fingers releasing the ball in order to develop a certain pitch, for example. He can see and hear the lesson, but his body must practice and record the activity before it is learned. "Feel the weight on the inside ball of the stride foot," "Feel your weight over the rubber," and "Reach out and feel where you should release the pitch," are the kinds of phrases that should be used for the kinesthetic learner.

In many ways, the kinesthetic learner is fortunate because pitching mechanics, control, and velocity all are based on feel and touch. In whatever way the information is received, it must be assembled and developed through the kinesthetic process. The other types of learners are not necessarily at a disadvantage, however. The visual learner often gathers details in mechanical movements by simply imitating what someone else does. If he is highly developed in his ability to mimic, learning will be relatively fast. Some audio learners are adept at picking up the smallest details and properly prioritizing them into a sensible learning progression.

Good pitchers are in touch with their bodies. They know as soon as a pitch is released whether it is a good pitch. How many times have you seen a pitcher grimace at the release point because he knows at that moment it will not be the kind of pitch he intended? Or heard a cry of disappointment at release, expressing disgust over "hanging" a curveball? These pitchers are in sync with the movements of their body parts. Teaching pitchers to get acquainted with each part of the delivery will help the beginners and serve as a way to maintain or enhance the mechanical movements for even the more accomplished pitchers.

Closed-Eyes Training

Closing the eyes and feeling the activity is a method of getting the pitcher in touch with his body parts. This type of training is a sound method to help transfer information to kinetic production. Several by-products result from using this teaching technique. Balance, angles, and thrust are improved. Better understanding of the pitching mechanics is evident to both the pitcher and the coach. This closed-eyes method can be used at any age level and at any sequence in the teaching of mechanics. It is particularly good at the outset, or beginning learning stages.

Closed-eyes drills have many benefits. They provide a setting that emphasizes awareness of the details of the pitching motion and how each body part is involved. Touch and feel are enhanced. The inner eye is put to work. It sees and feels the activity from the inside out rather than from the outside in. The act of throwing a baseball to a given target must be conceived first and then executed. With the eyes closed, the pitcher can better isolate each segment and develop a feel for the given activity.

Try experimenting with blindfolding or having players close their eyes while simulating parts of, or all of, the throwing motion. Then, evolve into throwing to targets with the eyes closed. The purpose is to get the participant to become closely aware of balance, specific body parts, how movements are made, and the feeling of successful and unsuccessful motions.

The closed-eyes method, as an addition to the balance drills described in the previous chapters, is one of the best ways to help a pitcher get acquainted with body position, weight distribution, and the consistent placement of the push-off foot and stride foot. A real understanding and feeling for mechanics of pitching can be taught through practice with the inner eye.

Closed-Eyes Balance Drill on Push-Off Foot

To balance on the push-off foot, the stride leg must be lifted. The leg lift is easier to execute from the stretch position. Less movement occurs from that position, so that is the way the drill starts.

The purpose of the drill is to concentrate on, and feel, the proper balance position of the push-off foot. For the purposes of this drill, the pitcher should balance on the push-off foot for approximately three seconds, or to the count of three. At the outset, this maneuver may require help from a partner. Before allowing helpers, encourage each pitcher to be self-reliant and try to balance without help. For those having difficulty with balancing, or hanging, on the push-off foot, set a goal of balancing for one count or one second, building up to the three-count. After a few repetitions, the pitcher will be able to balance and meet the desired three counts.

Stretch position

Instruct each pitcher to "balance and feel the weight on the inside ball of the push-off foot." "Feel the weight transfer and isolate on the ball of the push-off foot," is a good way of making the point. Proceed with the following kinds of instruction:

- "Now place the weight on the inside ball of the foot, and take a mental snapshot of the foot position."
- "Repeat until you can feel the same position of foot placement that was in the snapshot."
- "Now balance and feel how stable you can make your push-off foot. Practice until the foot is completely stable."

Early in the lesson, some pitchers, if not all, may wiggle, or move the push-off foot. Practice until these problems are solved.

Balance on push-off foot

Once the foot is stabilized and the weight is properly distributed, repeat the procedure with emphasis on the push-off knee. Note: Pay attention when new challenges in a lesson plan are presented and make sure that the previous instruction is still being followed. As the pitcher balances on his push-off foot, the coach instructs him to isolate his thoughts and inner vision to the push-off knee, which should be unlocked and slightly ahead of the push-off foot. The following coaching instructions will help teach body awareness of the push-off knee:

- "As each of you lifts your leg, feel the weight shift to the push-off foot and let the feeling settle on the push-off knee."
- "Make sure the knee is unlocked (slightly bent) and is turned in toward the hitter."
- "Repeat, but this time make sure you feel loaded, balanced, and coiled. Feel the coil of the knee."

The push-off position is critical to maximizing the effort of the pitching delivery. Emphasis is on developing a good load position, which provides the pitcher with a functional and well-directed thrust. It affords him the balance that enhances his control of each pitch. Remember, the pitcher should be sound mechanically, but not be mechanical with the delivery. Pitchers arrive at a mechanically sound delivery in one of two ways—natural ability or practice. The majority of pitchers can only arrive there by practicing.

Stride Foot Drill with Closed Eyes

Because the leg lift from the stretch position requires less movement of body parts, start this drill in that position. Only work on this drill after the push-off foot drill has been completed satisfactorily. Proper feel and use of the push-off foot initiates the stride. From a balanced push-off position, the pitcher leads with his hip, keeps the weight on his push-off foot (back side over the rubber as long as possible), and then strides to the inside ball of the stride foot. Repeat this procedure a few times. Next, place emphasis on the stride foot.

Stride, balance, and hang on stride foot

Some good examples of instructional statements are the following:

- "Stride to the inside ball of the stride foot. Feel the weight transfer to that point."
- "Now keep your weight on the rubber as long as possible and stride to the same stride spot."
- "This time, I want you to be in complete control of the stride foot. Land it softly and then transfer the weight to it."
- "Feel the weight transfer to it while you are starting to deliver the pitch."
- "Feel the weight on the inside ball of the foot."
- "Now do a series of leg lifts, and strides, landing in the same stride spot each time."

When the pitchers are successful with this drill, move to the next part of the mechanical movement that needs work—the leg lift.

Leg Lift Drill with Closed Eyes

A controlled leg lift and the controlled motion toward and to the stride spot help the drive and direction of the body and the control of the pitch. The relaxed and controlled front leg helps to relax the upper body and allows the arm and upper body to move quickly. The angle of the lift leg is important and should be consistent. The distance of the stride foot from the body and its relaxation dramatically affect other body parts.

Examples of instructional suggestions include:

- "Bring the lift-leg knee toward the throwing-arm side of the chin."
- "Leave the lift-leg foot on the ground as long as possible. Let the knee control the foot."
- "Feel the knee and direct it at an angle to the chin toward the throwing arm."
- "Make sure you feel the angle and the control of the knee."
- "Repeat this procedure and develop a consistent angle with the knee."

When control and direction of the lift leg is satisfactory, turn the senses to the lift-leg foot. When that foot is at the zenith of the lift, it should be relaxed and extended, with the toe pointed downward. If the pitcher were to open his eyes, he could look down the thigh and see the tip of the stride toe, which should be just past the knee. Since he is not using his eyes, he should feel the foot in that area. Suggest that the pitchers "feel the toe relaxed, pointing downward, and extended," as previously indicated. Repeat this procedure several times, with attention paid to control of, angle of, and relaxation of the lift leg.

Leg lift

Leading with the Hip Drill with Eyes Closed

The next drill in the sequence involves the front hip. Leading with the hip, while keeping the weight distributed properly over the push-off foot, is the beginning of the leg thrust to deliver the pitch. Pitchers should avoid rushing, or opening up too soon. Use the following coaching suggestions:

- "At the top of the leg lift, elevate the front hip. Repeat the leg lift and the elevation of the hip several times. Feel the hip elevate. Make sure the push-off foot, or back side, stays over the pitching rubber."
- "Now, lead with the hip without gaining distance with the back side of the body."

The elevated hip should drop gradually toward the stride spot. The pitcher should be able to drop his hip toward the stride spot approximately four inches before the back side moves forward. Other teaching comments include:

Leading with the hip

- "Feel the hip moving downward to the stride spot. The angle is a direction in a diagonal line from the elevated hip to the stride spot."
- "Repeat this activity several times."

The push-off is explosive but must be coordinated so that the summation of forces is released in an effective manner. Developing balance and the ability to explode in sequence will be of great value to the pitcher.

Wind-Up Position Drill with Eyes Closed

Follow the fundamentals that have already been described in the earlier chapters, but with the eyes closed. Make sure the hands move up and down the midline of the body and separate at the same place each time. Also make sure the separation spot is identical to the stretch position separation spot.

Wind-up position

Start the drill with both feet pointed toward the target. Direct each pitcher in the dry run group to:
- "Place the push-off foot in the correct position on the rubber."
- "Turn the foot but keep the belly button facing toward the target."

- "Repeat steps one and two until they become automatic." (This step is where feel really comes into play.)
- "Determine the top of the hand movement." (Some pitchers use up-and-down movement, others move the hands over the head.)
- "Now, as the hands start down, begin the leg lift." (This move should be economical.)

The weight should not be required to travel very far to get in a balanced position. The movement of the hands coming down the midline of the body should be coordinated with the leg lift. Tell players to:
- "Sense the timing. Feel the weight shift."
- "Develop and feel the smooth transition from the starting position to the leg lift position."
- "Repeat until balance and coordination are achieved."

From the wind-up position, repeat all of the drills that were done in the stretch position. Develop the same leg lift and the same separation point in both positions.

Stationary Stride Position Drills with Eyes Closed

Almost all aspects of the pitching delivery can be practiced in the stationary stride position. Weight transfer and all upper body parts of the delivery can be stressed.

Stationary stride position

By eliminating the leg lift and the actual stride, emphasis can be more easily placed on all of the other aspects of the pitching delivery. Even the weight shift and the stride can be partially practiced from this position. Use the stationary stride drills that were described in the previous chapters and practice them with the eyes closed. In addition, try some of the following drills that can be done with closed eyes.

Stationary Stride Position—Separation of Hands Drill with Eyes Closed

Begin the drill with the pitcher in a stationary stride position, with the hands together at the midline of the body, and the elbows touching the fat pads of the sides, at the height of the belt buckle. The pitcher should have a ball in his throwing hand. Instruct the pitcher to do the following with his eyes closed:

- "Transfer your weight to the inside of the stride foot and then to the inside of the push-off foot, swaying back and forth. Keep the hands in front at the midline and do not move them up and down, yet."
- "Feel the weight transfer."
- "Now move the hands upward approximately 6 to 12 inches."
- "As your hands start down, begin to shift your weight to the push-off foot."
- "Drop the hands and separate them at the bottom of the drop. Just allow them to fall. They will separate and the hands will begin to swing apart if they are relaxed."
- "Repeat these four steps and feel the rhythm, weight shift, and separation of hands."
- "Now, concentrate on the hand separation at the bottom. Bottom out, separate the hands. The throwing hand will need a little help as it separates. The back of the thumb will be facing the outside thigh of

Separation of hands

the push-off leg. As the hand starts back, turn the thumb clockwise one-quarter turn and then lift." (This movement helps to prevent wrapping of the arm or excessively turning the body. Repeat this part of the drill until the separation and start of the lift can be felt and is consistent.)

Stationary Stride Position—Throwing-Arm Lift Drill with Eyes Closed

One of the most common pitching flaws is failure to get the throwing arm up and into a functional throwing position. This drill is designed to help the pitcher get the feel of a proper lift. The pitcher assumes a stationary stride position with a baseball in his throwing hand. With the hands held at the midline, the pitcher is instructed to:

- "Bottom out and separate your hands."
- "At separation, and as the weight is transferring to the push-off foot, turn the thumb clockwise one-quarter turn."
- "Reach back with the throwing arm and lift up with the fingertips pointed toward the ground."
- "Get the feel of lifting the arm with the wrist picking the hand and arm up to the sky."
- "Keep lifting until the hand of the throwing arm is higher than the head and in a ready, or load, position. Make sure the weight is now transferred to the inside of the push-off foot."

Repeat several times. The purpose of this drill is to practice and develop a feel for functionally getting the arm into a throwing position. It places the arm into a position to maximize angles and direction.

Throwing-arm lift

Stationary Stride Position—Trajectory Drill with Eyes Closed

The pitcher starts the drill in a stationary position with a baseball in his throwing hand and his eyes closed. Apply the following instructions:

- "Start with the throwing arm in the ready or launch position. Pause and feel that position."
- "The hand of the throwing arm should be above the head, fingertips pointing toward the ground and ready to throw the pitch. Make sure the wrist is relaxed. Feel the relaxation of the wrist."
- "Simulate a throw by reaching out to establish a good release point."
- "Finish the throw."
- "Repeat, but this time internalize and feel the direction of the ball. It should feel as though the throwing hand and the ball are traveling on a diagonal toward the plate. Get the feel of throwing down hill."

Trajectory drill

As the hand travels from the load position, with the fingertips facing the ground, and starts forward, the wrist will snap back with palm facing upward, with the backs of the fingers facing the forearm. This position loads and provides maximum use of the wrist, forearm, and fingers. This action will happen naturally if the hand of the throwing arm is loaded properly.

Stationary Stride Position—Right-to-Left (RHP) Drill or Left-to-Right (LHP) Drill with Eyes Closed

This drill helps with the pitcher's upper body alignments, arm extension, and focus. The pitcher should assume a stationary stride position with a ball in his throwing hand. His eyes should be closed. The purpose of the drill is to become consistent and fluid through the braking action of the throw. To do that, the right-handed pitcher's arm should follow a path to and through the release point area, traveling from right to left (left to right for a left-handed pitcher). Use the following instructions to improve this part of the throwing motion:

- "Use the same starting motion as in the previous drill."
- "Simulate a throw."
- "From the top of the arm lift, feel the movement of the arm as it takes a route from right to left, and finish with the outside portion of the forearm touching the outside portion of the thigh."
- "Simulate another throw. This time, feel the release point to the forearm touching the thigh."
- "Simulate another throw. This time, note the relaxation of the fingers, wrist, and hand at the finish of the throw." (If the throwing action is smooth and functional, the wrist, hand, and fingers will be relaxed.)
- "Make a number of simulated throws, working to isolate the thoughts and inner vision of one of the coaching points during each simulation."

Right-to-left or left-to-right drill

Stationary Stride Position—Front-Arm Drill with Eyes Closed

The purpose of this drill is to use the front arm in an efficient manner. Attention to the motion and timing of that arm will have a positive influence on the throwing motion. Pitchers should start in a stationary stride position with the eyes closed and with a ball in the throwing hand. The following instructions should be given in this drill:

- "Drop the hands and at separation of the hands, pay attention to how you direct and lift the front arm, then complete the simulated throw."
- "Simulate the first part of another throw by dropping the hands and at separation, point the back of the glove to the target as you lift with the wrist to a height no greater than the chin."
- "Repeat until a consistent direction and height are achieved."
- "Start the next part of the drill with the back of the glove extended toward the target and at chin level. Use this starting position for the following few movements."

- "Turn the thumb of the glove over so that the palm faces upward to the degree of the angle of the throwing arm." (Palm to palm.)
- "Raise the heel of the glove slightly above the fingers as you bring the front elbow in toward and brush against the upper rib cage."
- "Repeat until the move is made correctly and is understood."

When the first seven steps in this drill are done satisfactorily, the pitchers should move on to the next phase to perfect the front arm action. Use the following coaching suggestions:

- "Now go back and perform steps 2 and 3 using the inner eye to see and feel the activity. Repeat several times."
- "Now, do steps 4, 5, and 6 using the inner eye."
- "Simulate several throws, taking the front arm through the complete throwing motion, with the internal focus on that part of the delivery."

Front arm drill

Chest to Target Drill with Eyes Closed

The focus of this drill is on barreling the chest and extending it to the target. Pitchers should start in a stationary stride position with the eyes closed. Give the following instructions:

- "Pay attention to your chest as you simulate a throw."
- "Barrel the chest as you simulate the next throw."
- "As you simulate and barrel the chest during the next throw, direct the middle of the chest directly at the target, keeping the breasts level and parallel to the ground."
- "In your mind's eye, see and feel the chest extending closer to the target, keeping the breasts level, on the next several throws."

Chest to target

As the chest reaches toward the target, it is important to keep the bottom of the chin parallel to the ground with the eyes level and directed at the target. Practicing the positioning of the chin and the eyes could also be developed into two separate drills.

Target Throwing Drill with Eyes Closed

For this drill, each pitcher should have a partner. The partners should stand 45 to 60 feet apart. (In initiating this drill, the pitchers could be less than 45 feet apart.) For safety reasons, the pitchers should spread out, making sure to have plenty of room on both sides of each pitcher. The pitchers will begin the drill by playing target catch with the eyes open. The teaching language will be as follows:

- "Use your partner's mid-chest area as a target and with your eyes open, throw and hit that target."
- "Become aware of the release point."
- "Repeat this routine for several throws, developing a feel for the release point."
- "Now, with the eyes closed, throw and hit the same target."
- "Before opening the eyes, call out the destination of the ball, based on the feel of the release point."

A few pitchers will be able to successfully execute the drill quickly, especially after successful work in the preceding drills with the eyes closed. Others may struggle a bit. For those experiencing difficulty, have them open their eyes two out of every three throws. As they become more proficient with the eyes closed, advance to one throw with the eyes open and two with the eyes closed. They all will improve and have better body awareness.

As pitchers acquaint themselves with the concept of using the inner eye, they will be able to utilize the closed-eyes practice on pitches in the bullpen—an excellent way to improve the grip and rotation of various pitches. The limits to what can be done with the closed-eyes drills are only in the imagination of those who use them.

Conclusion

Practicing these pitching drills with the eyes closed is a good technique to help each pitcher get in tune with the mechanics of pitching, as well as to help each player to improve body awareness. The closed-eyes drills will work hand in hand with the teaching of visualization and concentration. The inner eye has excellent vision when put to use.

Fresno State Baseball Strength and Conditioning Program for Baseball

Steve Sobonya
Former Strength Coach
Fresno State

The following strength and conditioning program was designed by Steve Sobonya, the strength coach at Fresno State. Not only is it an outstanding program in terms of physical development, it is also mentally challenging and exciting.

Basic Weight Training Philosophy as a Coach

- Keep it simple for the athletes .... and leave the technical parts to the coach.
- Keep it fun and have goals and challenges built in to the program.
- Don't "Weight Train"........ train for baseball.

Fresno State Baseball
Yearly Outline

Phase	Month	Goal	Volume/Int
Summer #2/Fall Prep	August	Cont. Base Training	Mod/Mod
Fall Off-Season #1	Sept/Oct	Cont. Base Training Strength/End	High/Low
Fall Off-Season #2	Oct/Nov	Strength	Mod/High
Pre-Season	Dec/Jan	Strength/Power Spec Preparation	Mod/Mod-High
In-season	Jan/May	Maintenance	Low/Mod
Post-Season	June	Transition Active Rest	Low/Low
Summer #1	July	Begin Base Training Muscle Balance	Mod/Low

NOTE: At the completion of most phases, there is a short downloading phase— rest, low volume, or low intensity.

Basic Weight Training Guidelines for the Player

- Never compromise technique for more weight.
- Always perform technical baseball work before lifting.
- Try to play long-toss after each lift session and stretch!
- Perform shoulder program on regular basis.
- Use periodization (planning). Don't just lift.
- If the player is a two-sport athlete, train for the current sport, but make time for baseball skills.

Specific Requisite Qualities for Baseball Players (FSU's Program is Designed to Develop these Qualities)

- Power
- Speed
- Body Control—Agility
- Flexibility
- Strength
- Confidence of Ability

Several qualities influence the ability of a pitcher to be successful.

Exercises that Are Used to Develop the Requisite Qualities for Baseball Players

1. Power
- Training base of endurance and strength (works best with optimum muscle balance)
- Olympic lifts (high pull and clean—floor and hang)
- Plyometrics (upper and lower) in all directions (medicine balls, power jumps, reactive jumps)

2. Speed
- Running mechanics and positioning drills (emphasizing timing of segments)
- Strength speed (overload running)
- Over speed (downhill or release running)
- Game speed—absolute and reactive speed (flat short running, chase drills, reactive drills)

3. Body Control
- Traditional agility drills (6-ball drill, figure eight, juggling, etc.)
- Stabilization exercises (hurdle drills, ice skaters)
- Foot speed drills (speed ladder, rhythmical drills)

4. Flexibility
- Traditional stretches for the trunk, and the upper and lower body
- Dynamic flexibility (leg swings)
- Exercises that demand flexibility (hurdle drills; lifts that demand flexibility)

5. Strength
- Rotator cuff exercises
- Abdominal and low back exercises (both straight and twisting exercises)
- Leg exercises (one and two leg exercises—primarily double joint exercises)
- Specific strength exercises
  - forearm/hand circuit (rice, bats, bars, plates, rollers, alphabets, flippers)
  - tricep-bicep muscle balance (extensions and twists)
  - leg/hip circuit (hurdles, spiders, lunges, calves)
  - shoulder-back muscle balance (pull-over, presses, pulls)

6. Confidence of Ability
- Design a program which will challenge and reward.

Baseball Training: Off-Season Phase #2

Warm up: jog, bike or calesthenics for two minutes to heat body temp; abdominal crunch x 100; twist x 50; low back extension x 50 (25 twist); rotator cuff x 35 each of six main exercises

Stretching: focus on the muscles that the pitcher is going to use while throwing

Day 1

- *Explosive Training*
  —One-leg lateral jumps
- *Speed Prep Training*
  —Hurdle over/under
- *Strength Training*
  —Power clean
  —Four-way step-up
- *Auxiliary Training*
  — Single leg extension
  —Dumbell row
  —Rear delt fly
  —Throwers curl
- *Forearm Circuit*
  —As a team (5 stations)—hard
- *Pitchers Circuit*
  —As a team (5 stations)—hard
- *Trunk Stability*
  —As a team—moderate
- *Total Body Stretch*
  —As a team

Day 3

- *Explosive Training*
  —Bench strides
- *Speed Prep Training*
  —Knee ups/side
- *Strength Training*
  —Squat
  —Bench press
- *Auxillary Training*
  —Single-leg curl
  —Over head shoulder

—Pull-ups
—Tricep extension
- *Forearm Circuit*
  As a team (5 stations)—easy
- *Pitchers Circuit*
  —As a team (5 stations)—easy
- *Trunk Stability*
  —As a team—hard
- *Total Body Stretch*
  —As a team

Day 5

- *Explosive Training*
  —Ice skaters
- *Speed Prep Training*
  —Hurdle front/back, hurdle side
- *Strength Training*
  —High step-up
  —Incline press
- *Auxiliary Training*
  —Seated row
  —Dumbell pull-over
  —Tricep extension
  —Reverse curl
- *Forearm Circuit*
  —As a team (five stations)—hard
- *Pitchers Circuit*
  —As a team (five stations)—hard
- *Trunk Stabilty*
  —As a team—moderate
- *Total Body Stretch*
  —As a team—moderate

Sets and Repetitions / Progression

Week	Exp	Speed	Strength	Aux
1	1x10	1x20	Rep Sheet 4	3 x 8-12
2	1x12	1x20	"	"
3	2x10	2x15	Rep Sheet 5	3 x 6-10
4	2x10	2x15	"	"
5	2x12	2x20	Rep Sheet 6	3 x 10-14
6	1x20	1x25	"	"
7		Begin Ironman Testing		
8		Begin Preseason Phase on Wednesday		

Tuesday and Thursday Running Program: Off-Season #2

Day 1

- *Warm Up*
  - Stride 4 X 60 easy
  - Knee to front (side X 25 each leg)
  - Light stretch (hamstrings, quads, hips, butt, calfs, trunk, arm swings)
  - Leg swings (side to side X 20 each)
  - Leg swings (front to back X 20 each)
- *Mechanics (Rest 40 Seconds Between)*
  - Skip for timing 4 X 30 Yds
  - Skip for distance 4 X 30 Yds
  - Glide (step over knee 4 X 60—90% sprint)
- *Speed Training (Full Rest Between)*
  - Progression runs 4 X 60 Yds
  - Timing (length; arm speed)
- *Acceleration Training (Full Rest Between)*
  - Flying 30 (4 X 30)
  - Jog X 15 (sprint X 30)
- *Agility Training (1-Minute Rest Between)*
  - 20-Yd Shuffle (three each direction—timed and charted)
  - Position specific agility drills
- *Long Stretch*

Day 2

- *Warm Up*
  - Stride 4 X 60 easy
  - Knee to front (side X 25 each leg)
  - Light stretch (hamstrings, quads, hips, butt, calfs, trunk, arm swings)
  - Leg swings (side to side X 20 each)
  - Leg Swings (front to back X 20 each)
- *Mechanics (Rest 40 Seconds Between)*
  - Skip for timing 4 X 30 Yds
  - High knees 2 X 30 Yds; Side 1 X 30 each side
  - Marching leg cycle 2 X 20 each leg
- *Speed Training (Full Rest Between)*
  - Ramps X 6
  - Timed 60 X 4 (chart the time)
- *Acceleration Training (30 Seconds Between)*
  - 15 yd start and back X 6 (timed and charted)
- *Agility Training (1-Minute Rest Between)*
  - Ice skate X 50 and back
  - Hurdle walk X 50
  - Position Specific Training
- *Long Stretch*

Preseason Changes General

- All workout days are performed in the following manner:
  A. Warm-up
  B. Specific baseball skills
  C. Weight training or speed training
  D. Non-technical baseball drills
  E. Total body stretch
- Only one leg exercise is performed—no regular squats.
- Power cleans are done light or as high pulls.
- Many more dumbbell exercises are employed (no bar bench, no BNP)
- Very big emphasis on trunk and midsection.
- Many more closed chain exercises.

Sample In-Season Workout 2-3 Days a Week

Weight Room Workout
- Warm-up
  —Rotator cuff X 25
  —Twist abs X 100
  —Ab crunch X 50
  —Twist back X 50
  —Leg raise X 25
  —Leg circle X 25
- Explosiveness
  —Power jump X 6
  —Medball side X 20 Each
- Strength
  —Leg press 2 X 10-12
  —Lat pull 2 X 10-12
- Strength
  —DB bench 2 X 10-12
  —Bent fly 2 X 10-12
  —Tricep kick 2 X 10-12
  —Throwers curl 2 X 10-12
  —Over-under 2 X 10 each
  —Forearms 200 total
- Flexibility
  —Total body stretch

On Field Workout
- Station #1—Trunk
  —Ab/back circuit
- Station #2—Arms Back
  —Cords—tricep/bicep
  —Pulls
- Station #3—Cuffs
  —Tennis cans
- Station #4—Legs
  —Step—ups/lunges
- Station #5—Stability
  —Ice skaters
  —Hurdle qalk
  —Marches
- Station #6—Stretch

Supplement for Rep Sheet #1 — 3 X 10

Reps/Wt For		100	110	120	130	140
10			70	75	85	95	105
10			80	90	100	105	110
10			75	85	90	100	110

Rep Sheet #3 — 3 X 10 @ 65-72%

Note: Perform at least two work-up sets prior to each program

Reps/Wt	150	160	170	180	190
10	151	20	125	130	130
10	120	125	130	135	140
10	120	125	130	135	135

Reps/Wt	200	210	220	230	240
10	135	140	150	155	160
10	145	150	160	170	175
10	140	145	155	165	170

Reps/Wt	250	260	270	280	290
10	165	170	175	185	190
10	180	185	195	200	205
10	175	180	190	190	200

Reps/Wt	300	310	320	330	340
10	195	200	210	215	225
10	215	220	230	235	245
10	205	215	220	230	235

Reps/Wt	350	360	370	380	390
10	230	235	245	250	255
10	255	260	265	270	280
10	245	250	255	260	270

Reps/Wt	400	410	420	430	440
10	260	265	275	280	285
10	290	295	305	310	315
10	275	280	285	295	300

Rep Sheet #3 (Cont)

Reps/Wt	450	460	470	480	490
10	295	300	305	310	320
10	325	330	340	345	350
10	310	315	325	330	335

Reps/Wt	500	510	520	530	540
10	325	330	340	345	350
10	360	365	375	380	390
10	345	350	355	365	370

Reps/Wt	550	560	570	580	590
10	355	365	370	375	385
10	395	405	410	415	425
10	375	385	390	395	405

Reps/Wt	600	610	620	630	640
10	390	395	405	410	420
10	435	440	450	455	460
10	410	415	425	430	440

FSU Strength Pyramid
(70-85%)
Sheet #5

Reps/Wt	100	110	120	130	140	150	160	170	180	190
8	70	77	84	91	98	105	112	119	126	133
8	75	83	90	98	105	113	120	128	135	143
8	80	88	96	104	112	120	128	136	144	152
8	85	94	102	111	119	128	135	145	155	160

Reps/Wt	200	210	220	230	240	250	260	270	280	290
8	140	147	154	161	168	175	182	189	196	203
8	150	158	165	173	180	188	195	203	210	218
8	160	168	176	184	192	200	208	216	224	232
8	170	180	185	195	205	215	220	230	240	245

Reps/Wt	300	310	320	330	340	350	360	370	380	390
8	210	217	224	231	238	245	252	259	266	273
8	225	232	240	247	255	262	270	277	285	292
8	240	248	256	264	272	280	288	296	304	312
8	255	265	270	280	290	300	305	315	325	330

Reps/Wt	400	410	420	430	440	450	460	470	480	490
8	280	287	294	301	308	315	322	329	336	343
8	300	307	315	322	330	337	345	352	360	367
8	320	328	336	344	352	360	368	376	384	392
8	340	350	355	365	375	385	390	400	410	420

Reps/Wt	500	510	520	530	540	550	560	570	580	590
8	350	357	364	371	378	385	392	399	406	413
8	375	382	390	397	405	412	420	427	435	442
8	400	408	416	424	432	440	448	456	464	472
8	425	435	440	450	460	470	475	485	495	500

FSU Strength Pyramid
(75-88%)
Sheet #6

Reps/Wt	100	110	120	130	140	150	160	170	180	190
5	75	83	90	98	105	113	120	128	135	143
5	80	88	96	104	112	120	128	136	144	152
5	85	94	102	111	119	128	135	145	155	160
5	88	97	106	114	123	132	140	150	160	165

Reps/Wt	200	210	220	230	240	250	260	270	280	290
5	150	158	165	173	180	188	195	203	210	218
5	160	168	176	184	192	200	208	216	224	232
5	170	180	185	195	205	215	220	230	240	245
5	175	185	195	200	210	220	230	235	245	255

Reps/Wt	300	310	320	330	340	350	360	370	380	390
5	225	232	340	247	255	262	270	277	285	292
5	240	248	256	264	272	280	288	296	304	312
5	255	265	270	280	290	300	305	315	325	330
5	265	270	280	290	300	305	315	325	335	340

Reps/Wt	400	410	420	430	440	450	460	470	480	490
5	300	307	315	322	330	337	345	352	360	367
5	320	328	336	344	352	360	368	376	384	392
5	340	350	355	365	375	385	390	400	410	420
5	350	360	370	375	385	395	405	410	420	430

Reps/Wt	500	510	520	530	540	550	560	570	580	590
5	375	382	390	397	405	412	420	427	435	442
5	400	408	416	424	432	440	448	456	464	472
5	425	435	440	450	460	470	475	485	495	500
5	440	445	455	465	475	480	490	500	510	515

Baseball "Ironman Standards"
Must Score 65+ Points in 9 Categories to Earn a T-Shirt

- Some events are modified for individual needs (Db bench, leg press)
- Points are pro-rated

Cybexrotator Cuff (27,21)

4PTS above Norm	=	10 points
3PTS above Norm	=	8 points
2PTS above Norm	=	7 points
1PT above Norm	=	6 points
0PT above Norm	=	5 points
1PT below Norm	=	4 points
2PTS below Norm	=	2 points
5PTS below Norm	=	1 point

Mat Jumps

54	x	3	= 10 points
54	x	1	= 9 points
51	x	3	= 8 points
51	x	1	= 7 points
48	x	3	= 6 points
48	x	1	= 5 points
45	x	3	= 4 points
45	x	1	= 3 points
42	x	3	= 1 point

300 Shuttle (Avg. of two)

- :55 = 10 points
- :58 = 9 points
- 1:00 = 8 points
- 1:02 = 7 points
- 1:04 = 6 points
- 1:06 = 4 points
- 1:08 = 2 points
- 1:10 = 1 point

60-Yard Sprint

- 6.5 = 10 points
- 6.6 = 9 points
- 6.7 = 8 points
- 6.8 = 7 points
- 6.9 = 6 points
- 7.0 = 5 points
- 7.1 = 4 points
- 7.2 = 3 points
- 7.4 = 1 point

Power Clean

220	x	10	= 10 points
210	x	10	= 9 points
200	x	10	= 8 points
190	x	10	= 7 points
180	x	10	= 6 points
170	x	10	= 5 points
160	x	10	= 3 points
150	x	10	= 1 points

Squat

325	x	10	= 10 points
300	x	10	= 9 points
275	x	10	= 7 points
255	x	10	= 5 points
240	x	10	= 3 points
225	x	10	= 2 points
205	x	10	= 1 point

Bench Press				Sit-Ups (1 min)
225	x	10=	10 points	70 = 10 points
210	x	10=	9 points	60 = 9 points
200	x	10=	8 points	55 = 8 points
190	x	10=	6 points	50 = 7 points
180	x	10=	4 points	45 = 5 points
170x	10	=	3 points	40 = 3 points
160	x	10=	1 points	35 = 1 point

Platehold (100 lb)	Push-Ups (1 min)
1:30 = 10 points	65 = 10 points
1:20 = 9 points	60 = 8 points
1:10 = 8 points	55 = 6 points
1:00 = 7 points	50 = 5 points
:50 = 5 points	45 = 3 points
:45 = 4 points	40 = 2 points
:35 = 2 points	35 = 1 point
:30 = 1 point	

Nutrition

While training for baseball, the pitcher's body needs quality nutrients for energy and rebuilding muscle tissue. To ensure the intake of the required nutrients, he must make wise choices.

   Protein: Needed for building and rebuilding tissue. Considerable research suggests that individuals can only use small quantities of protein at a given time. This research indicates that only 15% of the total caloric intake should be protein. As a result, an athlete needs only about 1.0 to 1.5 grams of protein per kilogram of body weight.

   Example:
- 220 lb. body weight divided by 2.2 = 100 kilograms
- 100 kilograms x 1 gram of protein = 100 grams
- In reference to the chart below, this amount would convert to approximately 10 oz of lean chicken (poultry).

   Accordingly, it is not necessary to eat protein every meal. The point that individuals should remember is that the body will either excrete excess protein or convert it to body fat. Therefore, excessive protein is not be in the best interest of baseball players.

Baseball players have several choices of protein, including turkey, tuna, x-lean beef, chicken, fish, egg whites, skim milk and beans.

Sources of Protein	Protein (g)	KCAL	%CHO	%Protein	%Fat
Cooked lean beef (3 oz)	25	156	6	65	29
Cooked poultry (3 oz)	29	161	5	72	23
Cooked fish (3.5 oz)	30	202	0	60	40
Mozzarella Cheese (l oz)	8	72	0	44	56
Lowfat cottage cheese (l cup)	28	164	0	68	32
Egg (one)	8	79	0	40	60
Skim milk (1 cup)	8	86	60	40	0
Dried beans, cooked (l cup)	13	240	79	21	0
Gatorpro (8 oz)	16	360	65	18	17

**(Note: Information based on data from Gatorade Sports Research.)

Fat: Small quantities of fat are needed by the body for many essential functions. However, most of the fat that an individual needs can still be consumed while eating very lean meats and some carbohydrate foods. In baseball, fat is the least important nutrient source and is probably the most common food that hinders a player's performance.
- Fat exits the stomach very slowly and may cause cramping.
- Excess body fat will increase weight and thus, decrease speed and mobility.
- Fat can seriously hinder an individual's general fitness level by increasing blood cholesterol levels and cardiovascular risks .

Baseball players should attempt to avoid foods that are high in fat content, including mayonnaise, butter, margarine, fried foods, ice cream, cheese, candy, potato chips, bacon and other breakfast meats, and egg yolks.

Carbohydrate: This food source is the most important nutrient for working muscles. Carbohydrate is also the fuel that an individual's brain and nervous system use for all functions. Carbohydrate is what the body will use most while weight training, running, or at practice. Accordingly, this nutrient is the food source that an individual needs to concentrate on. A player needs carbohydrates for energy replacement (after exercise) and energy fuel (before exercise).

The body stores very little carbohydrates. Therefore, it is essential to consume carbohydrates frequently if a player wants superior performance from his body. Research suggests that athletes need about 65% of their total calories from carbohydrates. Accordingly, an athlete should eat foods high in carbohydrates every meal.

- It is very important to consume carbohydrates in the morning (to get an athlete's body going and at dinner (to replace what he has burned.)
- After exercising, it is very important to consume carbohydrates quickly to replace what the athlete has used and to speed the recovery process. This action to ensure increased performance for future bouts of exercise or practices.
- Immediately after exercising, an individual's body can absorb an increased amount of carbohydrates (as compared to normal levels). According to research, this level of an increased ability to consume carbohydrates only lasts about 30 minutes. Therefore, it is wise to consume post-exercise carbohydrates in liquid form because liquids are more easily absorbed in the digestive tract.
- Baseball players have several sound options for choosing carbohydrates, including rice, noodles, pasta, vegetables, fruits, juices, crackers, breads, bagels, potatoes, and cereals.

The table below gives several examples of the calorie and nutrient content of various sources of carbohydrates.

Carbohydrate	Cho (g)	KCAL	%CHO	%Protein	%Fat
Bread (2 slices)	23	135	81	13	6
Bagel (1 whole)	31	163	76	16	8
Pasta (1 cup)	44	216	81	13	6
Rice (1 cup)	36	184	89	7	4
Potato (medium baked)	21	95	88	10	2
Muffin (med. blueberry)	19	126	61	8	31
English muffin (1)	25	135	77	13	10
Pancakes (3 medium)	42	210	80	13	7
Waffle (1 large)	36	285	50	7	43
French toast (2 slices)	34	306	44	15	41
Popcorn (3 cups)	32	162	79	13	8
Banana (1 medium)	27	105	99	1	0
Apple (1 medium)	20	81	100	0	0
Orange (1 medium)	64	65	100	0	0
Pear (1 medium)	25	100	100	0	0
Yams	48	210	91	9	0
Corn on the cob (small ear)	27	100	84	13	3
Carrots (2/3 cup)	7	31	90	10	0
Peas (1/2 cup)	11	62	71	29	0
Vegetable juice (8 oz. V-8)	11	53	93	7	0

Nutritional Suggestions

Small changes in a baseball player's diet and life-style may allow him to increase his opportunity to perform at an optimal level. At a minimum, making simple and wise choices can greatly enhance his energy level and improve his ability to recover from practice, competition, or training.

- Eat more frequent but smaller meals that consist of carbohydrates.
- Drink plenty of liquids during the day.
- Snack only on high-quality foods that will help performance.
- Remember that as an athlete, you must make the food choices that will help your performance. Why choose something that can hinder you?

The key point to keep in mind is that small sacrifices can really add up over the long haul. Athletes who want to "be the best that they can be" must make the sacrifice.

Gaining or Losing Weight

Gaining weight is often a problem for many athletes. Athletes who would like to gain weight should consider the following factors:

- Consume more calories then are expended.
- Eat a variety of sound food choices.
- Engage in a sound strength training program on a regular basis (i.e., 3 x a week).
- Get plenty of rest.
- Focus on gaining "good" weight (i.e., lean muscle mass) as opposed to "unproductive" weight (i.e., body fat).
- Remember an individual's genetic makeup may prevent him from gaining weight no matter what he does.

To lose weight, the athlete should be concerned with losing body fat and maintaining muscle mass. The athlete who needs to lose body fat should adhere to the following guidelines:

- Eat at least three meals a day
- Concentrate on complex carbohydrates (these are low in fat and very satisfying)
- Allow himself an adequate amount of time to lose the weight (i.e., don't start only weeks before the season).
- Eat protein in moderation (at least once a day)
- Drink plenty of water.
- Perform aerobic-type exercise at least three times a week for a session lasting a minimum of 20 min. (cycling, jog, Stairmaster, etc.).
- Engage in a sound strength training program on a regular basis (i.e., 3 x per week).
- Write down and analyze what is eaten. Make sure that a good balance of foods (high carbohydrates, moderate proteins, low fat and variety of nutritious fruits and veggies) is consumed.

Conclusion

Sound pitching mechanics should stand the test of time. Teaching methods, however, change. Through trial and error, teaching techniques evolve and improve. A good pitching coach should always be open to suggestions.

Teaching involves communication. If a better way of communication is developed, the coach should use it. Rather than feel threatened, the coach should listen to the new idea. If the new idea is sound and improves his teaching methods, it can be incorporated into the coach's teachings.

Teaching and learning is an exciting adventure. Coaching is more than just demanding and telling. It is listening, observing, and evaluating. If the methods used are not getting results, it is advisable to improve or change the methods. This objective can be accomplished without changing the fundamentals. Presentation is the key.

The value of listening to other coaches is immeasurable. Two coaches who agree on pitching mechanics may differ a great deal on their presentations. One presentation may be easier to understand than the other. One coach may emphasize certain points while the other coach glosses over those same points. Each presentation should be examined carefully. At every clinic, there is something to be learned. Key words and phrases to highlight a technique may be an important factor. Enthusiasm and interest in the subject may be even more important. Coaches should listen and watch carefully. One important point could make an improvement in a presentation.

The pitching program presented in this book took years to develop. It was developed by taking the ideas of many coaches and combining them with a few ideas of my own. The pitchers whom I have coached taught me as much as I taught them. They told me with words, body language, and results when the lessons were sound and when they were not sound. Learning is a shared process; many people shared this learning journey with me.

This book has explained the fundamentals of pitching and a method of teaching those fundamentals. The sequential approach, the pitching language, and the drills are designed to help the pitcher and the pitching coach. Beginning with the feet and working upward through the head gives the pitcher and the pitching coach a concrete learning program. The dry-run drills were devised to augment the teaching program.

This text is really a guide book. Coaches should use it as it is written or make those changes that will enable the information presented in this book to be better adapted to their needs. For example, the terminology presented in this book is my language to my pitchers. Other coaches may have better descriptions that create better images for both them and their pitchers.

Fundamentals are lasting, but the methods used to teach them constantly change. Coaches should never stop looking for better ways to teach. They should always keep watching, listening, and learning. When a method or technique is uncovered that improves the learning process, a coach should use it. I plan to.

About the Author

Bob Bennett is the former head baseball coach at Fresno State University and one of the winningest Division I coaches of all time. His career record of 1302-759-4 ranks among the top 10 on the NCAA Division I all-time victory list.

Photo: Justin Kase Conder/Fresno State Media Relations

During 34 seasons (1970-2002, plus a year as FSU's interim head coach in 1967) at Fresno State, Bennett led his teams to extraordinary success, winning or sharing 17 conference titles, earning 1302 victories (an average of 40 wins per season), and making two trips to the College World Series. For his achievements, Bennett was honored several times, including being named Conference Coach of the Year 14 times and NCAA Coach of the Year in 1988. He also received the Lefty Gomez Award for his lifetime contribution to baseball.

Bennett, who was inducted into the American Baseball Coaches Hall of Fame in 1992, was also heavily involved in baseball at the international level, serving as head coach of the U.S. National Team in 1983 and 1986 and serving on the National Team's coaching staff in 1977 and 1979.

Bennett and his wife, Jane, have three children, Karen, Brad, and Todd, and eight grandchildren.